Armistead Maupin was born in Washington, D.C. in 1944 but grew up in Raleigh, North Carolina. A graduate of the University of North Carolina, he served as a naval officer in Vietnam before moving to California in 1971 as a reporter for the Associated Press. In 1976 he launched his daily newspaper serial, *Tales of the City*, in the *San Francisco Chronicle*. The first fiction to appear in an American daily for decades, *Tales* grew into an international sensation when compiled and rewritten as novels. Maupin's six-volume *Tales of the City* sequence – *Tales of the City*, *More Tales of the City*, *Further Tales of the City*, *Babycakes*, *Significant Others* and *Sure of You* – are now multi-million bestsellers published in eleven languages. The first two of these novels were adapted as a pair of widely acclaimed television mini-series: the third, *Further Tales of the City*, is currently in production. Maupin's 1992 novel, *Maybe the Moon*, chronicling the adventures of the world's shortest woman, was a number one bestseller. As a librettist he collaborated in 1999 with composer Jake Heggie on *Anna Madrigal Remembers* for mezzo-soprano Frederica von Stade and Chanticleer, the classical choral ensemble. *The Night Listener* is Armistead Maupin's latest novel. He lives in San Francisco, California.

Official Author Web Site:
www.ArmisteadMaupin.com
For further information about books by Armistead Maupin contact:
nightlistener.com and talesofthecity.com

Also by Armistead Maupin

TALES OF THE CITY
MORE TALES OF THE CITY
FURTHER TALES OF THE CITY
BABYCAKES
SIGNIFICANT OTHERS
SURE OF YOU
MAYBE THE MOON

and published by Black Swan

THE NIGHT LISTENER

Armistead Maupin

BLACK SWAN

THE NIGHT LISTENER
A BLACK SWAN BOOK : 0 552 14240 9

Originally published in Great Britain by Bantam Press,
a division of Transworld Publishers

PRINTING HISTORY
Bantam Press edition published 2000
Black Swan edition published 2001

1 3 5 7 9 10 8 6 4 2

Set in 11/13½pt Melior by
Falcon Oast Graphic Art Ltd.

Black Swan Books are published by Transworld Publishers,
61–63 Uxbridge Road, London W5 5SA,
a division of The Random House Group Ltd,
in Australia by Random House Australia (Pty) Ltd,
20 Alfred Street, Milsons Point, Sydney, NSW 2061, Australia,
in New Zealand by Random House New Zealand Ltd,
18 Poland Road, Glenfield, Auckland 10, New Zealand
and in South Africa by Random House (Pty) Ltd,
Endulini, 5a Jubilee Road, Parktown 2193, South Africa.

Printed and bound in Great Britain by
Clays Ltd, St Ives plc.

For Terry Anderson
and
for Armistead Maupin Sr.,
with abiding love

I am certain of nothing
but the holiness of the heart's affections
and the truth of imagination

John Keats

And almost everyone when age,
Disease, or sorrows strike him,
Inclines to think there is a God,
Or something very like him.

Arthur Hugh Clough

One

Jewelling the Elephant

I know how it sounds when I call him my son. There's something a little precious about it, a little too wishful to be taken seriously. I've noticed the looks on people's faces, those dim, indulgent smiles that vanish in a heartbeat. It's easy enough to see how they've pegged me: an unfulfilled man on the shady side of fifty, making a last grasp at fatherhood with somebody else's child.

That's not the way it is. Frankly, I've never wanted a kid. Never once believed that nature's whim had robbed me of my manly destiny. Pete and I were an accident, pure and simple, a collision of kindred spirits that had nothing to do with paternal urges, latent or otherwise. That much I can tell you for sure.

Son isn't the right word, of course.

Just the only one big enough to describe what happened.

* * *

I'm a fabulist by trade, so be forewarned: I've spent years looting my life for fiction. Like a magpie, I save the shiny stuff and discard the rest; it's of no use to me if it doesn't serve the geometry of the story. This makes me less than reliable when it comes to the facts. Ask Jess Carmody, who lived with me for ten years and observed this affliction firsthand. He even had a name for it—The Jewelled Elephant Syndrome—after a story I once told him about an old friend from college.

My friend, whose name was Boyd, joined the Peace Corps in the late sixties. He was sent to a village in India where he fell in love with a local girl and eventually proposed to her. But Boyd's blue-blooded parents back in South Carolina were so aghast at the prospect of dusky grandchildren that they refused to attend the wedding in New Delhi.

So Boyd sent them photographs. The bride turned out to be an aristocrat of the highest caste, better bred by far than any member of Boyd's family. The couple had been wed in regal splendor, perched atop a pair of jewelled elephants. Boyd's parents, imprisoned in their middle-class snobbery, had managed to miss the social event of a lifetime.

I had told that story so often that Jess knew it by heart. So when Boyd came to town on business and met Jess for the first time, Jess was sure he had the perfect opener. "Well," he said brightly, "Gabriel tells me you got married on an elephant."

Boyd just blinked at him in confusion.

I could already feel myself reddening. "You weren't?"

"No," Boyd said with an uncomfortable laugh. "We were married in a Presbyterian church."

Jess said nothing, but he gave me a heavy-lidded

stare whose meaning I had long before learned to decipher: *You are never to be trusted with the facts.*

In my defense, the essence of the story had been true. Boyd had indeed married an Indian girl he had met in the Peace Corps, and she had proved to be quite rich. And Boyd's parents—who were, in fact, exceptionally stuffy—had always regretted that they'd missed the wedding.

I don't know what to say about those elephants, except that I believed in them utterly. They certainly never felt like a lie. More like a kind of shorthand for a larger, less satisfying truth. Most stories have holes in them that cry out for jewelled elephants. And my instinct, alas, is to supply them.

I don't want that to happen when I talk about Pete. I will try to lay out the facts exactly as I remember them, one after the other, as unbejewelled as possible. I owe that much to my son—to both of us, really—and to the unscripted intrigues of everyday life.

But, most of all, I want you to believe this.

And that will be hard enough as it is.

I wasn't myself the afternoon that Pete appeared. Or maybe more severely myself than I had ever been. Jess had left me two weeks earlier, and I was raw with the realization of it. I have never known sorrow to be such a physical thing, an actual presence that weighed on my limbs like something wet and woolen. I couldn't write—or wouldn't, at any rate—unable to face the grueling self-scrutiny that fiction demands. I would feed the dog, walk him, check the mail, feed myself, do the dishes, lie on the sofa for hours watching television.

Everything seemed pertinent to my pain. The silliest coffee commercial could plunge me into profound Chekhovian gloom. There was no way around the self-doubt or the panic or the anger. My marriage had exploded in midair, strewing itself across the landscape, and all I could do was search the rubble for some sign of a probable cause, some telltale black box.

The things I knew for sure had become a litany I recited to friends on the telephone: Jess had taken an apartment on Buena Vista Park. He wanted space, he said, a place to be alone. He had spent a decade expecting to die, and now he planned to think about living. (He could actually do that, he realized, without having to call it denial.) He would meditate and read, and focus on himself for once. He couldn't say for sure when he'd be back, or if he'd ever be back, or if I'd even want him when it was over. I was not to take this personally, he said; it had nothing to do with me.

Then, after stuffing his saddlebags full of protease inhibitors, he pecked me solemnly on the lips and mounted the red motorcycle he had taught himself to ride six months earlier. I'd never trusted that machine. Now, as I watched it roar off down the hill, I realized why: It had always seemed made for this moment.

The solitude that followed sent me around the bend. Or at least into the Castro once a day, where I foraged for pork chops and porn tapes, just to be among the living. It was weird doing this after a decade of cocooning with Jess. All those bullet-headed boys with their goatees and tats. All those old guys like me shambling along in their dyed mustaches and gentlemen's jeans, utterly amazed to still be there, still out shopping for love.

And the creeping genericism of it all, the Body Shops and Sunglass Huts of any American mall. The place had become a theme park for homos, where the names of icons were writ large upon the wall of the flashy new juice bar. I couldn't help checking, of course, and there I was, GABRIEL NOONE—just to the left of the wheat-grass machine—between OSCAR WILDE and MARTINA NAVRATILOVA.

Even in my depression, I got a rush out of that, and the way my name would surface softly in my wake as I walked down the street. Once I was stopped by the tour guide for an operation called "Cruisin' the Castro." With genial decorum she offered me up like a resident artifact to a dozen visitors from Germany and Holland. They applauded politely, standing there in the midst of the busy sidewalk, and one of them asked how Jess was doing. I said he was fine, that the new cocktail was working wonders, that his energy levels had never been higher, that he had a real chance to live, thank God. And they were all so happy to hear that.

I left before anyone could see what a fraud I was. Or notice that the video under my arm was called *Dr. Jerkoff and Mr. Hard*.

Then one afternoon my bookkeeper, Anna, came by the house to drop off checks for my signature. I had explained things to her on the phone, since Jess had always handled our finances. She took it in stride, but I detected a trace of motherly concern. This felt odd coming from a twenty-one-year-old, but I accepted it gratefully.

It was Anna who made the Pete thing possible. Without her intervention that morning, he would never have found his way into my rapidly shrinking orbit. She and I were holed up in the office—Jess's office—sorting receipts and combing the mail for bills. I could have managed this on my own, but Anna, I think, had noticed my red-rimmed eyes and was trying to keep me company. Her own eyes, glossy black in a heart-shaped face, would study me solemnly when she thought I wasn't looking. I remember noticing a faint resemblance to Olivia Hussey in *Lost Horizon*, a reference so hopelessly antediluvian I didn't even bother to express it.

"That looks interesting," she said, pushing a parcel my way. It was a padded envelope, about eight by ten.

"Don't bet on it," I said. "It's just galleys."

"Photos?"

"No. Galleys for a book. Some editor wants something blurbed."

"You can tell that from the package?"

"In the dark," I said, "and blindfolded." I pointed to the colophon on the envelope. "It's from Argus Press, see?"

I might have also told her how the cover letter would read. How it would acknowledge the many demands on my time and the number of manuscripts that must come my way each week. How it would go on to point out that just a few kind words from a writer of my stature would help this searing memoir, this tender coming-out novel, this fabulous celebrity AIDS cookbook, find its way to "the audience it so richly deserves." Meaning, of course, fags.

But I kept quiet. I didn't want Anna to see how poisonous a broken heart could be. I wanted her on my side. I wanted everyone on my side. So I gave her a crooked smile and lobbed the package into the wastebasket.

"Hey," she said, looking mildly affronted. "Aren't you even curious?"

"No."

"Why not?"

"Because I can't handle someone else being brilliant right now."

She mulled that over. "Maybe it'll be shitty."

"Then why read it?"

"I dunno. To cheer yourself up?"

"It doesn't work that way. I identify with the shitty stuff."

"You do?" She looked utterly perplexed.

"It's hard to explain," I said. "It's a writer thing."

"I guess so," she murmured, giving me up for lost as she turned back to her labors.

I was tempted to blame this nonsense on the crisis at hand, but the truth is I've always been unsure about my literary powers. My work, after all, was originally intended for radio: grabby little armchair yarns that I would read for half an hour every week on a National Public Radio show called *Noone at Night*. My characters were a motley but lovable bunch, people caught in the supreme joke of modern life who were forced to survive by making families of their friends. The show eventually became a cult hit; listeners would cluster en masse around their radios in a way that hadn't happened since the serials of the forties. While this fulfilled me hugely as a storyteller, it left me feeling illegitimate as a writer, as if I'd broken into the Temple of Literature through some unlocked basement window.

Never mind that the books compiled from those

shows have never stopped selling. Or that Barnes & Noble and Amazon.com now use my name in their promotions. In my heart I remain a clever impostor, a sidewalk magician performing tricks for the crowd outside the opera house. A real writer makes star turns at conferences and summers at Yaddo and shows up in the *New York Times Book Review* as someone to Bear in Mind. A real writer would never have stopped writing when his life collapsed around him. He would have caught every last detail. He would have pinned his heart to the page, just to give his readers a closer look.

But the fight went out of me when my marriage began to unravel. I lost a vital engine I never even knew I had. Those gracefully convoluted plotlines my listeners cherished had been driven by a bedrock optimism that vanished overnight. And once that was gone my authorial voice deserted me in the most literal way possible—in the midst of a recording session.

We were taping that day, as usual, at the local public-radio station, which fed the show, via satellite, to the rest of the system. (As a space-struck teenager I'd kept a scrapbook on *Sputnik*, so I'd always loved knowing that one of its grandchildren was beaming my stories to the nation.) I hadn't been able to write for several weeks, but I still had a backlog of five or six episodes that would buy me some time until I could get my head together.

But ten minutes into the session, when the engineer played back a troublesome passage, I made an unnerving discovery.

"What's the matter?" he asked, reading my confusion.

"It doesn't sound like me," I told him.

18

He shrugged. "The levels are all the same."

"No, I mean . . . *I* don't sound like me."

This time he widened his eyes and deedled out the theme from *The Twilight Zone*.

"I'm serious, Kevin."

"Do you wanna take a break?"

"No. Let's just start from the top of the page."

So I began again, but my voice felt even more phony and disembodied. I found myself tripping over the simplest words as I attempted a lighthearted domestic scene. (The couple that most resembled me and Jess were fighting over the sovereignty of their remote control.) After half a dozen takes I'd run so far beyond my allotted time that the panelists for the next show—a trio of Silicon Valley pundits—began to mill about in the control room with obvious irritation. Wary of witnesses to my self-annihilation, I apologized to the engineer, took off my headphones, and left the room, never to return.

The following week, without explanation, NPR began to treat its listeners to *The Best of Noone at Night*.

So there I sat, useless, while Anna worked and a flock of winged toasters flapped across the face of Jess's Mac. That had always been his favorite screen saver, so there was no reason to believe he had left it there as a parting comment. Still, the irony was inescapable. Those jaunty appliances seemed the very essence of our lost domesticity, the dependable homeyness that had come and gone. I felt a clear sense of relief when Anna hit a key and made them disappear.

"Have you updated the Quicken files?" she asked.

"No," I told her. "I don't know how to get into that thing."

She batted her eyes at me dubiously.

"I'm an IBM person," I said. "Jess always handled this."

She began clicking the mouse. "Save all your receipts, then. I'll take care of the rest."

"Great," I said feebly.

"Why don't you go kick back?" she said.

"You mean get out?"

"Yeah."

The difficult child had been banished to his room.

So the dog and I went for our walk. The street we took—the one we always take—was dubbed an avenue early in the century, though it barely qualifies. True, it's paved with red bricks and lined rather grandly with red-leafed plum trees, but it runs for only a block, dead-ending at the edge of Sutro Forest. The houses along the way are old shingled places with copper gutters bleeding green, but their foolproof charm wasn't working that afternoon.

I reached the woods well ahead of Hugo. Below me lay a gorge furred with fog, where eucalyptus trees creaked like masts on a galleon. I stared at them for a moment, lost in their operatic gloom, then turned and looked for the dog. He was yards behind, too blind and dotty to get his bearings. When I whistled, his floppy ears rose to half-mast, but he promptly trotted off in the wrong direction. Poor old geezer, I thought. He seemed even more befuddled since Jess had left.

"Hey, beastlet! Turn your ass around."

My voice was sounding disconnected again. I was

halfway down the block before I realized why: I had sounded just like Jess. That gruff but folksy tone was precisely the one he had always used with Hugo. And no one else, I can assure you, had ever called the dog "beastlet." There was nothing mystical about this, just a cheap trick of the mind that reconstructed Jess the only way I could manage. How pathetic, I thought. And how like me to play the dummy to my own bad ventriloquism.

The fog was much thicker as I headed home. Out of habit, I approached the house from the sidewalk across the street, where I could see it in context: three narrow stories notched into the wooded slope. Its new cedar shingles were still too pallid for its dark green trim, but another season or two of rain would turn them into tarnished silver. I'd been eagerly awaiting that. I'd wanted the place to look ancestral, as if we had lived there forever.

Upon moving in, three years earlier, we had thrown ourselves into a frenzy of renovation. Fences and decks sprang up overnight, and the garden arrived fully grown, an instant Eden of azaleas and black bamboo and Australian tree ferns the size of beach umbrellas. We had already lived for seven years with Jess's dwindling T cells and had no intention of waiting for nature to catch up with us.

Jess used to joke about this. Sometimes he called me Mrs. Winchester, after the loony old lady on the Peninsula who believed that constant home improvement would keep evil spirits away. And that was pretty close. My frantic agenda for the house had been my only insurance against the inevitable. Jess was bound to get sick, one of these days, but not until those shingles had mellowed and the new fountain was

21

installed and the wisteria had gone ropy above the lych-gate. That was the deal: Jess could leave, but only when the dream was complete, when we were snug in a fortress of our own creation, barricaded against the coming storm.

It didn't occur to me there were other ways of leaving.

But about that package:

It awaited me upon my return, having risen like a phoenix from the wastebasket to a place of prominence beside the fax machine. Anna was gone, bound for another client, but her dry smile still lingered in the room. I sat at the desk and picked up the padded envelope, turning it over slowly in my hands. It had the feel of Christmas somehow, peculiar as that sounds, the brown-paper promise of wonders to come. Anna had been right, I decided; it wouldn't do to stop being curious. Especially now.

I pulled the little tab and out fell a set of bound galleys with a light blue cover. The book was called *The Blacking Factory*. Its author was Peter Lomax, a name I didn't recognize. According to the cover letter from Ashe Findlay (a stuffy but pleasant New York editor I'd seen several times at book fairs), this was indeed another memoir. But one with an arresting difference: its author, a survivor of long-term sexual abuse, was thirteen years old.

I flipped through the galleys, as I invariably do, sampling passages here and there. When I had seen enough, I brewed a pot of coffee and climbed to my attic office. Hugo followed on my heels, whimpering anxiously, as if his only remaining human might also be on the verge of leaving. I made a nest for him on the sofa, using one of Jess's unlaundered T-shirts. The scent calmed him right away, and he was soon fast asleep at my feet, snoring with gusto by the time I had opened the galleys. It was six o'clock, not yet dark. It would be past midnight when I next looked up.

It's not an easy thing to trim Pete's story to its barest bones, to trot out the horror for your examination, minus Pete's wisdom and courage and disarming humor. But that's what I have to do if you're to understand how fiercely those galleys consumed me, and why I slept so uneasily that night, and why, above all, I went straight to the phone the following morning.

Pete was born in 1985. His father was a foreman in a hosiery factory, his mother a housewife. To their neighbors in Milwaukee Pete's parents were nothing out of the ordinary, just average people who ate at the mall and shopped at the Price Club, and showed up at Mass with their cute kid in tow. They were a nice-looking couple, apparently, far too wholesome and all-American to be suspected of anything ghastly.

At home lay the truth. In the backyard was a sound-proof shed where Pete was routinely sent for "discipline." His father began beating him at two and raping him at four. His mother knew this; she video-taped the sessions, in fact, and shared them with other grownups who liked that sort of thing. And when money got tight, Pete himself was shared. People would drive across three states just to involve an eight-year-old in their games. Pete remembers waiting for them in the slushy parking lots of Holiday Inns. He remembers their grownup toys and the scary sounds of their pleasure and the rotten-fruit stink of amyl nitrite. And the way that afterward his mother would buy off his bruises with plastic dinosaurs.

It stopped when he was eleven. Two days after Christmas, in the midst of a snowstorm, he left the house and ran eight blocks to a public library with his backpack stuffed full of videotapes. There he phoned a child-abuse hot line and waited in the stacks until a lady doctor came to meet him. Her name was Donna Lomax. She wore jeans with a blazer, he remembers, and had brown eyes and listened quietly while he told his story. Then she took him to her office, where he read a *Star Wars* comic book and she and another doctor watched the tapes in a different room. That was it. He ate supper at Donna's house that night, and slept there, too, in a room with clean sheets and a door he could lock from the inside.

Pete's parents were arrested and jailed. They never saw their son again, unless you count the videotape on which he testified against them. Though Donna was divorced and had never particularly wanted children, she saw something remarkable in this child, something that reached a part of her that had never been reached before. When she offered to adopt Pete, he accepted almost immediately, but without a trace of emotion. Compassion was still alien to him; he had no precedent for trusting anyone, even this lanky angel who promised him safety and expected nothing in return.

So Pete became a Lomax, but in name only. He stayed locked in his room for weeks, leaving only for meals, and even then he would eye his new mother across the table like some dangerous wild thing. Donna didn't push; she let him wander out of the woods on

24

his own, and in his own time. And when he finally did, she was there to meet him, the tenderest of certainties, rocking him in her arms while he cried.

It should have ended there, but didn't. When Pete's body had healed at last, when he had learned to laugh along with Donna, when he had begun the journal that would eventually become his book, he developed a troubling cough. Donna had to tell him what she already knew: that he had tested positive for AIDS.

At the hospital they treated Pete's pneumonia and drained his lungs with tubes. As soon as he was able to sit up, he asked Donna to bring him his journal. She did more than that: she brought him a laptop computer. It became his obsession, then his salvation. He would write on it for hours at a time, oblivious to everything around him, dizzy with the discovery that words could contain his suffering.

And sometimes, when the ward was dark, he'd listen to the radio. There was a TV above his bed, but he never turned it on. He had seen his own torment on such a screen, so its unrelenting literalness was not his idea of escape. But radio let his mind roam to a secret place where no one's face reminded him of anyone else's. His favorite show was a man who told stories late at night, stories about people caught in the supreme joke of modern life who were forced to survive by making families of their friends. The man's voice was low and soothing, the voice of an understanding father.

And often, though Pete knew better, it seemed to be speaking to Pete alone.

Two

The Noones

"Well," said Ashe Findlay on the phone the next morning. "I thought I might be hearing from you."

The editor's voice was just as I'd remembered it: the tart nasality of a Yankee blue blood. I could all too easily sketch in the rest: the frayed pink oxford-cloth shirt, the crooked bow tie and brambled eyebrows, the whole tiresome Cheeveresque thing.

"That kid is amazing," I said.

"Isn't he, though?"

"I'd be glad to do a blurb."

"Splendid." He paused significantly before continuing. "I take it you got to the end."

"I finished it, yes."

"So you know what a fan you have."

"Yes," I said evenly. "I was touched."

"Pete asked especially that you be sent the galleys. He's never missed one of your shows."

I fought the urge to bask in this flattery. I wanted

Findlay to know that the boy's talent alone was enough to sustain my interest. "Is he okay?" I asked. "His health?"

"For the moment. He's a tough little fellow. A survivor, if ever there was one."

I told him that's what I loved about the book: the way Pete never stooped to self-pity, even in his bleakest moments. And he was so funny about it sometimes, so bluntly matter-of-fact about the most horrendous hardships. Who would have thought that the late discovery of love by a boy facing death could ever be construed as a happy ending?

"How in the world did you come by it?" I asked.

The editor indulged in a chuckle at his own expense. "An utter fluke. His AIDS counselor knows one of the secretaries in our trade division. It just landed on my desk."

"Did it take a lot of editing?"

Another chuckle. "Hate to break it to you. It was one of the cleanest manuscripts I've handled all year."

"Jesus."

"I had to pull him back here and there. He'd use a ten-dollar word when a ten-cent one would do. But children do that, don't they?"

"I'm completely in awe," I said. "Actually . . ." I found myself faltering for reasons I couldn't identify. Modesty? Embarrassment? Some ancient, ingrained fear of rejection?

"What?" prompted the editor.

"Well, I just wondered if it would make sense for me to tell him this myself."

"You mean call him?"

"Yeah."

"I should think he'd be thrilled. Certainly. Let me

check with Donna first. I'm sure it'll be okay, considering . . . you know, how he regards you."

"If it's a bad time or something . . ."

"No, they'd be delighted. I'll ring you in a day or two."

"Great."

"He's a good kid. And you'll like her, too."

I told him I couldn't imagine that I wouldn't.

"How's your own writing coming along?"

This was a query born of etiquette, not interest. Findlay's literary taste ran to Updike and Lessing, the (old) *New Yorker* and the *Paris Review*. He couldn't have cared less about my feel-good penny dreadfuls. Ours was just a marriage of convenience. If he valued me at all, it was because some clever person upstairs had decided to angle Pete's book to "the AIDS market."

The fact that Findlay's curiosity wasn't genuine made it easier to answer him candidly. In fact, I confessed something that I had yet to tell my own editor: that I'd grown less and less in love with the act of arranging words on a page. And that it might be a permanent condition.

"You mean you're blocked?"

"That's a little optimistic," I said. "It assumes there is something to block in the first place."

"Oh, Gabriel, come now!"

"It's the truth," I said, oddly touched that he had used my name. It seemed such an intimate act for him.

"You just need a break," he insisted.

I told him I'd had one for almost four months.

"Then drive down the coast with . . . Jamie, is it?"

"Jess."

"Yes. You two just charge off into the wild blue yonder. And don't think about writing at all. I think you'll be surprised how swiftly the urge will arise again."

"Maybe we'll do that," I said.

"Is he okay, by the way?"

"He's fine," I told him. "He feels better than he has in ages. He has to stay on top of things, of course, because you really never know . . . but . . . he's doing fine . . ."

As I droned away, my gaze straggled across the cityscape. Jess's new place was an upended sugar cube against the primeval green of Buena Vista Park. Framed neatly in the window, it was visible from the bed— from *our* bed—the first thing I faced in the morning, the last thing I pondered at night. Such a deft stroke of melodrama, I thought; I might have concocted it myself.

"I'm so glad," said Ashe Findlay.

I'd lost my way in the conversation. "Sorry, Ashe . . . about what?"

"That Jamie's doing well. I mean Jess. Damn it, why do I insist on calling him that?"

I told him Jamie was the name of one of my characters.

"Ah."

"He isn't actually Jess per se. But I borrowed heavily."

To put it mildly. When Jess and I met, so did Jamie and Will, the happy homo couple on *Noone at Night*. And when Jess tested positive, Jamie did the same— and used the same beeping pillbox for his AZT. Though Jamie is a coppersmith, and physically the opposite of Jess, people tend to confuse the two. Even Ashe Findlay, who was hardly a devotee of my work, had made the graceless leap from fact to fiction.

"It's a natural mistake," I told him.

Whereupon he veered into a speech about the nature of fiction. I remember very little of it except the rousing conclusion, when he urged me to remain stalwartly in the moment, for that would be the place from which my writing would flow.

"And it will flow, Gabriel. I promise you."

Sure thing, I thought, gazing out the window again.

"And give my best to Jess, will you?"

That afternoon my depression got worse, so I took Hugo to Golden Gate Park, where I came across a Hare Krishna festival on the lawn behind the tennis courts. The revelers were kids mostly, pale-skinned and pimply in their saffron robes, but I envied them their stupid bliss. I sat cross-legged on the grass and watched for a while, feeling like an impostor. I wanted to be one of them, to vanish in that vortex of gaudy color and burn out my grief in the sun, but I knew far too much about myself to make it happen.

When I got back to the house, Anna was in the office. "I had to check some stuff," she said, gazing up from the computer like a burglar caught with a sack of silverware.

"Check away," I told her. "You never have to call ahead." It would have shamed me somehow to speak the whole truth: that I loved finding someone else at home, keeping my wobbly life on course the way Jess had always done.

"Your father called, by the way."

This was the last thing I'd expected. "He did? When?"

"Little while ago."

"Did you pick up?"

She chuckled. "Had to. He kept saying 'Are you theah, are you theah? Pick it up, goddammit, I know you're theah!'"

"That's him," I said.

"He's a nice ol' coot."

I told her strangers always liked him.

"What's not to like?" she asked.

"If he knew you," I said, "he'd call you a cute little Chink gal behind your back."

She grinned and turned back to the computer. "I *am* a cute little Chink gal."

I didn't press it. My father has always been a hit-and-run charmer, so most people just don't get it. You have to know him for half a century before you can see how little he's really giving you. "Why did he call, anyway?"

"He saw you on *Jeopardy*."

For a moment I wondered if Pap had finally succumbed to the delusions that had consumed my grandmother back in the sixties. Dodie used to see the whole family on television. I was largely to blame for this, since I was a reporter then for a Charleston station, and the side of my head could sometimes be glimpsed during off-camera interviews. Dodie had been alerted to watch for me, and in no time at all she'd improved on the concept. In her cinder-block room at the Live Oaks Convalescent Home she saw my sister, Josie, on *Bewitched*, my great-uncle Gus on *The Defenders*, my mother on *Connie's Country Kitchen*.

Once she told me tearfully that my father—her son— had been killed by "a mob of radical nigras." She'd seen this on TV, she said, and could not be convinced otherwise. Even when I brought her martyred child to the rest home, where he yelled at her like a man accused: "Goddammit, Mama, I'm not dead! Look at me! I'm here, goddammit!" But Dodie couldn't stop crying, so Pap snatched a plastic lily from her dresser and reclined on her bed. "Okay," he bellowed, erecting the lily over his chest, "I'm dead! Are you happy now, Mama?" After a moment or two, Dodie giggled like a girl, her demons expelled by her lingering grasp of the absurd. Sanity escaped her, but she knew a good laugh when she saw one.

"*Jeopardy?*" I said, blinking at my bookkeeper. "I've never been on *Jeopardy*."

"You have now," she replied. "Two days ago."

"What do you mean?"

"You were a question. Or an answer, I guess. However they do it. You know, like: 'This city is the setting for Gabriel Noone's stories on *Noone at Night*.' Your dad saw it. Him and your stepmom."

"No shit?"

Anna wiggled her eyebrows. "Way cool, huh?"

I had to admit it was. I could see Pap slouched in front of the quiz show, his trousers undone at the waist, munching Triscuits out of the box. I imagined the little grunt of amazement he made when he heard Alex Trebek speak my name—his own name, in fact—and saw it spelled out on the screen in blazing blue and white. My Peabody Award had barely fazed him, but *Jeopardy* was different. *Jeopardy* swam freely in Pap's mainstream, next to *Patton* and Roy Blount Jr. and *The Sound of Music*.

"Plus," said Anna offhandedly, "he's coming to town."

"He said that?"

She nodded. "On their way to Tahiti."

"When?"

"Two weeks, I think. He wants you to call him."

"Fuckshitpiss."

"Hey," said Anna, turning back to the computer. "Don't shoot the messenger."

It was Jess, in fact, I wanted to shoot. How could he not be here for this—my champion and co-conspirator, my happy ending, my living proof that men could love each other deeply? My father would see this house at last, but with a vital piece missing: the one that had charged it with passion and politics. And I knew how he'd react to the separation. I could hear him already, telling me I was better off without the sorry bastard, ticking off the faults of a man he had never bothered to know. His long-stifled distrust of my "lifestyle" could flourish again in the name of taking my side.

"This is not good news," I told Anna.

"How old is he?" she asked. "He must be ancient."

I gave her a look. "Because I am, you mean?"

"Well . . . yeah."

"There *are* other bookkeepers, you know."

She wasn't at all ruffled. "I just meant, I hope I'm over my parents by the time I'm your age."

"Good luck," I said.

Anna's parents, as I remembered, were both women. She had a birth father in the East Bay who ran a chain of convenience stores, but she'd met him only once, just for curiosity's sake. Her twin brother, who seemed as straight as she was, worked weekends at a center for Lesbian, Gay, Bisexual, Transgendered, and Questioning Youth. None of this struck her as especially unusual. She was a recent invention, placidly free from entanglements. Unlike me, she had never experienced the dark tidal pull of the past.

*   *   *

When I was little, I knew almost nothing about my grandfather, who died before I was born. In another family this might not have been odd, but ours was obsessed with the trappings of kinship. My father briefed us daily on our ancestors. We knew that a Noone had died of dysentery at Fort Moultrie, that another had been a dashing bachelor governor, that Granny Prioleau had been forced to quarter Yankees during Sherman's March. Some of these figures, so help me, we could have picked out of a lineup, but not my father's father. To my memory, I'd never even seen a picture of him. He was just a grayish blur, an abstraction without a lore.

This didn't change until I was twelve, when my friend Jim Huger buttonholed me on a school field trip to tell me what the rest of Charleston had known for decades: the original Gabriel Noone had blown his head off with a shotgun. There were several versions of this, Jim said. One held that my grandfather had done the deed in my father's bedroom. Pap, scarcely out of his teens, had come home from a camping trip on Kiawah Island to find an old black retainer—Dah, they called her—mopping gore off the wallpaper.

Another version placed the suicide in the garden after supper, when children were at play, and all of Meeting Street could hear the blast. Jim's aunt Claire was out jarring lightning bugs at the time and remembers Dah's terrible keening. Whichever rendition was true—if either—my father had been known to discuss the event only once in his life: with my mother, very briefly, on the night before their Eastertime wedding at St. Michael's.

34

When I asked my mother why Grandpa Noone had killed himself, she told me he had lost money in the Depression. "And," she added darkly, "there were too many women around." (A mother-in-law and a maiden aunt had lived under the same roof with Dodie and Grandpa.) This, my mother suggested with breezy misogyny, was reason enough for any man to lose interest in living. But none of that mattered, she said. All that mattered was that Pap not have to think about this terrible thing again. So I joined her confederacy of silence, standing sentinel to a secret that wasn't a secret at all.

I remember a night, not long after that, when my father and I were watching *Playhouse 90* together. The show, I realized to my horror, was about a man coping with his father's suicide. (Forty years later, I can still invoke the title: *The Return of Ansel Gibbs.*) Too mortified to leave the room or change channels or even glance in my father's direction, I held my breath for an hour and a half. When I finally dared look, his face told me nothing. The man who always talked back to the bad guys on *Gunsmoke* sat as mute and unblinking as a corpse.

I began to wonder if suicide, like everything else in the family, was hereditary. Pap kept a captured Japanese pistol in his desk that I regarded with mounting dread. It was there, he said, in case he had to "stop some crazy nigger from breaking in," but it was *his* craziness that worried me. Whenever he stormed off to his study after one of his tantrums I would listen for gunfire. I think he knew this, too. "Don't worry about me," he was fond of saying. "I won't be around much longer." This could have been a reference to his famously high cholesterol, or just the onset of middle age, but I took it to mean he would someday become his father's son.

I guess he felt outnumbered. The four of us—my mother and brother and sister and I—had united in the face of his helpless fury. And the thing we could never mention had dredged a gulf so wide that none of us could bridge it. Pap tried, in his own way. He surprised us with pet ducks one Christmas. He drove us to Quebec in the Country Squire, belting out the same two sea shanties all the way. But he was always the outsider, the Caliban we fled when things got scary. My mother was our harbor. She was all we needed to divine—and forgive—my father's mysteries. He loved us, of course, but in a growly, jokey, ceremonial way, since real feelings had already been proven to hurt too much. And this got worse as time went on. I remember being held by him when I was six or so, but not much later. When he and my mother met me at the airport after my first semester at Sewanee, I tried to hug him, but his arm shot out instead for a blustery handshake, as if to say, *Please, son, no closer, no closer.*

After that, I stopped trying.

"You have reached the Noones. At the tone, you have sixty seconds to leave a message."

Pap's new machine threw me. It was weird to hear his antebellum voice in such a postmodern context. And weirder yet to think that "the Noones" meant him and Darlie Giesen, a classmate of mine in high school, circa 1962. December had met and courted May several years after my mother died of breast cancer in 1979. Now they owned a condo on the Battery in Charleston, the very spot where the first shots of the Civil War were fired. The very spot, I might add with no small degree of irony, where the third

Gabriel Noone first discovered the pleasures of sucking cock.

"Hey," I told the machine, "it's Gabriel. Anna says you're heading west. That's great. It's a real busy time for me, but maybe we can have dinner or something. I'm here most of the time, writing away, so . . . call when you can."

When I put the receiver down, Anna was smirking at me.

"Not a word out of you," I said.

"They don't know about Jess, do they?"

"No."

"Are you gonna tell 'em?"

I shrugged. "What's to tell? I don't know myself."

"Won't they wonder, if he's not here?"

I told her they might not be coming to the house, that we might just meet somewhere for dinner. But what I was thinking was: Jess could be home in two weeks, and everything could be fine.

Back then, when the pain was new, I let myself believe that.

Three

Life Isn't Radio

Two days after his twelfth birthday, a fortnight before his father was jailed for debt, Charles Dickens was sent to work in a blacking factory. There, in a rat-infested room by the docks, he sat for twelve hours a day, labelling boot polish and learning the pain of abandonment. While he never spoke publicly of this ordeal, it would always be with him: in his social conscience and burning ambition, in the hordes of innocent children who languished and died in his fiction.

Pete thinks we all have a blacking factory: some awful moment, early on, when we surrender our childish hearts as surely as we lose our baby teeth. And the outcome can't be called. Some of us end up like Dickens, others like Jeffrey Dahmer. It's not a question of good or evil, Pete believes. Just the random brutality of the universe and our native ability to withstand it.

Is that true? I couldn't say. I do know it was Dickens who sprang to mind when I first heard Pete's voice on the phone. It was more childlike than I'd imagined, but scrappy as all get-out, like some latter-day urchin pick-pocket. The Artful Dodger by way of Bart Simpson.

"This is Pete Lomax. The guy who wrote that book? My mom said I should call you."

Thrown by his voice, and unsure of the tone I should take, I poured out my praise for *The Blacking Factory*. I was probably stiffer than usual—I'm sure I was, in fact—but I did my best to be specific, citing themes and passages, the rhythm of his language: the sorts of things I like to hear. I wanted him to feel the impact of what he had done, the enormity of it.

But there was no response at all.

"Pete?"

"Yeah?"

"Did I lose you?"

More empty air, and then: "You swear it's you?"

I chuckled. "It ain't Tallulah Bankhead."

"Who?"

"Just . . . somebody. Why would it not be me?"

"I dunno. You don't sound like yourself."

How odd to think that radio had already given Pete some concept of how I should sound, some feel for what "myself" should be. And odder still that he might have noticed the same hollow note that had sabotaged my last recording session. I wasn't at all prepared for such scrutiny.

"Life isn't radio," I said, condescending shamelessly even as I evaded him. "I'm slightly less dramatic in person."

"Oh."

"I sound . . . different to you?"

"Yeah."

"Like . . . how?"

39

"Like hammered shit."

I laughed uneasily. "That pins it down pretty well."

"No offense."

"'Course not."

"I just . . . I can't fucking believe it's you."

"Well," I said, after a moment, "you'll just fucking have to."

Pete released a torrent of childish giggles that belied all the grownup language that had come before. "Sorry," he said eventually. "My mom says I got a trashy mouth."

"She's fucking right."

He giggled even harder, then pleaded with me to stop.

"Why?" I said. "Gimme one fucking reason." I was enjoying myself immensely.

Then I heard a muffled clunk, which I took to be the phone dropping. And movement of some sort. And the sound of labored breathing.

"Pete?"

Nothing.

"Pete?"

"It's okay," he said. "Stupid tubes."

An image came instantly into my head: a small, ruined body strung up like a marionette, struggling desperately to breathe while I was busy being clever. "God, Pete, I'm sorry."

"No. It's cool."

"You sure?"

"Yeah."

I listened for his breathing. It seemed to be regular again. "What happened?"

"I just knocked the damn thing, that's all. They're draining my lungs."

"I see."

"Sounds worse than it is."

"What is it? Pneumocystis?"

"Yeah. As usual."

"What about a prophylaxis? Septra or something?"

"Not for somebody my age."

"Oh."

"That shit's so boring, anyway. Let's talk about something else. Do you have an E-mail address?"

"I don't, actually."

"But you've got your own Web site."

"Yeah, but Jess does that. I don't even know how to find it. I use my computer as a word processor."

"But E-mail is so easy, man."

"I know, and I plan to learn very soon. Just not right now. There's not enough room in my head."

"I could teach you," Pete offered eagerly. "I taught Warren, and he's pretty out of it, too."

"Thank you," I said dryly. "Who's Warren?"

"My AIDS counselor."

"Oh, sure." Pete had written at length about this man, a social worker in his forties—gay and HIV positive—who had helped to ease him back into the land of the living.

"Warren's a big fan of yours, too. We listened to *Noone at Night* together all the time."

"At the hospital, you mean?"

"No. Later. When I was home. The first time I heard you I was . . . you know . . . alone." His voice quavered on the last word, speaking volumes in the silence that followed.

"You okay?" I asked.

"I can't believe it, that's all."

"What?"

41

"That I'm talking to you, man."

His worshipful tone unsettled me, so I tried to de-personalize the moment. "That's what books do, you know. They put you out there to the world. You never know who you're reaching. Wait'll your book's published. You'll see. You'll be hearing from everybody."

"Right."

"I mean it. Who would you like to hear from?"

"I dunno."

"C'mon. There must be somebody you've always wanted to meet." I was talking down to him, I realized, but I couldn't help it. It was safer somehow to deal with a child than to address the wise and battered old soul I had met in *The Blacking Factory*.

"I wouldn't mind hearing from Cal Ripken," he said.

"Awriight."

"You know who that is?"

"Well, yeah. Sure. Sort of."

"Who, then?"

"He's a . . . sports guy."

Pete snorted. "You big homo."

"Excuse me?"

That schoolroom giggle erupted again. "What sport?"

"Jeez," I said. "Get picky on me now."

"Don't you even *look* at the sports section?"

"No," I said. "I throw it out first thing, along with the business section."

"Man."

"I tell you what else. I would order a paper *without* a sports section if they had one."

"Well, 'scuse the fuck outa me."

Now I was laughing.

"Warren's the same way," he said.

"Is he?"

"I told him: 'Just 'cause you're a dicksmoker don't mean you can't watch a ball game sometimes.'"

"A what?" I asked.

"A ball game."

"No. Before that."

"What? Dicksmoker? You never heard that?"

"No," I said, chuckling.

"Shit, man. Where you been?"

"I dunno. Smokin' dicks, I guess."

He giggled again. "I got lots of stuff like that. Really cool stuff. Expressions and all."

"I bet you do."

"Okay, okay," he said, and for a moment I thought he was still talking to me, but then came another wheezy interlude and the cold squeal of metal, and I realized some sort of adjustment was being made, either to him or his bed or the apparatus draining his lungs. I asked if this was a bad time to talk.

"My mom is here," he explained. "Bein' a big pain."

"Hey," came a woman's voice softly scolding him.

"This is him," he told her. "Say something."

Whereupon Donna came on the line. "Hello, Him," she said. Her voice was honeyed oak, as sturdy as it was warm. Odd as it seems now, I felt instantly at ease with her, as if we'd been gabbing on the phone for years, sharing everything.

"Thanks for arranging this," I said.

"Oh, please. You did *me* the favor. I'll be hearing about this for months, believe me."

"Well . . . glad to be of service."

"We're doing the yucky stuff now. If I'd known he was gonna call you I would've told him to hold off a tad longer."

I said I understood completely.

"You're his favorite writer, you know."

"Well, he's mine," I said. "From now on."

"C'mon."

"I mean it. Ashe didn't exaggerate a bit."

"Oh, God, really? That's so great."

She was clearly pleased, but she sounded distracted. In light of "the yucky stuff" at hand and the complications I'd already caused, I thought it wise to sign off. "Look," I told her, "I'll call back later."

"You don't have to. You've done plenty."

"I'd like to. If it's okay."

"Of course. If you're sure it isn't . . ."

"I'm sure," I said.

Donna gave me their phone number. I read it back to her twice, slowly, as if it were a private line to Camp David, or, back in the old days, the unlisted number of some really hot guy I'd met at the baths.

There are moments, I think, when you actually *feel* your life changing, when you can all but hear the clumsy clank and bang of fate's machinery.

Four

Roughhousing

"Guess I was right, huh?"

My bookkeeper was up in the window, calling down to the hot tub, where I floated naked and bereft, feeling sorry for myself in the least pitiable of places. It was four o'clock and foggy; the shampooey spice of the eucalyptus trees was drifting down from the woods.

"About what?" I asked.

"That book."

"Oh, yeah. You were, actually." I didn't have a clue as to how she'd deduced this.

"There's a message on your machine," Anna explained, "from somebody who's gotta be the author. Except that he sounds about ten."

My sodden heart stirred like some half-dead creature on a beach. "What did he say?"

"Want me to play it for you?"

"Yeah. If you would."

Anna left the window and returned moments later

with the answering machine, which she set on the sill. I noticed something flicker in her dark hair: a streak of electric magenta that hadn't been there on her last visit. It seemed out of character somehow, even for someone so certifiably young; Anna was such a no-nonsense sort of person.

Then Pete's voice settled on me like the song of a small, gray bird: "Hey, dude. I just wanted to thank you for reading my book. I hope you're doin' okay. You sounded kind of weird on the phone. No offense or anything. You don't have to call back, unless you want to, but you better want to, you big dicksmoker. You know where to find me, unless I'm out Rollerblading with the Spice Girls. Yeah right, Lomax, dream on. Okay, that's all, take it easy, man."

Silence consumed the garden again. Anna just stood there, gazing down at me expectantly.

"Thanks," I said.

She blinked at me a moment longer, then left the window. I knew I owed her an explanation, but I just couldn't do it. Even now, it seemed patently disloyal to launch a new story with anyone other than Jess. I needed him here to make it real for me, to trim its ragged edges and file it on the proper shelf, before I could offer it for general consumption.

I sank into the velvety curve of the wood and let the warm water hold me. The little beige bromine floater drifted by, then nudged my shoulder like a puppy wanting attention. I pushed it away, lost in a sudden flashback. We had been here together, a year or so earlier, soaking under an out-of-focus moon, when Jess turned and studied the slope behind us. "This is where I want my ashes to go," he said. His tone had been casual and informative, the one he would use in bookstores, say, when pointing out some other author's enviable new dump bin. So I looked into those buried blue eyes and tried to divine their message. Don't make a fuss over this, they seemed to be saying, and I understood immediately. For he had given me something so huge and enduring that nothing less than silence could ever contain it.

"You got it," I said, and we left it at that.

As I passed the office in my bathrobe I complimented Anna on her snappy new hair color. She turned from the computer with a crooked smile, as if to accept my subterranean apology. "It's the same as Pam's," she said.

"A friend?"

"No. On *The Real World*."

I still didn't get it.

"You know. Pedro Zamora's housemate? MTV?"

"Oh, yeah. Of course."

"It's D'or's idea mostly."

I drew another blank.

"My other mother. My mom's partner? She was a model back in the seventies, and she's always giving me fashion tips. Whether I want 'em or not. She makes me feel like Eurasian Barbie."

I shrugged. "You could say no."

"Oh, I don't care. It's no big deal. It's just hair and stuff. And she just started doing it. I wasn't, like, you know, JonBenet Ramsey or anything."

Her breezy gothicism made me smile, then sent my thoughts hurtling back to Pete. Amazingly, it seemed to do the same for Anna. She paused, apparently weighing her words, then cast me a look of sweet contrition.

47

"I guess I shouldn't have checked your machine?"

I felt like such a bully. My ham-handed effort at saving the story for Jess had apparently come off like an accusation of eavesdropping. "Oh, no," I said. "Check anything you want. It would help, really. I'm not on the planet right now. There aren't any state secrets on that thing. Trust me."

Anna was still looking chastised. "Jess thought there might be a message from your accountant."

My breathing must have come to a standstill. "You talked to him?"

"Your accountant?"

"No. Jess."

"Yeah," she said cautiously.

"When?"

"This morning. That was okay, wasn't it?"

"Of course."

"He was worried about your quarterlies. They're coming up next week."

My heart turned to goo at the thought that Jess was still looking out for me, even from a distance. Oh sweetie, I thought, you know this is forever, so just stop this bullshit and come home before we break something that can't be fixed. I was tempted to grill Anna further, but I resisted on her behalf. "That would be a help," I said finally. "If you'd talk to my accountant, I mean." I started to leave and then stopped. "He's thirteen, by the way."

"Your accountant?"

I smiled. "The boy on the phone."

Her eyes widened. "Really?"

"He lives in Milwaukee and he's had a really shitty life and he writes like an angel."

"It didn't depress you?"

"What do you mean?"

"You said it depresses you when other people are brilliant."

I'm sure I must have reddened a little. "This is different."

"Why?"

I hesitated. "I don't know exactly." You do too, I told myself. Tell her at least part of the truth. It won't queer things with Jess if you share this with somebody else. It won't affect the outcome one way or the other.

So I spilled a few of the beans: "I guess he sort of has a thing about me."

Her brow furrowed gravely. "A thing?"

"Oh, God, no," I said, catching her train of thought. "He's one of my listeners."

"Oh."

"He thinks of me . . . kind of like a father."

"Why?"

It was embarrassing to explain things in my own words, but I did my best. "He was laid up in the hospital during a bad time, when he was sort of shut off from the world. And the sound of my voice was like . . . you know, the father he never had. Well, he had one, actually, but he was a monster."

Anna, to my discomfort, was still frowning. "He told you all that?"

"Not on the phone. In the book."

"Oh." She weighed that for a moment. "That's kind of intimidating."

"How so?"

"I just mean . . . well, it's a big compliment, Gabriel, but it's really intense for somebody to lay that on you."

I resisted the notion that some worrisome new burden had been dumped in my lap. Pete himself had never come close to suggesting as much. "He didn't lay anything on me," I said calmly. "I know he sounds like some tragic waif, but he's not. He's really bright and funny, and he can hold his own with grownups. The father thing was just something he shared, that's all. It didn't come with any strings attached. Really." Even to my own ears, this declaration sounded anxious and overstated, so I abandoned it immediately. "I'm done with the galleys," I said, "if you'd like to look at them."

"Thanks," said Anna, turning back to the computer. "I've got too much reading for school already."

That night I cooked myself a real meal—my first since Jess had left. Hugo smelled the chicken roasting and made his way stiffly down the stairs, obviously expecting to share in this bonanza. I could hardly refuse him; taste was his last surviving sense, the only cheap thrill he had left. I tossed a chunk of meat on the porch and watched as he tore into it like a *T. rex*, mumbling lasciviously under his breath. Then I collapsed on the sofa and lit my first joint in weeks.

It wasn't like me to have gone without grass that long. I've been a confirmed pothead half my life, finding release in my nightly joint the way the other Gabriel Noones have found it in their bourbon. But I also know that dope erases nothing, merely underscores that which is already there. Now that Jess was gone I was wary of facing my solitude stoned. Who knew what fresh terrors might emerge in the widescreen version of my grief?

But something had changed already. My one conversation with Pete had brought me the childish consolations of laughter and spontaneity. I wanted more of that, I guess, so I convinced myself—only moments before I called him—that a toke or two couldn't hurt.

He answered on the fourth ring, his voice small and tentative, like an engine that hadn't yet warmed up. "Hello."

"It's Gabriel, Pete."

A pause and then: "Oh, hi, Gabe."

"Make it Gabriel, okay?"

"What?"

"I'm not real big on that nickname."

"Well, 'scuse the fuck outa me."

"Hey," I said, "I wouldn't tell you if I didn't want us to be friends." I explained to him that the people closest to me never call me Gabe, that the surest indicator of a complete stranger is anyone who flings that nickname around as if we've known each other forever.

"But half the things I've ever read . . ."

"I know. They're wrong."

"What does Jess call you?"

"Gabriel."

"No he doesn't."

"Pete . . ."

"He calls you Sweetie or Babe." The boy's tone was triumphant. "Am I right?"

"Well . . . yeah. Sometimes." Not lately, I thought. Not for this hellish eternity of a fortnight. And here we were on the subject I had desperately hoped to bury—at least for the evening. Already I regretted that joint.

"Wanna know how I know?" asked Pete.

"Know what?"

"That he calls you that."

"How?"

"Because Jamie calls Will that on *Noone at Night*."

51

"Clever."

"I thought so."

"Except that those guys aren't us."

"Says who?"

"Says the guy who wrote it."

"But you met him on a tour of Alcatraz, right? With all those little Catholic girls?"

"Not really."

"That didn't happen?"

"Well . . . it happened, yes . . . but after the fact."

"What do you mean?"

"I thought it would be a fun way for Jamie and Will to meet. So Jess and I took the tour and got locked up in solitary together. And we were in there with all these schoolgirls in their silly little plaid skirts, which I thought was perfect, so I used it. I just let it be what happened."

"Well, fuck."

"Hey, it's a *story*, Pete."

"How did you meet, then?"

"Up at his college." A formidable sheepshank was tightening in my chest. "Why?"

"No reason. I just like real stuff, that's all."

I thought I detected a whiff of reprimand, but I let it pass. "He was running a gay group," I said, "and he invited me up to speak to them."

"Up where?"

"Oregon. Eugene."

"He's younger than you, right?"

"About fifteen years."

"No shit."

"It's not that big a difference." Oh, really now? I thought. How would you know, you deluded old thing? You didn't even see this coming.

"Oh, yeah," said Pete. "I remember now. It doesn't matter because you guys are the same gay age."

This was really something, I thought. And it bordered on intimidating. The kid knew my life so well he could toss my own tired catchphrases back at me. "Where'd you hear that?"

"I read it. In the *Journal* last fall. Warren showed it to me. It's kind of a cool theory."

The "theory" had been around for years, a well-worn chestnut in my media repertoire. It went like this: Jess and I were *technically* fifteen years apart, but we had come out at roughly the same time. (Jess had been sixteen; I'd been thirty.) This meant we'd reached the same level in our personal growth—that is, the same "gay age"—which was far more pertinent to our compatibility than our chronological difference. It was Jess, I think, who invented this little spiel, but I had embraced it completely. We would trot it out for reporters on a moment's notice, locking eyes in the process with a tenderness that seduced everyone, ourselves most of all.

"What *don't* you know about me?" I asked Pete.

"Fuck if I know."

"What do you mean?"

"Well, you make up so much shit."

"Right," I replied. "And there's a warning about it in the front of all my books. It says, 'This is a work of fiction.'"

"Don't you ever wanna write about your own life?"

"Sometimes," I said. "Then I get over it."

"Why?"

I thought about this for a moment. "Too many responsibilities, I guess."

"To what?"

53

"To telling the truth . . . to not hurting people."

"Who would you hurt?"

"The truth always hurts somebody."

"But it's *your* life."

"So?"

"Well, that means you have the right to claim it. If it happened to you, then it belongs to you. No matter what it is. That's what Mom said."

We had moved onto dangerous ground, I realized. The boy must have clung to this adage as he hammered out the details of his own torment. I didn't want to undermine his fragile new belief system. "Your mom was right," I said. "It does belong to you. But it takes courage to own it in public. Maybe more than I have. That's why I admire what you did, Pete."

"You could do it, too."

"I don't think so."

"Your life was worse?"

"God, no. Not even close."

"Why not, then?"

"Because I'm always too aware of the effect I'm making. I'm afraid people will lose interest if I don't keep tap-dancing. My whole mechanism is about charming people. And fixing things that can't be fixed. That's why I tell stories: it helps me create order where none exists. So I jiggle stuff around until it makes sense to me and I can see a pattern. Then I split myself up into a dozen different people and let *them* tell the truth. It's not very brave, Pete. In fact, it's pretty cowardly."

"You wrote about being gay. That wasn't cowardly."

"And what a perfect little fag I was, too. With the perfect witticisms and the perfect relationship."

"You weren't so perfect to me."

"Oh, really?"

"No . . . you were like . . . really insecure. You thought everything was about you, even when it wasn't. And you treated Jamie . . . or Jess or whoever the fuck it was . . . like he was already dead or something."

This hit me like a two-by-four across the face. "You don't say."

"Yeah. And that shit gets old, man."

"I guess so."

"But it felt like the truth. It felt like I knew you."

There was barely a breath left in me. "Maybe you knew somebody I didn't know."

"C'mon."

"I mean it. I don't see myself very clearly."

"Then look at the people who love you. That's what Mom says when I get . . . you know, confused and shit. Look into their eyes and see what they're seeing; that's all you need to know about yourself."

By now there were tears scalding my cheeks, and there was nothing I could do but let it happen. I had arrived without ceremony at the place I had feared the most. Holding the phone away, I took broad angry swipes at my eyes and tried to collect myself.

"Gabriel?"

"Yeah, I'm here."

"You okay, man?"

"No. Not really."

"If I said something that—"

"No, Pete, no. It wasn't you."

"Then why . . . "

"Jess moved out last week. He wants to be by himself for a while. I'm not really sure if . . ." I couldn't finish, as well as I knew this speech. My grievances seemed so paltry and self-indulgent when recited to a thirteen-year-old who'd been fucked by his father and sold into prostitution. There he lay, scaffolded in chrome and entangled in tubes, while a melodramatic old queen whimpered away about losing his warm-and-fuzzy. It wasn't the way it was supposed to be.

But Pete was already on the case. "Do you know why he left?"

"No," I said. "Not completely."

"What *do* you know?"

I couldn't let him take me there. "Pete, look . . . this is sweet, but—"

"Fuck you, I'm not sweet! Talk to me, man."

I hesitated a moment. "I'm just not comfortable with that, Pete."

"Why?"

"I just . . ."

"Because I'm not a dicksmoker?"

I startled myself with a noise that resembled laughter. "No. It's just that it's kind of personal and . . . you know, sexual. I don't think it's really appropriate, considering."

"Considering what?"

I didn't have an answer ready.

"Are you calling me a kid or something?"

"No. Well, yeah, I guess I am."

"You think I don't know about that shit?"

"Pete . . ."

"I bet I know more than you do."

This was more than boyish bluster, of course. I'd read Pete's book, after all. My sex life was a mere skirmish compared to the world war he had endured for the past six years. Why was I trying to protect him? And from what? My feeble little French-vanilla existence?

56

"Anyway," said Pete, "I might as well be gay. My ward was nothing but gay guys. And half those other jackoffs *thought* I was gay."

"Who?"

"At the hospital. The pediatric AIDS people. They got all these shrinks and social workers, and they ask you all this shit, but all they wanna know is if you liked it."

"Liked what?"

"Takin' it up the butt."

"Jesus, Pete."

"I'm just tellin' ya."

"They didn't *ask* you that, did they?"

"Not like that, no. But that's what they wanna know."

"But why on earth would it—"

"Get a clue, man. They want their little AIDS babies to be pure and innocent. Transfusion cases and IV mothers, shit like that. It makes 'em nervous when you get it the way I did. They gotta make sure you weren't havin' a good time. Put you in the right fuckin' room."

As medieval as this sounded, I could believe it. "What did your mom say?"

"She said I was twelve, and I didn't have to be anything, or tell 'em anything. Except to give me my fuckin' meds and fuck off."

"Good answer."

Pete laughed. "Except she didn't say fuck."

"I figured."

"So they put me in the fag ward with six other guys. And I was next to this big queen named Chico who thought he was Mariah Carey or somethin' and made bras and shit out of his pillowcases."

"I think I know him."

57

"No way!"

"I'm joking, Pete."

"Jesus, man. Don't do that to me."

"Sorry."

"I hated that dude. He stole my chocolate pudding."

"I see what you mean."

"He didn't like you either."

"*Me?*"

"On the radio. He hated your show. He always wanted me to turn it off. He thought you sounded like Colonel Kangaroo."

"Captain."

"What?"

"It was *Captain* Kangaroo. He said that, huh? That I sounded like him?"

"Yep."

"What an asshole."

Pete giggled. "I'm tellin' ya, man. He was bad news. So why did he leave?"

"Who?"

"Jess."

I hesitated, then told him there were a number of reasons.

"Name one."

I drew a breath wearily, then took the plunge. "He wanted rougher sex."

"S and M, you mean?"

"Yeah."

"He wanted you to hurt him?"

"No. Just make-believe. It's not at all like . . . Look, Pete, I just don't think . . ."

"But you're good at make-believe."

"Not that kind . . . all those props and poses. I don't disapprove or anything; grownups can do what they

58

want. I just can't take it very seriously. It's not what I'm after in the long run."

A silence followed, then Pete asked: "You cryin' again?"

"No."

"What else?"

"With Jess, you mean?"

"Yeah."

"Oh . . . it's just me, I guess. The truth is, I'm not that versatile in the sack."

"Meaning?"

"Let's just leave it . . ."

"Gabriel!"

"I'm not into fucking, all right?"

That stopped him cold for a moment. "What do you do, then?"

I found myself turning defensive on the spot, since even this abused child seemed baffled by my sexual deficiencies. "Lots of things," I replied. "Well, not lots, but . . . Pete, I'm not ready to . . ."

"Dicksmoking, huh?"

"Yeah. Absolutely."

"What else?"

"Jerking off and touching. And lots of kissing. I love kissing."

"*Kissing?*"

"Yeah. Sure."

"During *sex*?"

It made terrible sense that this would seem odd to Pete. He'd been nothing more than an object in all those pedophile games. A living sex toy.

And no one kisses a toy.

* * *

59

It was kissing I'd missed the most. His lips were so full and sculpted, and they could fine-tune every part of me until I was goofy with pleasure and gasping in his arms. Sometimes, to my amazement, I'd end up jerking off with my toes in his mouth, those faded-denim eyes gazing up at me with slavish devotion. Or he'd work my nipples like a ravenous baby, murmuring, "Sir, yessir, yessir," until I came with a fury, feeling the rough hemp of his chest across my belly, that silken cock against my leg, or in my astonished hand. It was leisurely, custom-made lust, the kind that can happen after years of knowing someone. But my fulfillment was so important to Jess that I found it all too easy to mistake it for his own.

In the beginning my excuse was safe sex. Jess cared deeply that he not infect me, so I took the easy way out. Long before we met I had accepted my disinterest in fucking, though I had always felt something less than a true fag for my failure to achieve either top- or bottom-hood. Suddenly there was a reason to keep things oral and manual, a solid *political* reason to formalize my limited repertoire. And Jess played along. Whenever we discussed our sex life in interviews, we invariably sounded like poster boys for Responsible Behavior. The human mind, we would say, was the greatest sex organ of them all. People who required penetration at any cost were merely lacking in imagination. Visuals were the key, after all, and the act of withholding could be extremely erotic.

And so on.

It wasn't that Jess didn't mean it. He did; we both did. Our sex life *was* extraordinary, and all the more so because Jess usually chose the most highly charged moment to tell me he loved me. But there must have been times when he longed for the unedited rough-housing of his early youth, the very acts of raw abandon that had given him the virus in the first place. I could have provided that certainly, one way or another, with little danger to either of us, but I chose to wallow in my own contentment.

When the transformation came it was almost a Jekyll-and-Hyde thing. Jess had been taking testosterone for energy, and the hormones had begun to forge his softly sensual body into an exoskeleton of muscle. Then he shaved off all his thinning baby-chick hair and grew a beard. And got a tattoo. And began to assemble a formidable leather wardrobe. And while such makeovers are common around here, this one filled me with dread, because I knew that Jess wasn't reinventing himself for me; in fact, my opinion in the matter was never solicited. When I stumbled across a thin gold ring at the base of his scrotum and wondered out loud why he hadn't mentioned it, he shrugged it off as unworthy of comment, as if he'd merely had his sideburns trimmed. I, in turn, felt old and disconnected. And slightly ashamed for having implied, however unintentionally, that his body was under my jurisdiction.

Meanwhile Jess had assembled a whole new circle of friends. Guys he had met at ACT-UP and his HIV support group. Guys with daunting four-gauge earrings like his, who joined him for coffee at the Pasqua in the Castro to discuss Jung and Joseph Campbell. They were nice guys, Jess told me, but I rarely met them, since Jess never brought them to the house. Until now our friends had been largely mutual; we had cultivated them together as couples often do. This new arrangement unsettled me, but I struggled against my doubts.

Jess, after all, had been my satellite for ten years without complaint. I knew that he needed a crowd in which he could be judged on his own, beyond the distracting glare of my celebrity. And he certainly needed the company of others who had defied a death sentence. I could never give him that, I knew, no matter how much I loved him.

Then one day, when we were driving home from lunch in Berkeley, Jess turned to me with a sickly little smile I had never seen him use. "What would you say," he asked, "if we started having sex with other people?" My reaction alarmed even me: a flood of tears that wouldn't stop. Jess's expression, I saw to my horror, became one of pained compassion. How difficult this moment must have been for him, I thought, and how terribly important. And I knew with a certainty there was no taking it back; the desire once voiced was as good as the deed. Our fortress had been stormed, right there on that gray stretch of freeway, and the damage was irreversible.

Worst of all, I didn't know myself anymore. Who was this fool weeping over sex? I had been a regular tart until I met Jess. A night of dick worship at the glory holes had meant less to me than a handshake. Only straight people, I believed, confused lasting love with a good time. Gay folks—or most of the men, at least—knew better, and were therefore capable of owning the whole package: adventure *and* commitment. Jess and I had even flirted with the idea of three-ways early in our relationship, snickering drunkenly over prospective candidates at a restaurant in Key West one balmy night. We had certainly never committed to monogamy in any formal way; it was just something we fell into with deceptive ease. All we'd ever promised, really, was honesty. So when an overly earnest reporter used the M-word to describe our relationship in the "Couples" section of *People*, Jess flew into a righteous rage: "Where the fuck does she get off?"

"But we *are* monogamous," I said, laughing.

"She doesn't know that. We never told her. And she has no fucking right to *presume*."

"You're right," I said. "It's a vicious libel. Call the lawyers."

It was funny at the time: two homos in a huff over the disgrace of monogamy. But I remember feeling uncomfortable, too. For, beyond all that sex-positive posturing, Jess seemed unduly concerned that someone might hold him to a contract he had never agreed to sign. Which was what I was doing, I guess.

Oh, I tried like hell not to. Before that ghastly car ride was over I had promised to give the matter serious thought. I needed time to adjust, I told him. I knew it *should* be possible, if two people really trusted each other. And if rougher sex was required, then maybe Jess could have an occasional night out at a club. I forced myself to imagine such a scenario; it was almost manageable as long as I kept the place heavily populated and overly stylized: whips and dildos and masters barking orders like robots.

But what if there was more to it? What if there was cuddling afterward? Or a dinner date the following night?

Or *kissing*, for God's sake?

"You know what?" said Pete. "None of this means shit."

63

I was back in the conversation again, but I wasn't sure where. "None of what?"

"This sex stuff. Forget about it."

"I wish I could."

"He's coming home, Gabriel."

"I can't say that for sure."

"Maybe *you* can't. But I can."

"Pete . . ."

"He's your buddy, man. He's family. I know you guys. And I know when somebody loves somebody."

This was the simple truth, without frills, offered up in a tone of mild annoyance. I began to cry again, in spite of myself.

"Jesus," he said. "Will you stop?"

"I'm just agreeing with you."

"Well, argue a little, then."

"You know," I said, "you and Jess are a lot alike."

"Pissed off, you mean?"

I laughed. "Not just that."

"I feel like I know him."

"In a way," I said, "you do."

Pete snorted. "I thought he wasn't the guy in your books. Okay, okay, in a minute."

This response confused me until I realized he wasn't addressing me.

"The boss lady is on my case," he explained.

I glanced across the room and tried, unsuccessfully, to read the digits on the VCR clock. "Oh, God, it's late, isn't it? I forgot. I'm sorry. How much later is it there? Three hours?"

"Two," he answered. "And I stay up late all the time. I listen to your show, remember?"

"Tell your mother it's my fault."

"She doesn't care. She's cool about everything."

I heard Donna utter a comic growl.

"Go to bed," I said. "We'll talk later."

"Promise?"

"Scout's honor."

Pete giggled and hung up.

The next morning, when I was cleaning out the coffee machine, Donna called back.

"Hey," she said pleasantly. "Sorry I cut it short last night."

I told her she had no reason to apologize.

"He'd had an awfully long day of it. We were up at five with the lungs again. They just don't want to stay clear."

"God, Donna . . . I'm so sorry."

"Well, what can you do? He had a bad case of syphilis when he was ten, so his lungs are like Swiss cheese. If it weren't for that, we'd have a much easier time with the pneumonia. He's pretty hardy otherwise." She paused for a moment. "He's not being a pain, is he?"

"What do you mean?"

"You know . . . calling you."

I told her I was the one who had called him.

"Well . . . just tell him to cool it if it gets too much for you. He can be pretty overbearing sometimes."

I wondered how much she'd heard of our conversation, or how much Pete had told her afterward, but I really didn't care; I felt as comfortable with her as I did with Pete. "It's no problem," I said. "He's good company."

"Funny little dude, isn't he? So brash and grownup, but just a kid underneath. One minute he's reading

Kübler-Ross, the next he's throwing mashed potatoes at the dog."

Kübler-Ross. The expert on dying.

"This must be so hard," I said, feeling a surge of sympathy for her situation.

"Oh, there's a lot of payback," she said. "Pete gives as much as any kid I've ever known. There are days when I can't believe my luck."

"But isn't it hard doing it on your own?"

"Without a husband, you mean?"

I was suddenly red-faced. "Well, no . . . not specifically a *husband* . . . I just meant . . ."

She laughed huskily. "I know most of the staff at the hospital by their first names. And my friend Marsha across the street helps out. Husbands, in my experience, are more trouble than they're worth."

As I recalled from Pete's book, Donna had divorced her only husband after three years. He had been a psychologist as well—in couples counseling, no less. How agonizing would that be, I wondered, to have two professional minds analyzing the same breakup? I didn't ask, though, for fear that Donna would ask about *my* husband. I felt much too raw-nerved to discuss it that morning.

"I guess you spend a lot of time at the hospital," I said.

"Some," she said, "but I've arranged for home care, too. It's such a long haul into Milwaukee."

"I thought you lived in Milwaukee."

"Not anymore. I wasn't comfortable with it."

"How so?"

"Too many chances for Pete to run into . . . them."

It took me a moment to absorb this. "Jesus, you mean his parents are still . . ."

"No. God, no. They're history. They're locked up. But most of their clients are still out there getting their jollies. And some of them are pretty pissed off that he broke up their party."

"But, couldn't the police . . ."

"Oh, get real, Gabriel!"

I laughed, since her tone had been friendly, and she laughed right back. That lovely golden rumble.

"The world's not as tidy as your stories," she said.

"Guess not."

"I wish it *were* . . . for what it's worth."

There was silence while this thought ascended.

"So here we are in lovely Wysong, Wisconsin—home of Neilson's Antique Auto Barn."

I laughed. "Culture shock, huh?"

"It's not terrible," she said. "There's a lake just down from the house, and a nice anonymous mall that has everything we need."

"Are you worried that . . ." I didn't know how to finish this.

"That they might find him and . . . do something?"

"Yeah."

"Sometimes. Not often, really. But I have to remember it's possible. They're a club, you know. With their own chat rooms and everything. And they don't like it when people snitch."

"Do you know who they are?"

"No. Pete could identify *some* of them, I'm sure, but he shouldn't have to. Not now, not anymore. He did his job when he turned his parents in. That was enough hell for a lifetime. Now I just want him to feel safe."

"But when the book is published . . ."

"Well, that's why he never mentions Wysong. Or his birth name, for that matter. We've worked all this out with Ashe Findlay. I think we've covered all the bases."

Another silence, and then: "Anyway, the point of moving here was *not* to be paranoid. To get the scary stuff behind us."

"I understand."

"I'm glad you're in his life, Gabriel. You're a good man. I want him to know that grownups can be trusted."

Two days later, a manila envelope arrived from Wysong. I studied it like some sacred artifact, turning it over slowly in my hands, savoring the jangly Midwestern consonants of their address: 511 Henzke Street.

When I opened the envelope, out tumbled a kitschy postcard of Neilson's Antique Auto Barn, apparently photographed in the seventies, judging from the pantsuits on the tourists. On the back Donna had scrawled: "Okay, so it ain't the Guggenheim."

The other item was a photograph of Pete. He was standing in front of a garage door in jeans and a gray sweatshirt, a small-boned boy wearing a crooked smile beneath a tangle of black hair.

His eyes were his most arresting feature: a pale, glowing green that stopped you cold with their sheer unlikelihood. Like those pretty stones you find on the beach sometimes that prove, upon closer examination, to be fragments of a pop bottle, roughed up by the ocean.

Five

Semaphore

For my father and stepmother's visit I chose a fancy
new pan-Asian place on the Embarcadero. I chose it for
its big pink blowfish chandelier and the fact that the
maître d' would almost certainly make a fuss over me.
I was showing off, God help me, to a man I had battled
royally for half a century and a woman I barely recalled
from a high school trig class. They were *family*, for
what it was worth, Pap and Darlie; I wanted them to
see who I'd finally become, all these years later, since
I was no longer sure myself.

But the maître d' had called in sick that evening, so
we were greeted instead by one of those haughty,
terrified tartlets who guard the door at places like
Planet Hollywood. "Newman?" she asked with a
frown, scanning her reservations list.

"Noone," I said as genially as possible. "Gabriel."

"Oh. Gabriel is the last name?"

"No. Noone is the last name." Get me a homosexual,

I thought. Find me a cocksucker immediately.

"Oh," she said at last. "I think there's a note here."

There *was* a note there, and she read every bit of it, too, as evidenced by the faint movement of her lips. Finally, she smiled and told us to follow her, her heels clicking smartly on the tile floor as she explained about the maître d's illness. I saw to my relief that we were headed for the far end of the restaurant, where two banquettes—the best in the house—commanded a stunning view of the Bay Bridge.

"Goddamn," said my father, when the bridge was all his for the evening. "Just look at that, would you?"

"It used to be blocked," I explained.

"What?" asked Darlie.

"The view. There was a freeway here, so all this was a cave, and you couldn't see the bridge at all. And these places on the waterfront were really scuzzy, the cheapest real estate in town. But the earthquake messed up the freeway so badly that they had to—"

"Oh, God," said Darlie. "When all those people were crushed?"

"No, not that one . . . same time, but not here. That was the Nimitz freeway. Across the bay."

"Thank God," she murmured. An odd reaction, but I knew what she meant. I had always been rather relieved myself that those ghosts had been confined to Oakland. We had enough ghosts as it was.

"What people were crushed?" asked my father.

"You know," said Darlie. "In the earthquake."

"Hell, how old do you think I am?"

"The *other* one," said Darlie, rolling her eyes at her husband.

"The other what?"

"Earthquake."

"There was another one?"

"In eighty-nine," I offered, growing uneasy. I hadn't seen Pap in three years. Maybe he'd finally begun to lose it; lots of folks did at his age. "You were here just after it happened. After your trip to—"

"*Eighty-nine?*" My father's face clenched in confusion. "Mama was born in eighty-nine, for God's sake! I sure as hell wasn't around then."

"Oh, just quit it, Gabriel." Darlie shot a non-poisonous dagger at him, then turned back to me. "He's just teasing. He's doing his Alzheimer's routine. It's his favorite new joke."

One glance at Pap proved the truth of this. His eyes were lit with sly conspiracy, a sight that filled me with unexpected nostalgia. Joking had always been his way of avoiding intimacy, when anger wasn't available. He looks just like me, I thought, studying his old face as if he were a newborn in my arms. He had my jawline and jowls, my droopy blue eyes, the same full silky head of hair, only white instead of gray. Here sat my past and my future, my inevitable twin, the face I was melting into with fierce efficiency. God help us, I thought. Someone left the cake out in the rain.

I turned back to Darlie, widening my eyes melodramatically. "Maybe it's not a routine. Maybe it's the real thing."

"Oh, go to hell, both of you!" The old man was in his element now, home free at last, swapping insults instead of endearments. "I remember that earthquake better than you do. We'd just got back from Kenya, and Darlie was wearing those ridiculous nigger clothes . . ."

"Gabriel!"

"Well, that's what they were. That ugly damn sarong thing with the turban." Pap turned to me. "And you

71

had that little place with all the stairs . . . over there with all the funny fellas."

I arched an eyebrow at my stepmother. "Gee. Wonder how I ended up *there*." In my father's eyes, his stalwart son would always be one thing, the funny fellas quite another.

"And Whatshisname showed us that big crack above your fireplace."

Whatshisname. The love of my life.

"I'm sorry he's out of town," said Darlie, looking at me so directly that I wondered if she sensed something was wrong.

I did my damnedest to stay casual. "Oh, I know. He is, too. It was a last-minute thing."

"You do a lot of business in L.A.?"

"A fair amount, yeah."

"And this was for what, you said?"

"A TV deal. He's producing a special for us."

"Sounds great," she said pleasantly.

"A special what?" My father, no longer the focus of our attention, was cruising for some friendly friction.

"I'm gonna do a reading on TV," I told him. (This part was true, at least; Jess had been planning the special for months.) "Sort of a dramatized thing. With an armchair and a set. Like Alistair Cooke on *Masterpiece Theatre*. People will actually get to see me this time."

"Well, lucky them."

There was a trace of malice in this, but I let it go with a tart smile. I knew it wasn't easy for Pap, having his name co-opted by such a conspicuous homo. I had been programmed to be *him*, after all: a partner in his bank, a conservative, a practicing aristocrat. But now, by his own account, he had become a road-show

72

version of me. Dewy-eyed shopgirls and waiters, clocking the name on his credit card, would ask him for his autograph only to discover he wasn't *the* Gabriel Noone. I liked to imagine this happening during one of his lunches with Strom Thurmond, when ol' Strom had been ranting away about the evils of the Gay Agenda. But the senator probably avoided the subject altogether, recognizing, in his gentlemanly way, the cross his old friend had to bear.

"We saw your books in Paris," my father said. "Big pile of 'em. Right there . . . you know . . . in that virgin place."

Darlie provided the translation: "The Virgin Megastore."

"Ah."

"I wanted the new Jimmy Buffett," she explained.

I gave her a private twinkle. "I thought maybe he was looking for Nine Inch Nails."

Darlie chuckled; my father's eyes narrowed. "What the hell does *that* mean?"

"Nothing, sweetness. It's just a musical group."

"Thank God. I thought you were talking about my prowess."

"No, believe me, nobody's talking about that."

"Did you tell the boy about . . . ?"

"No, I did not."

"Good."

"Why on earth would—"

"Remember ol' Hubie Verner?" My father leaned closer, clearly intent upon telling me himself. Whatever the hell it was.

"Yeah," I said carefully. "Your doctor. Or used to be."

"Still is," said Pap with a chuckle. "Must be ninety, if he's a day, but I'm still goin' to him."

Darlie rolled her eyes. "He's seventy-one, for God's sake. He's a lot younger'n you."

"Well, he *looks* ninety, poor bastard." My father leaned closer in a moment of man-to-man lechery. "Wrote me a prescription for that Viagra stuff. Damnedest thing you've ever seen."

"Gabriel . . ."

"Oh, hell, Darlie, he's a grown man."

"Nobody cares if—"

"*You* sure as hell cared. You were pretty damn impressed." He turned back to me, his face rosy with revelation. "Took me one when she was out shoppin' on the Rue de Rivoli. Had a big ol' surprise waitin' for her when she got back to the George Cinq."

My stepmother's expression was flawlessly deadpan. "Now *there's* an image we could all live without."

"Tell me," I said, offering her a crooked smile.

Darlie looked good for fifty-three, I thought. She had trimmed down considerably, and her strawberry-blond hair was cropped stylishly short. We had never been close, but I admired the way she let the old man's crap roll off her back. My mother had spent her marriage tiptoeing around his anger and intolerance, making endless excuses and hoping, I suppose, for a miraculous conversion. Darlie just saw Pap as something elemental and unavoidable, like hurricanes and pluff mud, to be endured with stoic humor.

Maybe it helped that Darlie wasn't one of us. She wasn't white trash, or even "common," as we used to say, but had I brought her home during high school, she would surely have been assessed as someone whose family didn't "go to the ball." Darlie's father had been a chief yeoman at the naval base, her mother a bank teller. Perfectly respectable, unless you grew up south of

Broad, where "nice folks" were ruthlessly delineated by their attendance at the St. Cecilia Ball. Nowadays Darlie was nice by marriage, but Pap behaved as if she'd been born to the job, and defied anyone—from any class—to suggest otherwise. No one in *his* family could ever be less than aristocratic, just as no one could really be gay. When the truth locked horns with my father's prejudices, it was always the truth that suffered.

"Sometimes," my sister, Josie, once remarked, "I wish I'd given him a black grandchild, just to see how he'd make it white."

Our food had arrived, but my father's eyes had wandered out to the Embarcadero. A line of signal flags—plastic and strictly decorative—was snapping in the night air like forgotten laundry.

"India, Echo, Charlie," I said.

"What?"

"Those three next to the lamppost. Right?"

Pap and I had both served in the navy, once upon a time. This was our common currency, so I doled it out judiciously whenever I wanted to feel closer to him. Thirty years earlier, I had written long letters home from Vietnam, shamelessly dramatizing my circumstances, just to make him proud of me. Nothing could soften his heart like the memory of war.

He squinted at the signal flags for a moment, then grunted. "Who the hell knows? That's why you got signalmen."

I turned to my stepmother. "He found out about me that way, you know."

Darlie looked puzzled. "That you were gay?"

"No," I said with a brittle laugh. "That I was born."

"Christ." My father flinched in delayed reaction to *that word*.

"He was on his minesweeper in . . . where was it, Pap?"

"Guadalcanal. Well . . . no, Florida Island, Tulagi . . ."

"Anyway, he got word from the flagship that I'd been born. And they had to use semaphore to do it."

"No kidding," said Darlie.

I always loved the romance of this: the blue water and blazing heat, a strapping young signalman in his white sailor suit, brandishing flags with the news of me. It was the South Pacific of Nellie Forbush and *Mr. Roberts*, a showbiz entrance if ever there was one.

"What was the message?" asked Darlie.

"Hell," said my father. "I don't remember."

"Yes, you do," I said. "'Baby born, mother and son fine.'"

"Yeah. Somethin' like that."

I wondered if I'd embarrassed him with the mention of my mother; he rarely brought her up around Darlie. For years, I think, he'd felt guilty about remarrying after Mummie's death, judging from the number of disclaimers he made to his children. "You know," he would tell us, "this doesn't change how I feel about your mother." We understood that perfectly, and we approved of Darlie—age difference and all—in a way that much of Charleston did not. Pap was high maintenance, after all; we were just glad that someone young and vigorous had committed to the job.

I changed the subject by inviting my father's nostalgia. "It must have been a hell of a time."

"Oh, yeah," he said, shaking his head.

"Did he tell you about the billboard?" asked Darlie.

She had taken the old man's arm with easy affection. They really do love each other, I thought.

And the sight of their obvious coupledom stung in a way that I hadn't expected. Was it possible that they'd outlasted me and Jess?

I did remember that billboard, but I pretended otherwise, just to give him some material to work with. "Don't think so," I said.

"What billboard?" asked Pap.

Darlie squeezed his arm. "In the harbor. You know."

"Oh." My father chortled at the memory. "Damnedest thing you ever saw. The fleet commander was this tough ol' son-of-a-bitch who knew how to get the job done. Named, uh . . . damn, what the hell was his name?"

"We don't care, hon." Darlie was inspecting her lamb flatbread.

"He was somethin', though. A real kick-ass ol' cuss. Had the Seabees build this enormous billboard at the entrance to the harbor at Guadalcanal. First thing we saw when we came sailin' in. Said: 'Kill the bastards, kill the bastards, kill the yellow bastards.'"

I kept my expression blank. "An idealistic sort o' guy."

"Hell, it was war."

"It was war," I echoed, exchanging a wry look with Darlie.

"Can't hear that story too much," she said.

"Oh, go to hell, both of you," said my father, and he plunged into his butterfly prawns.

We were all a little high on wine by the end of dinner. Pap was the first to show it.

77

"You know what, son?"

"What?"

"I'm damn proud of you."

"Well . . . good." I tried to look into his eyes, but it was almost impossible. For both of us.

"I mean it."

"I know."

"You're gettin' rich, I guess."

"Well . . . comfortable."

"*Comfortable?* Your books are all over Harrods."

"I know, but there's a lotta folks to pay."

"I hope you're puttin' some away. Not spendin' it like a nigger, like you usually do."

"Jesus, Gabriel. Give it up." Darlie shot me a sympathetic glance.

"You don't know," my father told her. "Son-of-a-bitch bought a London taxicab when he was at Sewanee. Cost him more to ship the damn thing home than he paid for it. Broke down all the time, too." He winked at me rakishly to convey his harmlessness.

"I'm a little more careful now," I said.

"That boy's keepin' you in line, I hope."

He meant Jess, who had been cast as the Responsible One in our household. I had actually promoted this, since it was largely the truth, and it gave Pap an excuse to respect, however marginally, the funny fella who was sleeping with his son.

"He's pretty conscientious," I said.

"I'm sorry we missed him." Pap connected with me briefly to show what he really meant: that he liked Jess just fine, that he was glad I had company on the journey, just like he did. He was giving us his blessing at last, now that it could do nothing but hurt.

"He's okay, isn't he?" Darlie had that expression

some people use when they're talking about AIDS.

"Oh, yeah, very much so. The cocktail seems to be working."

The old man frowned. "Cocktail?"

"You know about that." Darlie scolded her husband with a glance.

No, he doesn't, I thought. He may have been told, but he didn't bother to store it, because it didn't matter to him that much. "It's a combination of drugs," I explained. "So far it's been fairly effective against the virus."

"I knew they'd find something," said my father. "Nobody believed me, but I said so all along, didn't I?"

"It's not a cure," I told him.

"Well, just the same . . ."

Pap's approach to mortal illness was to deny it outright, then accuse the world of unnecessary hysteria. He had done that the night my mother died in '79, when I'd been summoned to Charleston from California for reasons that were gruesomely obvious to everyone. "She's a whole lot better," he whispered, pulling me aside at the hospital. "These damn doctors are a bunch of nervous nellies." A decade later, when Josie found a lump in her breast, the old man had attempted a pathetic variation on the same theme. "You know," he told me. "Your sister's always been excitable."

I was sorry I'd provided another escape hatch. "A lot of people can't use the cocktail," I told him. "I know a thirteen-year-old who can't."

This made Darlie frown, then put down her spoon. "Who has AIDS, you mean?"

"Sure."

"From a transfusion or something?"

"No. The usual way."

"My God."

"This town," muttered my father.

"It wasn't here," I said with a trace of righteous satisfaction. "It was out there in Amurrica. His father had been screwing him since he was four."

"Jesus," said Darlie.

"Can we talk about something pleasant?" said my father.

But Darlie wanted to hear about it, so I assembled the story for her, sparing nothing as I gave it shape and color. I told her about the pedophile ring and the video-tapes that had convicted Pete's parents and the single mother who had come to his rescue when all hope seemed lost. I told her about a little straight boy who had felt like such an outcast that he had finally found fellowship in a ward full of AIDS fags. It gave me perverse pleasure to mess with the mythology of the nuclear family in my father's presence. And I couldn't help feeling proud of my role in Pete's life, proud that someone so extraordinary had seen me as father material.

"All because he heard you on the radio," said Darlie.

"It's a much more powerful medium than people think."

Pap's discomfort was palpable. "I'd be careful if I were you."

"What do you mean?"

"How many times have you talked to him?"

"I don't know. Six or seven, maybe. Why?"

"Does his mother know you're calling him?"

"Of course. She arranged it. What are you getting at?"

My father tore off a chunk of bread. "Well . . . you're a middle-aged man, and he's . . . well, people could get the wrong idea, that's all."

"Like what?" I had caught on finally, and I was bristling.

"I think you know."

"No, Pap. Tell me. What wrong idea will they get?"

Darlie had stopped eating entirely and was watching us with a look of slack-mouthed alarm.

"For God's sake," said my father, "use your damn head. The boy was abused by gays."

"He was abused by pedophiles. Have you been listening at all?"

"They were men, weren't they?"

"Yeah. *Straight* men."

"How could they be straight, if they were messing with a boy?"

"Because they called him a faggot while they were doing it."

Pap recoiled as if he'd been struck. For all his manly swagger, he was not about to venture into *that* territory. "Jesus," he murmured. "You can make anything disgusting, can't you?"

"Oh, I'm sorry," I said with the driest sarcasm I could muster. "Is that what I did? Let's get back to something pleasant. Like killing Japs."

"C'mon, guys." Darlie looked at her husband, then at me. "Be nice now."

"Somebody's gotta tell him it's not cute anymore."

"What the hell are you talking about?" My father's face was aflame.

"All this nigger and Jap shit. It doesn't make you a character, you know. It just makes you an asshole."

"Hey," said Darlie mildly.

"Do you think your children want *their* children to hear that kind of talk? They don't, Pap. That got old a long time ago. Billy dreads it every time he brings his

81

kids over, for fear you'll be pulling that racist shit again. Talk about a lousy influence on children . . ."

My father's eyes narrowed. "Who said anything about a lousy influence?"

"You implied . . ."

"I didn't imply shit. Jesus, you're the most sensitive fella I ever met. All I said was, people might get the wrong idea. That's all I said. If you wanna make it into somethin' else . . ."

"Why would they get the wrong idea? Because I'm gay?"

"Well . . . that complicates it, yes."

Darlie pushed her chair back and stood up. "Time for me to go pee." Neither of us acknowledged her efficient exit.

"How does that complicate it?" I asked.

"Just drop it."

"No. I wanna know. Would it be okay if I were straight?"

Silence.

"Or if Pete were a girl? Would that make it acceptable?"

"This is ridiculous."

"What's so ridiculous? The boy needs love. You don't have to be straight to do that. Children will take it anywhere they can get it. And you don't deny them just because you didn't get it yourself. Just because somebody betrayed you. Sooner or later, you have to break the cycle, or the damage is just passed on from one generation to—"

"Oh, blah, blah, blah. Where'd you get all that New Age crap?"

How absurd it was to hear the term *New Age* tumble from my father's lips. I was certain he'd never used it—

or even heard it, for that matter—until the frothing fundamentalists in his party had identified it as the Antichrist. He was just a social Episcopalian, and a lapsed one at that; he didn't give a damn about Christ *or* his Anti; he was simply baiting me.

"It's just common sense," I replied.

"You think I betrayed you?"

"No," I said quietly. "I think somebody betrayed *you*. And I'm the one who paid for it."

I was stunned by my own audacity. How had I summoned the nerve, or the sheer stupidity, to confront the unconfrontable? Without a moment's thought I had led us to the edge of a precipice, and a single misstep could send us both tumbling into oblivion. Pap's eyes were the true measure of our peril; them and his voice, which was so abnormally subdued that it scared me.

"You don't know what you're talking about," he said.

"I guess not," I replied. "How could I?"

Then we just stopped talking. We were both so embarrassed we might have been children caught white-handed in a flour-strewn kitchen. And we realized, too, that we were no longer alone; a presence hovered over us like some pale messiah who'd been sent to save us from ourselves.

"Can I tempt you with dessert?" he asked.

Somehow we found our way to safer footing. By the time Darlie returned from the john we were deep in a discussion about the charms of the Place des Vosges. Geography had often sheltered us. As a boy, I would sit in the garden while the old man mulched azaleas with pine straw, just to hear him rhapsodize about the

Skyline Drive, or the wild ponies on Ocracoke Island, or the boxwood maze at Middleton Plantation. I loved him most then, I think, when he was musing about other places. The earth was a source of wonder and sustenance to him; it was people who let him down.

Darlie settled into her chair with a chipper smile. "I just love a clean bathroom. Makes my whole day."

What a trouper she was, I thought, to have navigated the minefield of this family for so long.

"We ordered you a crème brûlée," Pap told her, then gave me a matey wink. "If it's on the menu, it's what she wants."

"You make me sound so boring," said Darlie.

"I'm that way about bread pudding," I told her.

"Foxtrot," said my father.

"What?"

"The one on the left."

I peered out at the flags on the Embarcadero. "I think you're right."

"I know I'm right. How 'bout the one next to it?"

"Alfa."

"Well . . . you got the letter right, but it's Able."

"Maybe in *your* navy. They changed it."

"Nah. When did they do that?"

"I dunno. After the French and Indian War?"

"Oh, go to hell," said my father, chuckling.

And so it went for the rest of the evening. Semaphore was just right for us, I thought, the perfect metaphor for how we'd managed to coexist all these years. Histrionic but mute, we had signalled our deepest feelings through broad strokes of pantomime, and always from a distance.

* * *

84

I dropped them off at the Huntington around eleven. We exchanged brisk, ritual hugs, and they promised to phone on their way back from Tahiti. Driving home in the fog, I had to ask myself why I'd chosen that night of all nights to tangle with the old man. After all, he'd mellowed a great deal in recent years, and I had long before stopped needing his approval, thanks largely to Jess. There was finally someone else to be proud of me, someone whose opinion mattered even more than Pap's. Was *that* the reason for my outburst, then? Was I just angry at Jess for making the ground shaky again?

And there was something else: Pap's curiosity about Pete had made it clear how much the boy already mattered to me. He was no longer just an interesting story; he was a habit. Our visits on the phone had become almost nightly now, which spoke far less to my charity than to my need. He was the perfect listener, the only confidant with whom I felt utterly secure. That I had chosen someone so young and far away, someone I might never meet who could well be near death, only made it easier to tell him the truth.

Six

Wayne

"Who's that?" I asked. "Anybody you know?"

There was a dog barking in the background. A large one, from the sound of it.

"That's Janus," Pete said. Then I heard him call out into the room, "Leave it, Janus! Leave it!"

"What's he got? A cat?"

"No, the vacuum hose. Janus, leave it!"

I laughed. "Ours used to do that. It's something to do with the sound. It makes them crazy."

"But it's not even on. He thinks it's an anaconda or something. Janus, you fuckhead!"

The dog barked once, for symbolism's sake, then stopped.

"He only listens to Mom," Pete said. "He totally behaves around her. She's had him for like a hundred years."

Unruly or not, the dog reassured me. I hadn't forgotten my last talk with Donna, and the people who might still hold a grudge against Pete.

"What is he?" I asked.

"A Lab."

"What color?"

"Yellow."

"Oh, they're the best. So loyal. We have an old mutt named Hugo. Part Australian shepherd and part jackal." The dog was curled up next to me, in fact, and his ear flicked in recognition of his name. I had detected a brand-new odor about him, sickly and disturbing, and wondered how much life he had left. Would he even last until Jess got home? I could remember a time, not that long ago, when I'd endured the certainty that Hugo would survive Jess. I'd written a poignant little essay about it, in fact.

"Hugo," Pete repeated. "As in *Les Misérables*."

"Close. He was named after Victor Hugo, but another one. A fashion designer in New York."

Pete grunted. "You like that fashion shit?"

"Not even slightly. That's one queer gene I missed completely."

"Then why did you . . . ?"

"A friend of mine named him." And where are you now, Wayne? Why aren't you here to get me through this? Almost nobody's dying these days. If you'd hung around a little longer you would have made the cut.

"He liked fashion, huh?"

"Not really. Just the designer. He thought he was sexy." Said sexy designer, if memory served, hadn't survived nearly as long as Wayne had.

"Man, is that all you guys think about?"

"Don't you think about girls all day?"

"Well . . . yeah."

"Well, there you go."

87

"That's *all* I can do, man. Think about 'em."

I pictured Pete on his endless loop between Henzke Street and the hospital, frail and barely able to breathe, stealing glimpses of pretty girls along the way, girls who would find him pitiable, or never even notice him at all. He had reached the age of crushes and budding lust, but he'd been robbed of all that. Having been denied it myself—or at least the license to act upon it—I felt my heart rush out to him.

"What about magazines?" I asked.

"What do you mean?"

"You must have a *Playboy* under your mattress."

"Are you nuts, man?"

"You do, don't you?" I chuckled knowingly.

"My mom would skin my ass."

No way, I thought. Donna Lomax was a thoroughly modern woman, unflappable as she was kind, and anything but a prude. If she disapproved of skin magazines—which I doubted—she would still greet such a discovery with worldly amusement, not alarm or disgust.

"Well," I said mischievously, "it's not the sort of thing moms have to be told, is it?"

"Right. I'll remember that the next time a magazine salesman comes by my oxygen tent."

I bowed to his grim humor. "Don't get out much, huh?"

Pete growled.

"Tell me about your room, then."

"My *room*?"

"What does it look like? I wanna picture it."

"Well, there's a cocktail lounge . . . and a mud-wrestling pit . . . and a trapeze over the Jacuzzi, which is where the strippers usually—"

"A straight answer, please."

"Then gimme a straight question."

"I'm serious. You're a writer. Describe it."

"Well . . ." He paused, seemingly to survey the room. "There's a bookshelf on the wall next to the window . . ."

"What sort of bookshelf?"

"I dunno. Chrome or some shit."

"What's on it?"

"My *X-Files* tapes, the *Encyclopedia Americana*, some old *National Geographics*, your books, Tom Clancy . . ."

"He's a big right-winger, you know."

"That's what Mom said, but I like him. So tough shit."

"Your mother is an exceedingly wise woman. Tell me what you see from the window."

"Not much. Just a bunch of trees. The house across the street. And an old water tank above the trees. It's completely rusted and dangerous as all fuck, but they leave it up so they can hang a star on it at Christmas. It's like a tradition or something."

"Sounds nice, actually."

"Except the star faces the wrong way. All we get is some of the light on the side of the tank . . . you know, like spillover. It just makes the graffiti easier to read."

I chuckled. "Festive."

"Yeah. The rest of the town gets Bethlehem. We get 'Roberta Blows.'"

"C'mon."

"I swear. They painted it out last year, but it came right back."

"She must *really* blow," I said.

Pete exploded with laughter, which delighted me until it led to a bout of coughing that I thought would never stop. "Fuck, man," he said, gasping for breath. "You gotta give me warning."

"Sorry." I waited for him to compose himself. "You okay?"

"Yeah."

"I think you should go with it, you know. Start your own tradition."

"What?"

"'Roberta Blows.' Just say that instead of 'Merry Christmas.'"

"Right."

"Really. Think about it. It's got a great sound to it. Euphonious. It's like something out of Poe. And it would put some meaning back in the season: 'Roberta Blows and a Happy New Year!'"

"Man, you are weird."

"What else?"

"What else what?"

"Is in your room?"

"Oh . . . lotsa nasty medical shit."

"Okay. Go on."

"That's it, except some lamps and stuff. And some comic books in plastic milk crates."

"You like comics?"

"Not anymore."

"Grew out of it, huh?"

"Yeah."

"I had a friend who loved comics, and he was forty."

For two weeks, Wayne, remember? You were forty for two crummy little weeks, and that was all the middle age you could take.

I met Wayne Stevens at Harvey Milk's memorial

service. Wayne had slept with Harvey three times in the last month of Harvey's life. The day the supervisor was assassinated at City Hall Wayne heard the news at work and stumbled home in disbelief to find a flirty message from Harvey that Wayne's roommate had taken that morning. At the memorial service, Wayne knew no one (including the three official "widows" in attendance), so he took the seat next to me. "You're Gabriel Noone," he said, and I held his hand for the next hour. A week later, when I ran into him in North Beach, I felt as if I'd always known him.

Wayne was blond and twenty-five then, with the face of a happy rabbit and a sleek superhero chest that startled you when his shirt came off. He was very bright in an obsessive adolescent sort of way. He filled composition books with annotated lists of his favorite things, which invariably included what he called the Four B's: Batman, Bette Davis, Busby Berkeley, and Bette Midler. I know how that sounds, but Wayne was no dreary queen doing bad Baby Jane impersonations. He had a serious gift for criticism, and he could analyze in depth the very essence of the artists he admired. Including, I should add, me.

We were lovers in the beginning, but it never took. Wayne wanted The Great Dark Man, and I, typically, wasn't up to it. We lived together for a while in a flat below Coit Tower—"in its pubic hair," as Wayne put it—and even after the sex had died we indulged in sentimental gestures. I would wake late, long after Wayne had left for one of his clerical jobs downtown, to find an index card propped on the kitchen table bearing some fragment of a thirties song and a line of X's and O's. It was Wayne's way of honoring the big romantic love that neither of us had ever achieved.

And it was I who ended this gentle charade, suggesting cautiously one night that we might both find what we wanted if Wayne took a recently vacated studio across the Filbert Steps.

I worried that I'd destroyed something precious, but we grew even closer. Wayne became my best friend and disciple, my randy little brother. We would hang out all night, smoking doobies and excoriating the celebrity closet cases we could spot on television. Or we'd head off to our separate hunting grounds (Wayne to a leather bar, I to the glory holes), knowing that later we would offer each other our exploits—if I may quote myself here—"like a small dog who drags a dead thing home and lays it on the doorstep of someone he loves."

Wayne's new digs across the garden were a study in monastic simplicity. He adhered, he said, to the Andy Warhol dictum that all you needed for happiness was one of everything: one bed, one chair, one spoon, one mug. Wayne's one book-of-the-moment (Wilkie Collins, say, or Isherwood or sometimes Nancy Mitford) was always placed symmetrically on his coffee table, often in the company of a lone comic book. I felt peaceful when I sat in that musty little room with its treasured Batman lithograph and its pristine row of tea boxes above the electric kettle. Wayne lived hand-to-mouth, bouncing checks until they finally landed, but he had learned to revere the ordinary. He was almost English in that regard; he had distilled the dailiness of life until it was pure as a sacrament.

And he was such a sunny guy. He could find the humor in catastrophe, thereby romanticizing it and robbing its power. I could do that myself, but Wayne was the acknowledged master. I knew he had his dark moments, but he played them offstage, until the worst had passed. His instinct was to connect with others, to make them characters in his lifelong comic book, to find some comfortable common ground, however tenuous, and inhabit it completely. A lot of people—Jess among them—would call that conflict avoidance, but I never understood what was wrong with that.

I worried about hurting Wayne's feelings when Jess and I became a couple. Wayne, after all, had been my companion for seven years. He had been my steady date for the movies, my confessor when a romance hit the rocks. He had joined me on a cruise ship to Alaska and later on my first British book tour, a laughably down-market affair we conducted out of a gay boardinghouse in Earl's Court. And still later we had rented a cottage in the Cotswolds, where we lived for six weeks without a car, so we could feel like a couple of loopy villagers out of E. F. Benson.

As usual, my fear of hurting someone had made me overestimate my own importance. Jess and Wayne got along fine, and their bond grew even stronger when they both tested positive. As the decade came to a close the three of us were braced against the beast, intent upon collecting memories while we could. To that end, we rented a villa on Lesbos one fall. We wanted to feel like Coward and company lolling on the lawn at Goldenhurst, or maybe Auden on Ischia, ogling boys among the ruins. (We were already aspiring to the proud nobility of twentieth-century queers.)

I can still see that old stone house: its tangle of dusty wisteria, the amber light that shot through its shutters during afternoon naps. We had brought along a compact disc player—this nifty new thing—and we would lie on our terrace above the Aegean, adrift in a musical we had just learned to call *Les Miz*. It never failed to break our hearts, since we had made it about us: loving comrades huddled at the barricades. One lyric in particular demolished me: "Oh, my friends, my friends, forgive me, that I live and you are gone. There's a grief that can't be spoken, there's a pain goes on and on."

Jess and Wayne contracted pneumocystis at the same time. We saw this as the first of many trials, so we were frugal with our distress. I learned to take their coughing in stride, waiting calmly without comment for it to stop, so as not to honor its message. They both lost a lot of weight. Jess had always been buxom—there is no better word—but now you could see the planes of his skull, the disturbing way his butt had begun to deflate (a fact I refused to confirm for him). And there were the usual ills: the fatigue and neuropathy, the night sweats and diarrhea. So we adjusted again; talked of plays we had yet to see, trips we had yet to take. Wayne even visited my sister, Josie, in Charleston, and walked the beach with her on Sullivan's Island, since they had become friends over the years.

Then a sort of edgy competition began. I thought of it at the time as a "sicker than thou" thing, with Wayne as the instigator. He would stack up his symptoms against Jess's, matching him hardship for hardship, then do him one better with a look of flinty triumph. He seemed to be saying: "Stop pretending we're equals; I'm going to die before you do." And so help me, I remember regarding him as a troublemaker, a bad sport.

As it happened, they both recovered from their pneumonia, but Wayne got KS and began to lose ground. He grew thinner and thinner, and during his third prolonged stay in the hospital they drove a shunt—this gleaming vampire stake—into his

94

beautiful chest, as if intent upon proving him mortal. His parents came out from Florida several times, armed with false cheer and new editions of the toys Wayne had loved as a child. He seemed to glory in it, this last chance to be babied and fussed over, after so many years of brave bachelorhood. He would hold court in bed, encircled by his plastic trains and Lincoln Logs, beaming like some skeletal holy man.

He wanted to go home after that, to refine his solitude again. But his frailty and that alpine stairway made shopping, or even leaving the house, a near-impossibility. Then one week he stopped returning my messages. Jess and I went to the Steps and found him in a stupor amid the fouled sheets of his sofa bed. When we rolled him over, he smiled at us with sheepish apology, as if we'd just stopped him from snoring, or woken him from a bad dream. The ambulance attendants didn't know the Coit Tower approach, so they had to haul him down through the garden to Montgomery Street. Later, when Jess and I were on a book tour in Britain, Wayne collapsed in the bushes. Our friends Seneca and Vance discovered him by chance when they arrived with groceries, then took him back to their place on Potrero Hill, where they cared for him like a wounded robin until he was stronger.

We looked into hospices, but Wayne resisted. This was just another bad patch, he said, and it would pass. But he had run out of money and was months behind in his rent, and there was no way a caregiver could operate in that cramped warren. Even after he agreed to a hospice (swayed by its vegetarian meals and the Zen Buddhist staff), he spoke of his return to the Steps. There was no *need* to give up his apartment, he argued;

his landlady had agreed to charge him a nominal sum until he was better. This was a flat-out lie, one of his rare ones, but easy enough to fathom: to surrender that little room, however useless it had become, was to acknowledge the end.

So we moved him to a hospice in the Castro called Maitri and made cheerful noises about its homey atmosphere. (I remembered doing the same when we moved my grandmother into the Live Oaks Convalescent Home.) There was greenery outside his window, after all, and they let us cover his walls with talismans from home, his Rocky and Bullwinkle cel, his etching of Telegraph Hill in the thirties, that Batman lithograph. It was there we held his fortieth birthday party. His parents were on hand for it, and Seneca and Vance brought lots of silly little presents, for the joy of the unwrapping. Jess and I had pulled strings with a friend in L.A. and scored an advance copy of Bette Midler's latest movie, *Hocus Pocus*. Twenty minutes into it, Wayne issued his last review in a tone of wide-eyed disbelief. "This is really shitty," he said.

We made up for it the day before he died. Jess and I brought him our tape of Midler's *Art or Bust* concert, Wayne's favorite. He could no longer speak, but we propped him up in bed, and when the Divine appeared on-screen bouncing a giant inflatable boob over her head, a beatific smile bloomed on his face. Toward the end of the concert, Jess and I held each other and wept. "Here comes the flood," Bette was singing, and it felt like a dirge for our friend, the saddest song we had ever heard. But Wayne's death was easier to take because Jess was there, and because, in the depths of my calculating heart, it was only a rehearsal for something much worse to come.

I had been so angry at Wayne those last few weeks. Anger was the easier emotion, and Wayne had left a snarl of unfinished business and petty debts that intruded bluntly upon our grief. And when we cleaned out his apartment, his life of Spartan simplicity had proven a fraud. In a basement storeroom beneath his monk's cell lay every scrap of paper Wayne had ever received: every dinner bill, every playbill and postcard, every thought he'd ever scribbled on a cocktail napkin. There were thousands of comics, too—*Batman* mostly— stored in decapitated cereal boxes. I'd always assumed he'd traded one comic for another, but they were all there, every last one of them, there and in a rented space downtown, where Jess and I spent days sifting through the litter that Wayne had left as an autobiography. We ended up saving the comic books and anything that resembled a journal, then dumped the rest.

I felt as if I'd finished him off with a pillow to the face.

"Did you ever like comics?" Pete asked.

"Not really. Not the kind my friend liked."

"What kind was that?"

"Oh . . . guns and explosions and big butch guys in tights."

Pete laughed.

"Little Lulu was more my speed. She operated by her wits, and she wanted no part of the boys and their stupid games. Even when they put up a sign on the playhouse that said 'No Girls Allowed.' "

"You didn't like boys?"

"Not many of them, no."

"Why not?"

97

"I don't know. We just weren't wired the same way."

For the rest of the day I thought about Wayne, the grownup boy who had brought me childhood again, minus the usual terrors. At dusk I drove to Telegraph Hill and parked in the lot at Coit Tower. The sky was conch-shell pink over the Golden Gate, and there were surprisingly few tourists around to spoil it. (I remembered how cross Wayne would get whenever the line of cars stretched down as far as his place.) I followed the rock-walled path to the Steps and stood watching the sunset as it winked off the windows in the East Bay, like a thousand little wildfires. Beneath that lay Treasure Island, a source of wonder to Wayne, since it had been built for a world's fair in 1939, and that particular year, in his opinion, had been the high point of the century. Deco had been in bloom then, he said, and it was the best year ever for movies: *Gone With the Wind, Dark Victory, Rebecca, The Wizard of Oz.*

I opened the gate to his garden. There were several purple petals on the Princess tree, but the rose we had planted over his ashes (in homage to the Midler ballad) was looking less than divine. I hadn't been here in at least two years, this sacred spot that had once been central to my life. I had always been on the move, a serial renter leaping from hilltop to hilltop in search of home. Now the Steps were another realm completely, which was odd, considering how little they had changed. I was the one who had changed, growing grayer and sadder in the midst of this immutable beauty. But I was alive and well. Shouldn't that be enough?

I turned on my heels and walked down to

Montgomery, then descended to the neon hubbub of Broadway. Night was falling, but the sky was briefly on hold at purple. There were tourists streaming down to the strip joints from the cafés on Columbus, so I wove my way through them with mounting irritation, intent upon my mission. At the first newsstand I could find I approached a clerk and asked a question so unlike me that it seemed to be coming from somewhere else:

"Where do you keep your *Playboys*?"

Seven

A Guy Thing

Looking fretful, Anna took the parcel from me with unnatural delicacy, as if it might contain a letter bomb.

"You sure you want to?"

I thought she'd see my gift to Pete as something harmless and fun, a generous hands-across-the-sea gesture from old to young, gay to straight. She was not someone I'd expect to be prissy about a skin magazine, especially one as tame and mainstream as *Playboy*. Then I remembered her lesbian parents and wondered about their sexual politics—if they were followers, for instance, of Andrea Dworkin.

"You think it's degrading to women?"

She looked down at the padded envelope as if the women in question were actually inside. "They're grownups," she said, "and they can do what they want. I just don't think in *his* case . . . oh, never mind."

"C'mon? What is it? He's too young? What?"

She shrugged. "My brother Edgar used to have those when he was twelve."

"Then why on earth shouldn't I . . ."

"He used to *do* porn, didn't he, this boy? He was in all those videotapes, right?"

That stopped me cold for a moment. "Well, yeah, but . . . this isn't remotely like that. That was hardcore and violent, and it was kids, and they were doing it against their will. This is just glossy fantasy stuff. It's not that much racier than the swimsuit issue of *Sports Illustrated* or . . . hell, he could download a lot worse off the Internet."

"I just thought the *idea* of it might . . . you know, bother her."

"Donna?"

"Yeah."

"She's not like that. She knows what the difference is. She's a shrink, you know . . . and sort of an old hippie, I think."

"Does she open his mail?"

"I can't imagine that she would. The first thing she promised him was his privacy."

"But if she's trying to protect him . . ."

"Oh, okay, fine." I reached for the package, but she pulled it away.

"No," she said. "I'll mail it. I was just asking."

"It's just sort of a guy thing. I thought it would make him feel like he had . . . you know . . . a big brother." I had almost said father, until I remembered Anna's misgivings about such a responsibility.

Anna turned the package over in her hands, squeezing it once or twice. "Why is it squishy?"

I explained—with some embarrassment—that I'd wrapped the *Playboy* in a *Noone at Night* T-shirt.

101

She didn't remark on that. She just stuffed the package into her shoulder bag, thereby closing the discussion, then removed another bundle and handed it to me. "I brought up the mail."

"Oh, thanks." I perused the usual oddball array of correspondence: a bank statement, a flyer from the Seattle gay chorus, an announcement of a PEN meeting at a Guatemalan poet's house in Berkeley, a catalog from my publisher in Sweden, and a hand-delivered notice informing me that Juanita and Gail of the Church of the Savior's Suffering had stopped by briefly, without invitation, to pray for my house. I handed the latter to Anna, who received the news of our benediction with a beguiling smirk.

"Gee," she said dryly, "that's good to know."

"Isn't it?"

"There's a letter there for Jess, too."

I shuffled the mail again and found it. The return address was 312 Ebenezer Church Road, Leesville, Alabama. It was apparently from Jess's father—not exactly an everyday occurrence.

"I could take it to him," said Anna, "if you want."

I mulled that over, then amazed myself with my reply: "That's okay. I'm gonna see him myself."

This had been coming for a while. Jess and I had been separated for almost a month, and I knew it was time to connect again. Some of my friends (the straight women mostly) had warned against it. Cold turkey was the only way to go, they said, if I really wanted him back. How else could he feel the full weight of what he might be giving up? If I hung around like some love-starved puppy, he'd only have his cake and eat it too.

For wasn't that what men wanted anyway: total freedom *and* total security?

I wasn't as sure as they were. For one thing, it's impossible to generalize about what men want if you're a man yourself. Men *know* what a conflicted species we are, how many emotions can war in our heads at any given moment. So even in the depths of my pain I could imagine Jess's pain, and every part of me wanted to soothe it. He was alone and confused; this was no time to cut him off. He needed to know I was still on his side, still his comrade, even in the midst of chaos. And I guess I needed to know that from him, whatever the outcome might be. I could part with our romantic life—for the time being, at least—but not the balm of our friendship.

And there was something else: I wanted to share Pete with Jess. I was certain the two of them would get along beautifully, given their scrappy temperaments and their common HIV status. They could discuss drug protocols and gripe about insurance companies and swap tales of their shitty childhoods. Pete's unshakable faith in Jess and me might somehow rub off on Jess, or at least give him a fresh perspective. Pete could be our go-between, our facilitator, our guardian angel.

For there was something magic about this boy.

And nothing less than magic was required.

"Hi."

"Oh . . . hey."

"Is this a bad time?"

"No. It's fine. How are you?"

"Not great, actually."

"Yeah. Know what you mean."

Do you? I thought. *Then why the fuck are we doing this? If you're hurting as much as I am, you could fix us both in the blink of an eye.*

"Just thought I'd check in," I said.

"Good."

"There's a letter here for you," I said. "From your father, I think."

"Oh, yeah?"

"Miracle of miracles, huh?"

"Not really. He just wants to have his hand held."

Jess's mother had died eight months earlier in a car wreck in Alabama, a trauma that had driven Jess's father to finally seek connection with his children. Jess deeply resented this latter-day conversion. Here was the man who had beaten him routinely as a child, who had thrown him out of the house at sixteen, who had all but ignored Jess's medical death sentence. He had no right to expect intimacy on demand, in Jess's reckoning of things.

"I thought I might bring it over," I said.

"Bring what?"

"The letter."

"Over here?"

"Yeah." His apparent hesitation went straight to the pit of my stomach. "Unless, it's not . . ."

"No. That'd be great."

"You sure?"

"Yeah. I'd like you to see the place. It's a mess right now, but . . ."

"God, Jess, I don't care about that."

What I cared about, in truth, was not the state of his apartment but the fact that he already had enough pride in it to make apologies. This place was supposed to be an interim measure at best, a neutral space in which he could read and think and be alone.

It made me crazy to hear him talk about it as if it were home.

His lobby was one of those gilt-and-green caverns from the twenties, somewhere between Mandarin and Mesopotamian, with a dinosaur of an elevator at the far end. Next to the elevator stood the mailboxes, where a man was wriggling his key out of its lock. The guy was as stubby and well built as a Shetland pony, and completely upholstered in leather. I couldn't help wondering if he'd met Jess yet, if they lived on the same floor, or even if they had fucked each other. To make matters worse, he dismissed me with the briefest of glances as I crossed the lobby.

Jess's apartment was on the sixth floor, the top one. The corridor had new carpeting and sturdy industrial light globes that were a little too late-eighties for their deco setting. Despite this recent attention, a palpable shabbiness remained: too many ancient paint jobs clotting the corners, a frenzy of rust on the fire escape, the stinging smell of disinfectant. The place wasn't nearly as fancy as I'd imagined, which both depressed and relieved me.

Jess was waiting at his door, his head recently shaved to a high shine. He was wearing an old mint-green sport shirt he had bought for our cruise to Cozumel. It seemed in conflict with his Mr. Clean–from–Hell look, but it was nice to see this remnant of his earlier, softer self. I couldn't help wondering if he knew that, if he'd consciously chosen the shirt to put me at ease.

"Hey," he said quietly, and gave me a hug.

I held him longer than I should have, hoping that our touch still had a language of its own, embarrassing myself in the process. So I shifted our focus to the apartment. "Well, this is nice."

"Yeah," he said, "the view's good."

The huge iron window was the room's best feature, lending it the air of a Parisian garret. But it was on the wrong side of the building to form a sight line with my house; the view was toward the southeast: SOMA and China Basin and the dull pewter plain of the bay. The window I'd imagined as his was somewhere else around the corner.

"Can I get you anything?" he asked. "Juice or tea?"

"Juice would be nice," I said.

I followed him through a stucco archway to his tiny galley of a kitchen, where I saw to my distress that he'd already begun to arrange snapshots on his refrigerator door. I spotted Hugo first, standing alone in our garden, his blind old eyes looking especially supernatural in the camera's flash. ("Mongrel of the Corn," Jess had dubbed that shot.) Then there was Seneca and Vance in a studio photo they'd had done as a Christmas present. And our godson, Jared, up in Inverness. And the silhouette of a man standing on a bluff at Big Sur. That had to be Frank, I realized, Jess's so-called "motorcycle buddy."

There was nothing of me.

"Orange, okay?"

"What? . . . Oh, yeah, fine."

Why would he leave that photo there if he knew I was coming? Wouldn't it be common decency to take it down? Or did he want me to see it? Was this his way of making something official?

"I was at Barb's yesterday," he said, handing me the glass of juice.

"Oh, yeah?" Barb was his doctor, a gentle, dapper dyke who wore men's suits and retro wire-rimmed glasses. Jess adored her.

"My viral load is zero."

He said this so quietly, so tentatively, that I wasn't sure at first how much weight to give it. "You mean it's . . . ?"

He nodded. "It seems to be inactive. I'm actually growing T cells."

I'd like to believe there was a moment when I received this news with unalloyed joy. Here, after all, was the miracle I'd never dared permit myself. But if that moment occurred, it was swept away in a flood of bitter irony. For the great love I'd longed for all my life had been a certainty only while Jess was dying. Now that he had a future again—or the hope of one, at least—all deals were off. How loudly was I expected to rejoice?

"God, babe," I said. "That is so wonderful."

"Isn't it?"

I gave him a clumsy hug, still holding the glass of juice.

"Barb says I'm a poster boy for the cocktail."

"Jesus, that is just great." I should have elaborated, I know, or asked a few pertinent questions or hugged him again or *something*, but I couldn't pull it off. Not in my current state. Not with Frank staring at me from the refrigerator.

Jess seemed to study me for a moment, then headed into the living room. "I got a call from Passavoy. He says it's a go."

Passavoy was an executive at Curtain Call, the cable network that wanted to film me reading my stuff. Or *had* wanted to, once upon a time. Despite what I'd told my father—that brazen invocation of Alistair Cooke—the project had been stalled for over a year. Money was tight, and producers had moved on, and dozens of encouraging phone calls had come to nothing. We had all but given up several times.

"You think he's for real?" I asked.

"Who the hell knows?" Jess dropped to a second-hand sofa I didn't recognize. Had he bought it himself? Or borrowed it from one of his HIV/leather buddies? "I'll believe it," he said, "when I see the contract."

I sat next to him, but not too close to presume anything.

"I wondered what I should do," he said.

"What do you mean? It's what we want, isn't it?"

"No . . . I mean . . . do you still want me to handle things?" He was looking directly into my eyes.

"God, babe, sure . . . of course."

He shrugged. "I wasn't sure what you wanted to do."

"Sweetie . . ." I hesitated for a moment, then risked a hand on his knee. "I can't imagine any of this without you. We did it all together. It wouldn't be any fun anymore."

"I liked it, too."

"Good." I squeezed his knee. "Then don't make it past tense."

His face was unreadable, but he eventually gave me a small, tentative smile. "I've got an idea for the set."

Already I felt such a flood of relief. "What?"

"Well . . . sort of a *Nicholas Nickleby* thing that rotates around you. Your chair could be in the middle and remain . . . you know, fixed. But the rest of the set could change slightly as the chapters change. You know, different rooms on different levels. Or trees for the outdoor stuff. It could be really beautiful, if we get the lighting right."

It was so calming to hear him say "we" again, to know he'd been thinking about this, planning our future. I thought how lucky I was to have found him, this man who cared about my vision of things, who wanted to make it grander and richer, more accessible to the world. I felt such tenderness toward him. "I love that," I said, meaning "I love you."

"It would work, wouldn't it?"

"Oh, yeah. Absolutely."

"But not too gimmicky. Like that Spalding Gray movie with those ugly psychedelic gels."

"No. God, no. I hated that."

"And I want us to be in charge. We're gonna get your name in the title—not above it but *in* it—so you can raise hell if they try to censor the queer stuff. I know these Hollywood pricks. They'll cut your guts out when you're not looking, and expect you to be grateful. We're not gonna let that happen."

The color had risen in Jess's cheeks. I couldn't help smiling at his old Shiite zeal. He had always been a control freak with a short fuse—a reality I found nerve-racking in most circumstances (in traffic, for instance, and in crowded airports) but curiously comforting when it came to my career. His tough territorial nature made me feel protected, I suppose. Loved, even.

"Did Passavoy go for that?" I asked.

"What?"

"My name in the title."

"Damn right. They wanna do this thing."

"They're that serious, huh?"

"Get this," he said, and plunged into a rundown of the agents and producers who had swapped calls and taken meetings in recent days. While he talked, my eyes crept about the room, ransacking the place for clues. The pieces he'd brought from home (where they'd been in the basement) had assumed an odd new vitality in this setting. There was the bedside table Wayne and I had used on Telegraph Hill. And the little mica-shaded lamp I'd bought during my bachelor days. And some paisley pillows that hadn't been compatible with the sofa Jess's aunt had given us. They had all been disposable items, since this was to be a disposable room.

Jess had bought a table, I noticed: blond and brand-new, but reassuringly flimsy. He could give that to a friend, I figured, or leave it on the street corner, when this was over. The same was true of his new fiberboard bookshelf, now the home of his vast array of self-help books, most of which had the word *soul* in the title. I saw some Jung there, too, and several scholarly books on masochism with creepy-sounding titles. And down near the floor, a homemade shrine with votive candles and a Tibetan Buddhist deity. Jess had renounced fundamentalism as a boy, but the need for religion had never stopped dogging him. I myself had lost that years earlier; our marriage had become the only deity I required.

"Sounds great," I told him, when he'd finished his rundown. "Go for it."

"I'm gonna need my computer."

"Fine. Whatever. It's your office."

"No. I mean . . . I'm gonna need it here."

My heart sank. Until that moment, I'd found re-assurance in the knowledge that—to Jess, at least—home was where his computer was. The clothes and furniture he'd brought here were of little import,

110

but his computer was his central nervous system, his roaring hearth.

I tried to stay nonchalant. "Won't that be more trouble than it's worth? Moving it, I mean?"

He shook his head. "I can manage. When you're at the gym or something."

"No . . . I don't mind helping. I just meant . . ."

"It's no problem, really."

A silence followed that grew into a gaping void before I found the nerve to fill it. Finally I asked: "Do you have any sense of . . . how long this is going to take?"

"The deal, you mean?"

"No . . . your being away."

"Oh. No."

"I just wondered if . . ."

"It's gonna be a while."

"And how long is that?"

"I don't know, babe. I have a lot of sorting out to do. I barely know who I am right now."

I nodded.

"I told you that before."

"I know, sweetie. I just thought that . . . maybe by now . . ." I couldn't finish; I was sounding too pathetic to myself.

"I know you think I'm going to an orgy every night. But I'm right here most of the time."

Okay, I thought, but what about that picture on your refrigerator?

"Would you like to see a movie sometime? Or have dinner out?" He was asking me for a date, I realized, this man who'd shared a bed with me for a decade, who'd cried in my arms over his mother's coffin. Whether the invitation signified a cautious renewal or

111

a gentle retreat I couldn't tell. And I was far too afraid to ask.

"That would be nice," I said.

I saved Pete for last. Jess listened to the story with his mouth slightly open, a double line forming on his forehead. I had reached him, I realized, in a way that I hadn't for months.

"He thinks of us as role models," I said.

He blinked at me. "He's gay, you mean?"

"No. He just . . . he sees us as two people who love each other."

"Based on what?"

I knew this wasn't meant to be ugly, so I chose not to respond that way. "The show I guess. And interviews and things."

"How many times have you talked to him?"

"Now you're sounding like my father."

Jess frowned. "Your *father* knows about this?"

I could've kicked myself. I'd intended to keep quiet about the old man's visit, knowing it would only cause additional tension. "I told him a little bit about it, yeah."

"He called you? He couldn't have called you."

"They came through town on their way to Tahiti."

Jess grunted. "She must've heard they have a mall there."

I smiled at this, predictable as it was. Jess had been hostile to Darlie since the late eighties, when she'd vetoed an offer for us to spend a night under her roof. The offer, amazingly, had come from my father, when I'd told him Jess and I would be passing through town. He and Darlie would be in Italy then, the old man said, but the house was empty and we should certainly feel free to use it. I was touched—deeply—but not for long; the invitation was retracted within days.

The official excuse was a previously arranged house-sitter, but my sister, Josie, told me that Darlie had told my father that she was afraid of "catching something off the sheets." So the old man had to renege. He called my brother, Billy, and ordered *him* to offer us a place to stay, and Billy called us to say that he and Susan had *two* bedrooms (the italics were audible) that Jess and I were welcome to use, even though we hadn't actually thought to call *them* first. We ended up staying at a hotel to regain our dignity. And Darlie moved to the top of Jess's shit list.

"She's gotten better," I told him. "She asked how you were doing."

Jess just grunted again, so I gave it up. I was tired of being the mediator between the wildly disparate people in my life. I'd learned that instinct from my mother, who seemed to believe that it was the only way she could ever be whole. Maybe she was right, but it took a toll on her.

"Did you bring that letter?" asked Jess.

"Oh." I pulled my jacket from the back of the sofa, retrieved the letter from Jess's father and handed it to him. "The moon must be in Patriarchy," I said with a rueful smile.

Jess didn't react. He just thanked me soberly and tucked the letter under a book on his coffee table. "So why did I sound like him?"

"Who?"

"Your father. You said I sounded like him."

"Oh . . . I just meant . . . when you asked me how many times I'd talked to Pete. But it wasn't for the same reason."

"What did he mean, then?"

I rolled my eyes. "He thought it might look funny if a middle-aged queer spent too much time on the phone with a boy who'd been abused."

"Jesus."

"I know." I acknowledged his indignation with a nod. "I let him have it, believe me."

"Good."

"It was more about appearances than anything else. He didn't actually think . . ."

"Oh, well, that's good to know. Your father doesn't think you're a child molester."

I could tell he wanted me to join him in a good venting, but I didn't feel like it. "The truth is," I said, "Pete badly needs a man to talk to. Imagine having so little trust in your own gender."

"Your own gender, hell. Didn't you say his mother was in on it, too?"

"In on what?"

"The abuse. The porn ring."

"Oh . . . his biological mother. Yeah, she was. But he's got Donna now."

"Does she have a boyfriend or anything?"

"Not that I've heard of."

"You think she's a dyke?"

"I kind of doubt it. She just sounds like . . . I dunno . . . a sort of world-weary straight woman. She had a husband once, I know. What does it matter, anyway?"

"I'm just trying to get a handle on it."

I could tell that, and I was more than ready to encourage him. "Well, whatever she is, she's one of us. The last time we talked she held forth on Trent Lott, and what a big homophobe he was, and how much she hated him. And *she* was the one who brought it up.

She's really great, sweetie. I'd like talking to her even if Pete weren't . . . you know, part of it."

"I hope she has him on the cocktail."

"I asked about that. He says he's too young for it."

"That's bullshit. Who told him that?"

"I dunno, babe. His doctors, I presume."

"That's total bullshit. Lots of kids are doing it now. He should be on it as soon as possible."

"Would you tell him that?"

"Me?"

"Why not? You know how good *I* am at that stuff."

This was an oblique admission of guilt, since I had long before stopped tracking the particulars of his health. Jess wanted to be in charge of that, I told myself; he *insisted* on it, in fact, taking pride in the way he challenged his doctors at every turn. After a while the matter of his survival became just another household duty that had fallen exclusively to one partner, like taking out the garbage or doing the taxes. I learned enough to give capsule updates to friends and reporters, but that was the extent of it. I told myself I was helping in other ways: providing the certainty of home and love, a respite from the grim rigmarole of staying alive.

"You're the expert," I said lamely.

"He doesn't even know me."

"Wanna bet?"

He gave me a sardonic little smile. "He thinks I'm a coppersmith, right?"

"No." I returned the same smile, and God it felt good to connect again. "He's not an idiot. He knows what fiction is. He read about you in the Milwaukee paper. And *Poz*, if I remember correctly."

Jess blinked at me.

"I think you'd like him," I added.

"What's not to like? He's Tiny Tim."

"You are *not* cynical about this," I said in reprimand. "Don't even pretend to be."

A look of mild amusement crossed his face. "Does he have a number? Or do I just rub a brass lamp or something?"

I reached for my jacket again and pulled out the scrap of paper I'd brought, handing it to him. "I'm not making this up," I said.

I must have stayed there no longer than twenty minutes. It hurt too much to see him on his new turf, to realize how much he was already part of it. I even told him so as I left, prompting him to frown in sympathy, which just made the pain official and sent it deeper into my bones.

I got really stoned that night, knowing it would send me to bed—and oblivion—that much sooner. I was woken at midnight by the sound of my own voice coming from Jess's office: "This is Gabriel. Please leave a message at the tone."

I rolled over with a groan, consulted the clock, waited for my caller to identify himself on the machine. The moon was fat and fluorescent that night, casting shadows in the bedroom.

"Gabriel . . . are you there?"

It was Pete.

I reached for the bedside phone. "Kiddo. What are you doing up?"

"I'm sorry, man. I couldn't sleep."

"That's okay. What time is it there? Three o'clock or something?"

"Yeah."

"Are you all right?"

"Oh, yeah. Just felt like talking."

"Cool."

Pete giggled. "You're totally asleep, aren't you?"

"No. It's fine. Is your mom awake?"

"Are you kidding? She sleeps like a log."

"Are you under the covers with a flashlight?"

"What?"

"That's what *I* used to do."

"When?"

"When I was your age. Well, younger, actually. Never mind."

"Shit, man. I didn't know they *had* flashlights back then."

"Okay. I'm going back to sleep."

Another giggle.

"I feel like hell, anyway. So cut me some slack."

"What's the matter?"

"I went to see Jess."

"Did you tell him about me?" There was a suggestion of hope in Pete's voice.

"Sure. He's gonna call you, I think. I gave him your number. He's got some ideas about your treatment."

A silence and then: "We don't have to talk about that, you know. That shit gets old."

"Not just that, Pete. He mostly wants to meet you."

"What's the matter, then? Did you guys have a fight?"

"No. We were very polite to each other. That's what hurt so much." I hesitated a moment, then added: "That and seeing a picture of his boyfriend."

"Fuck. You didn't tell me about that."

"I don't know *what* he is, really. Jess used to call him his motorcycle buddy. They went on little trips around

117

town together. Then they planned a *big* trip to Big Sur on the weekend of Jess's birthday. Which totally threw me because Jess had never wanted a fuss made over his birthday. He was always uncomfortable with that kind of attention."

"He wasn't with you on his birthday?"

"Well . . . he came back on the night of, and we had dinner together. He divvied it up between the two of us."

"Maybe he and this guy weren't . . ."

"No, they were. Jess told me so a month later."

"What happened?"

"Oh . . ." I sighed at the memory. "We were at a sidewalk café, and he told me, and I started crying and talking really loud. Which is *not* like me in a public place. He must have thought it would be safer there, with all those people around. I asked what this guy Frank meant to him, and he said they weren't seeing each other exclusively. This was just one of the people he was *dating*. I thought we were having a life together, and he was out *dating*."

"You didn't see this coming?"

"Well, he'd already asked if we could open up the relationship, but it hurt too much every time I thought about it. I asked him to give me time, which he did for a while. Hell, I *guess* he did. I never asked and he never told; we just turned into strangers. He started playing queer punk rock music really loud, which he knew I hated. And once he asked me to fasten his chaps when he was going out for the evening. I had never even *seen* those fucking chaps before. And another time I accidentally opened one of his letters . . ."

"Accidentally?"

"Yes. It looked like a flyer or something, and it was this leather club holding its big annual brunch. They were confirming his choice of an entrée. That's how I knew it wasn't just some random thing: he'd picked the chicken over the beef."

"Did you ask him about it?"

"Oh, yeah. He tried to laugh it off. He said one of his friends probably signed him up, until I pointed out the entrée thing." I paused for a dyspeptic laugh. "I know how that sounds, believe me. Betrayed by brunch."

"No . . . go on."

"That's all there is. I still can't believe it. I was more sure of him than anything I'd ever believed in. My parents . . . my work . . . Christmas."

"Christmas?"

"Yeah. Jess hated it, so we pretty much scrapped it. I could see his point, actually: why should one time of year be officially more happy than another? Christmas was just a contrivance next to what we had. Jesus, what am I babbling about?"

"Hey, I'm with you. Roberta Blows, remember?"

"Let's stop talking about me, okay?"

"Why? You have a right to your feelings."

That phrase was significant, I realized. Pete had been through months of psychotherapy—some of it with Donna, presumably—and the language of the couch had obviously colored his own. It touched me to hear him doling out some of the wisdom he'd already received. I had never been to a shrink, but I was beginning to understand the value of a generous listener. And what harm could there be, really, in playing the patient for him?

"The thing is," I said, "Jess was my only certainty. I hate the thought of losing that."

119

"What sort of certainty?"

"Oh . . . just something you feel sometimes. Like at night when you're driving somewhere, and it's dark and the lights of the highway are streaming past, and you're not even talking, and one of you reaches out and holds the other one's leg for a while. It's the truest moment in the world, Pete. And all it says is: There you are, and here I am, and we're here together. You get it in airplanes, too, when the lights are out and you're the last people awake. Or even in the middle of a bad party when your eyes meet across the room. It's the only miracle we get, I think."

"Did you ever have that before Jess?"

"Not long enough to believe in it. It takes time and a lot of work."

Pete hesitated. "Do you still love him?"

"Oh, yeah. I can't imagine not."

"Then you must be more certain than ever."

"Yeah, but . . ."

"So go with it, man. Hang on to it."

"It has to work both ways."

"Says who? Glinda the Good?"

"What?"

"She had it totally wrong, you know. That was really crummy advice she gave the Tin Man. The heart *is* measured by how much you love, not by how much you are loved by others. Fuckin' *Hitler* was loved by others."

"Yeah, but . . ."

"And you're one lucky motherfucker if you already love somebody that much. So just keep loving him. Love him across the city, if you have to. It doesn't leave room for the fear and anger and the rest of that shit. When my mom adopted me, she loved me for months

120

before I could love her back. And I wasn't even human until I learned how to do that. It really is inside, man. The whole thing. It's just something you do yourself, not something you get. Nobody's love ever saved anybody else."

I was at a loss for words.

"Anyway," Pete added, "you know that."

"I do, huh?"

"It's in your stories, man."

I heard a low crooning sound in the background. "What's that?"

"Just Janus. He heard me talking and came in. He wants to know what the fuck I'm doing."

"And your mother's gonna be asking soon."

"Nah, man. It's cool."

I could actually *feel* the indigo calm of 511 Henzke Street, the soothing lullaby of that darkened room, and I had no wish to disturb it further. "You should go to bed, kiddo. Get your beauty sleep."

"My *what*?"

I chuckled. "My mother used to say that."

"You'll have to tell me about her," Pete said.

121

Eight

Don't Even Go There

I felt so much better the next morning that I called Pete to thank him for listening. After six rings I reached Donna's answering machine—that bourbon-and-honey voice in its professional mode—so I left a message. He hadn't called by the time I'd left for the gym at four o'clock, and there was nothing on my machine when I returned two hours later. Nor did the phone ring for the rest of the evening.

A day passed. Then another.

And I began to obsess on the possibilities:

Maybe Donna had intercepted that *Playboy* when it arrived at Henzke Street. Maybe she'd been so appalled that she'd ordered Pete not to call me back.

Or maybe Pete had been so compromised by the arrival of the magazine that he was angry with me now and had *chosen* not to call me back.

Or—and here it got much worse—maybe the boy had finally had a talk with Jess and knew things now he didn't have the heart to tell me. Like the whole truth about Jess's motorcycle buddy.

There was another possibility, of course—a far more likely reason for Pete's silence—but I was too lost in my own pain to think of it.

The call came at two in the morning, waking me from a stony sleep, just as the previous one had.

"Gabriel, listen, I'm sorry. I know how late it is, but could you pick up, please, if you're there?"

I fumbled my way to the bedside phone. "Donna?"

"Oh, good. You're there."

Where else would I be? I thought.

"I was afraid you might have unplugged your phone."

"Oh. No. I don't do that. Is something the matter?"

"I don't mean to scare you," she said. "But Pete's been having a rough time of it. We've been in Milwaukee at the hospital for the past two days."

My first reaction—I'm loath to admit—was profound relief. Pete didn't hate me, after all; he'd just been very sick. It took me a moment to gather my wits and muster an appropriate response: "Is it his lungs again?"

"Yeah. They're just not draining the way they should be."

"Shit."

"We've been through this before, so he'll probably surprise us again, but I would never forgive myself if I didn't . . . it's just that the doctors aren't sure if he's strong enough to . . . Gabriel, I *know* what an imposition this is, but the little dude gets ideas in his head, and I have to respect them if . . ."

"Donna, I'm lost."

"I'm sorry." She uttered a strangled laugh. "He wants to talk to you."

"Oh. Well . . . I'd be glad to. Sure. I was actually wondering what had happened to him."

"I should have called. It's just been a madhouse around here."

"Don't worry about it."

"God knows he wants to talk to you. He's been on me about it for hours. And you're the *only* one he's asking for. He's got it in his noggin that he won't wake up tomorrow."

It took a while for this to register. "God, Donna . . . is that a possibility?"

"We don't know. His doctor says it's hard to call when they're this young. Like I say, we've been through this before and he's pulled through fine. It's just that he's so weak right now, and it's gotten worse all night. So it's . . . you know . . . his lungs could just . . . call it quits."

She let me absorb that, then added: "I want to be straight with you, Gabriel. You've been so sweet to him."

No, I thought. Mostly it's been the other way around.

"If this is too heavy for you, just say so, okay?"

"Donna . . ."

"No, really. He has plenty of support. My friend Marsha is here and she adores him. He's one popular guy. So I can tell him I couldn't reach you, if you don't feel up to—"

"Donna, don't be ridiculous. Put him on."

"Oh, God, you're so nice."

"Please. He's the easiest kid in the world to be nice to."

"It may take a while. He's in his tent with the tubes and all . . ."

124

"I'll hang on."

"You gotta come see us, okay? Let me cook my chili for you."

"That sounds wonderful."

"Hold on, okay?"

So I held on.

Three or four minutes later:

"Are you still there?" His voice was tiny and ragged, his breathing irregular.

"I'm here, Pete."

"Hey, dicksmoker."

"Hey, you little turd."

He giggled, though now it was more like the squeak of a tiny animal. "Back in the slammer again."

"They've got you in a tent, huh?"

"That's me. Big Top Pee-wee."

I chuckled.

"Sorry to wake you up, man."

"Hey. Cut it out."

"No, really. I know you need your beauty sleep."

I marvelled at how quick-witted he could be, even under these circumstances. "No sweat," I replied. "I'm beautiful enough already."

"Sure thing, Sherlock."

A silence followed that neither of us could fill. Who do we remind me of? I wondered. And the answer came quickly enough: my father and me, hiding our true feelings amid a flurry of jokes and jolly insults. Don't do this, I ordered myself. Say what you mean before it's too late.

"Look, buster. You better not be checking out."

No reply.

"I just want you to know, you can't. There're too many people here who need you, sport. Way too many of us. So don't even go there."

More silence, then several quick intakes of breath. He was crying.

"I'm scared, Gabriel."

"I know."

"I heard 'em talking this morning. When they were draining me."

"Who?"

"The doctors. They talk about me like I'm deaf or something. Like I'm not even there."

"What did they say?

"One of 'em sighed real loud when he saw me. And the other one said: 'Yeah, I know. Makes you wonder if it's worth it.' It was like they were lookin' at roadkill or something. Like there wasn't even a person there."

I was angry for Pete, but not especially surprised. Jess had told me plenty of horror stories about the body-shop mentality of hospitals. "Does your mother know about this?"

"Oh, hell, no. She'd bust their asses."

"Maybe you should let her."

"No. It would just upset her. She's got enough on her mind."

"You know those guys are idiots, don't you?"

"Maybe not."

"No, Pete. They are. They're looking at symptoms and not the person. Even *I* can tell how much life there is in you."

He began to weep again, bringing the conversation to a halt.

"I'm sorry," he said at last.

"For what? Cry all you want."

126

"I try to be strong, but sometimes I just can't."

"You don't have to be."

"Yes, I do."

"No, Pete, you don't. You can lean on the people who love you. You never really know if love is there, unless you let it carry you sometimes. This is one of those times, sport. Just lean on the rest of us. You don't have to be brave or smart or anything."

Another silence, and then: "Could I do that now?"

"You bet. That's what I'm saying."

"No, I mean . . . put my head on your shoulder?"

Children are such literal creatures, and Pete, of course, was still a child. While I'd been speaking figuratively, he'd been imagining the real thing: the warmth and reassurance of a father's arms, while it was possible. "Sure," I told him, struggling with my embarrassment. "Go ahead."

The odd thing was, I could feel it. The heat of his head against my shoulder, the faint cedary smell of those dark curls, his hand resting lightly on my chest. It was as if there'd always been an outline there, the suggestion of a child that had finally—miraculously—been colored in.

"Feels nice," said Pete.

"Good."

"Are you afraid of dying, Gabriel?"

"Oh, yeah."

"A lot?"

"More than anything, I guess."

"Why?"

I thought for a moment. "It's got something to do with not being the center of attention anymore."

A tiny laugh. "I mean, for real."

"That is for real. Sort of."

"Do you think there's a heaven?"

"Well . . . yeah. But I think this is pretty much it."

"What do you mean?"

"Just being close to somebody else. That's certainly a kind of heaven. It's the only one I'm going for anyway. Because you get to enjoy it while you're alive. And later on you can *really* live forever. In the hearts of the people who love you."

"What about when *they* die?"

I chuckled. "Well, at that point . . . I guess our books will have to do it. That's another reason to stick around, by the way: publication day. You've got lots of glory coming, son."

He was quiet for so long that I began to worry. "You don't believe me?" I asked.

"No. Not that. I was just wondering why you called me that."

"Called you what?"

"Son."

"Oh . . ." I laughed uneasily. "Just a throwback to my youth. In the South back then, grownups always called you son."

"Even if they weren't your parents?"

I chuckled. "Especially if they weren't your parents. Did that bother you?"

"No. I liked it." He waited a moment, then asked: "Could I call you Dad sometimes?"

I was so embarrassed that all I could manage was flippancy. "As opposed to Dicksmoker, you mean?"

Pete remained thoroughly serious. "I'd really like to."

"Okay, then . . . sure. Whatever."

"I've never called anybody that."

"Not even . . ." I censored myself, wary of opening that door.

"The sperm donor?"

I laughed nervously. "Is that what you call him?"

"Why not? That's all he ever did. Why should I have a name for *him* when he never called me anything?"

"What do you mean?" My flesh was crawling for reasons I couldn't quite pinpoint.

"He never used my name," Pete explained. "And neither did . . . you know, his wife. Sometimes their customers called me Little Boy Blue, but those two never called me anything. Just 'Hey, you' and shit like that. I didn't even know my name until I went to school and the teacher read it out during roll call. I couldn't believe it when Mom started using it."

I was thrown for a moment. "Oh . . . Donna, you mean?"

"Yeah. It was like I'd just been born, like she was the only mother I ever had."

"She was, Pete. She is."

"I know. Shit, man, I know that better than . . ." He couldn't finish this thought because of a coughing jag, one that grew in ferocity until it unnerved me. Then came a shrill wheezing sound, a noise I'd never heard him make. This is it, I thought. And I'll be the only witness.

"Pete, is your mom there? Or somebody who can—"

"It's okay," he gasped.

"Maybe you should ring—"

"No. I wanna be with you."

"I know, Pete, but—"

"I'm okay, now. See?"

His breathing had improved, but it was still labored, so I asked again where Donna was.

"Down the hall. I asked her for privacy."

"Don't you think you should—"

"No. I'm fine. There's a button here if it gets bad."

"But how do you know if—"

"I know, okay? I've been livin' with this shit."

"Well, catch your breath, then."

"Okay."

He didn't talk for a while, but I could still hear his tortured breathing. Finally he said: "I don't want you to go yet."

"I'm not going anywhere."

"Are you still holding me?"

"Sure."

"You know what I'd like?"

"What?"

"If we could do this for real."

I wasn't sure what to say. Pete had always been too straight with me to be humored like a child, and I didn't want to promise him something I couldn't deliver. On the other hand, if this was a last request . . .

"Actually," I said, "your mom did say something about her chili."

"Really?"

"Yeah. When you're feeling better."

"You mean, like . . . coming to Wysong?"

"That's what it sounded like."

"It's kind of a suckhole, you know."

I laughed. "I wouldn't be coming for the antique auto museum."

Pete giggled. "How'd you know about that?"

"Your mom told me."

"It's the boringest place in the world, but there's a pretty decent lake down the road. We could go fishing together."

A ludicrous image formed in my head: Andy and

Opie with their fishing poles, whistling their way down that country road. Pete was as much a fantasist as I was, but how could I begrudge him that? "Great," I said. "But why don't we just walk around the lake?"

"You don't like fishing?"

"Not really."

"Why not?"

"I've never been persuaded they don't feel pain."

I expected a teasing retort, but it never came. "I kinda know what you mean," he said.

"Good. It's a date, then."

"Cool."

"But you gotta stick around for it."

"I hear you," he said.

"You think you could get some sleep now?"

"Could you tell me a story first?"

"A story?"

"Don't gimme any shit, okay?"

I wasn't about to do that. It was painfully clear that Pete was claiming one of the missing rituals of his childhood while there was still time to do it.

"What sort of story?" I asked.

"Like one on the radio."

"Those are all written in advance, sport."

"So write me one now."

"I wish it were that simple. I spend days working on a page sometimes. And lately I haven't even done that."

"Yeah. They've all been reruns."

I issued a weary sigh. "Pitiful, isn't it?"

"Tell me about your dad, then."

A day or so earlier I would have offered a salty response, but so much about my relationship with the boy had already changed. Now it somehow seemed as

131

if he were inquiring into his own ancestry, so I couldn't very well disparage his grandfather. "What would you like to know?" I asked.

"Did you ever go fishing with him?"

I thought about that. "Maybe once or twice. I think he was the same way as me, actually."

"About the fish, you mean?"

"Yeah. I know he hated hunting. He had no respect for men who went off into the woods with guns. And sports were no big deal either. He never inflicted that one on me, thank God. Which was a good thing, since I was a miserable athlete."

"What did he like, then?"

"Oh . . . gardening, mostly, and worshipping our ancestors and being with my mother. He yelled at her a lot, but he adored her. He hated it when they were separated."

"Was he a writer, too?"

"No, not really. Well, he wrote a family history once. And he was an excellent storyteller."

"Before bed, you mean."

"Oh, no. It was more like . . . you know, to the whole room."

"Like you."

I laughed. "Yeah, I guess. Like me."

"He sounds great."

"Well . . . a lot about him was, yes."

"He's dead, you mean?"

"Oh, no. Not by a long shot."

"Do you talk to him like this? On the phone."

"Well . . . yeah, if there's a birthday or something. He's no good at the spontaneous stuff. He has to have a reason. And I get a little tired of always being the one who calls."

"Oh, man, if I had a dad . . ."

"Hey, I thought we'd just arranged that."

Another significant pause, and then: "That didn't weird you out?"

"No . . . well, maybe at first, but . . . I want you to call me that, okay? I want to be that person for you."

He started to cry again.

"I know," I said. "You could do a lot better."

"Fuck you," he said.

"Hey . . . that's 'Fuck you, Dad.'"

We talked for another five minutes or so. Trivial stuff mostly, since I wanted to lessen the urgency of saying goodbye. The end announced itself naturally enough, when Pete's voice began to dwindle. But he said "I love you" before we signed off, and I said it back to him.

And I remember thinking how easily those words had come, and how preposterously *true* they seemed, and how they would seem that way for years to come, even if they proved to be our last.

Nine

More Than Elephants

The sidewalk outside Pasqua was bustling with Bears: big guys in beards and suspenders who would have been called portly in an earlier age. Though they often gathered here in—what? packs?—their furry-shouldered presence was especially evident this morning. Was there a convention in town, I wondered, some mass migration from the hinterlands? There was a distinct tribal hum in the coffeehouse, the kind you hear on an airplane when every passenger but you is travelling to the same ball game.

I waited in line with a trio of grizzlies, then took my turkey pesto sandwich to a table in the corner, where I pondered my identity. At just under two hundred pounds I was certainly eligible for Beardom. What would it be like to abandon the gym, to say yes to jelly doughnuts, to buy a pair of roomy overalls and learn to eroticize fat? Bears were supposed to be free of attitude, weren't they? I liked the idea of that, and of reviving the carnal democracy of yore, before steroids and circuit parties had bullied so many men into seeking identical pneumatic bodies.

Then again, I already knew how it felt to be thirty pounds heavier. At the height of my domesticity with Jess I had lost my body-consciousness to such an extent that I stopped consulting the scales and started wearing sweatpants. Jess found me sexy in any size, he claimed, so I relaxed and ignored the obvious. I didn't realize how much had changed until I went on a book tour in Europe and read my own press profiles. Photographs can be denied as easily as mirrors, but even translated from the Finnish the word "fat" is sufficiently clear. So I joined a gym when I got home—not a gay one, which would have been too intimidating, but the gym down at the UC Medical Center, three blocks from the house. And I hired a trainer this time, adding financial commitment to my growing list of incentives.

My body changed in subtle ways—and slowly—but it changed. It was thrilling to discover the muscles in my back, to see my chest begin to expand, to feel that deep exquisite soreness the day after. And my thrice-weekly endorphin rush was an antidepressant like none I'd ever known. As Jess grew ever more distant and restless, my workouts became a routine bordering on a habit. (It was as if some part of me already *knew* I was about to require a much deeper reserve of self-esteem.) I was so pleased with my progress that I bought a pair of 501s—the first I'd braved in over a decade—though I snipped off that faux-leather label on the waist. Thirty-six was respectable, I told myself, but hardly worth advertising.

I was wearing my delabelled Levi's today, in fact.

And wondering for the first time in ages if my basket was presented to its best advantage. Or did guys in their thirties even give a damn about fifty-four-year-old baskets? *I* certainly hadn't, as I recalled. Once, for instance, when I was doing PR for a local hotel, the owner, a burly, white-haired guy in his fifties, asked me jovially if I had ever seen his cock. Before I could answer, he had reached into his desk and produced a plaster cast of the member in question, fully engorged. It was the proverbial baby's arm, ropy-veined and magnificent, and I was instantly drawn to it—but not, alas, to its proud owner. Looking back, I wonder why I didn't just drop to my knees and narrow my focus a little. But all I could manage then was a clumsy compliment, as if the nice gentleman, a much braver soul than I, had just shown me a snapshot of his grandchild.

I had been in the coffeehouse for at least ten minutes before I realized Jess was there. He was at a table near the window with a group of leathermen, most of them shiny-skulled and stacked like chorus girls. There was no clean escape without awkwardness, so I waited until I was sure he wasn't gripping the knee of anyone in particular, then made my way over. He was seated with his back to me, but he seemed to sense my approach and turned around. Or maybe someone had nudged him under the table.

"Hi," he said quietly, as if we were alone.

"I'm not stalking you," I joked, realizing he'd wonder a little, since Pasqua had never been a haunt of mine. I'd come here for the reasons he'd probably first come: the camaraderie and mild sexual energy, the chance to be alone in a crowd without alcohol.

He introduced me to his friends—as his partner, amazingly—then invited me to join them.

"Thanks," I said. "I gotta get back. I'm hopelessly behind on this episode."

Jess gave me a private smile, recognizing a glamorous lie told for the benefit of the others. "I'll walk you out," he said.

When we were on the sidewalk, he added: "I wanted to tell you that I called Pete."

I hadn't expected this. "Oh, yeah?"

"How bad off *is* he, anyway?"

"What do you mean?" I was fretting already, though Donna had promised she would call me if he got any worse. It had been at least three days since our last conversation.

"He sounds awful," said Jess. "Congested."

I told him that was business as usual.

"He's a spunky little fucker, isn't he?"

"What did you talk about?"

"Oh . . . Matthew Shepard, mostly."

"Who?"

"That kid in Wyoming."

"What kid in Wyoming?"

"You haven't seen a newspaper, have you? Look over there." He pointed to the corner of Eighteenth and Castro, where a makeshift shrine was already materializing on the sidewalk: burned-out rainbow candles and limp bouquets, a grainy blowup of a sweet-faced young man. "A couple of cowboys picked him up in a bar. Tied him to a fence and pistol-whipped him to a pulp. In front of their fucking girlfriends."

I winced. "He was gay, you mean?"

"What do *you* think? It was Wyoming." Jess's face

137

was flushed with outrage, but there were tears in his eyes. This was what I loved him for: the pent-up passion of that big, gentle, wounded heart.

"Is he dead?" I asked.

"Might as well be, apparently."

"Jesus."

"I didn't bring it up, by the way. He did."

"Who?"

"Pete. He was crying about it. About how mean the world can be."

"He knows enough about *that*," I said.

Jess wiped his eyes. "He said to tell you he's enjoying the magazine. Whatever that means."

I smiled. "Good. He got it."

"Got what?"

I explained about the *Playboy*, knowing Jess would understand. Another reason I loved him: he saw sex as everybody's blessing.

"Do you think he's hiding it?" he asked.

"I would imagine. It's required by the laws of puberty, isn't it?"

Jess couldn't let that one slip by. "Don't tell me you ever hid *Playboys*."

"No. But I saw them sometimes. And I was turned on."

"'Sex in the Cinema,' right?"

I laughed. "Some of those guys were hot. Not to mention naked. You didn't get a lot of that back then."

"So you've told me." The teasing look he gave me spoke to our age difference, and how long we'd been together, and how well he knew the particulars of my shopworn stories.

"Are you gonna talk to him again?" I asked.

"Pete?"

"Yeah. I'm not sure he's getting the best advice about treatment. And the doctors at that hospital act like he's dead already."

"I know. He told me."

"It's really unbelievable."

"Yeah . . . it is . . . as a matter of fact." There was a deepening crease in his forehead that disturbed me.

"What do you mean?"

"I mean . . . some of it really *is* unbelievable."

"In what way?"

"No doctors are *that* insensitive, you know. Not to a kid with AIDS. Not nowadays."

"Well . . . maybe not here . . . but he's in Milwaukee. It's probably a lot different back there. What are you getting at?"

"Just that he might be . . . revving it up a little. Telling you what you want to hear."

"What are you talking about? Why would I want to hear that he's being treated like a piece of meat?"

Jess remained calm. "It just makes for a better story. And it makes it that much easier to care about him."

"*A better story?*"

"He's a writer, isn't he? A pretty good one, you said."

"So he's making all of this up, just to give me a—"

"I didn't say he was making anything up. Don't put words in my mouth, Gabriel. You do that way too much."

We had stumbled upon a larger issue—and a much more threatening one—so I softened my tone. "Then what are you saying?"

"Think about it. Doesn't it strike you as a little too gothic? This poor little kid who's always being mistreated. By his evil parents and the evil pederasts and the evil doctors. People have shitty lives, but they're

139

not shitty *all* the time. This is like *The Perils of Pauline*. Don't you think it's *possible* he's exaggerating a little?"

"Jewelling the elephant," I said, nailing him with my gaze.

"Okay. Whatever." He smiled back at me carefully. "It's been known to happen."

"You know, I've enjoyed that joke as much as you have. But there's a lot more than elephants involved here. This kid is probably dying. If you toned down his life by half it would still be horrendous. And he's also somebody I happen to love." This just tumbled out heedlessly, like a deathbed revelation. My face grew blotchy with embarrassment.

Jess was gentle about it. "C'mon, sweetie. Love? After four phone calls?"

"It's more like ten. But yes."

"Well, that's what makes you who you are."

I knew he was trying to be nice, but I felt trivialized, dismissed as a sentimental fool.

"Are you mad at me?" he asked.

"Just a little disappointed," I said. "You know how this works."

"How what works?"

"What they always say about child abuse: the hardest part is getting adults to believe that it actually happened. People don't *want* to believe something that barbarous, so they find ways to deny it. That's exactly what you're doing, Jess. This kid has somehow screwed up the courage to lay it all on the line, to blow the whistle on his own parents . . . and all you can do is accuse him of exaggeration."

"I haven't accused him of anything. I just explained a feeling I had. If I can't do that with you . . ."

"I thought you guys would hit it off."

"We did. I like him a lot. He's a bright kid."

"You're one of his heroes, you know. He sees you as a much bigger hell-raiser than I am."

"Well . . . he's perceptive, too."

That made me smile.

"And politically he's right there with us. I was impressed by that."

"That's Donna's influence," I said, beginning to calm down. "And all that time in the AIDS wards. He knows what it's like to be an outsider. He's practically an honorary queer."

Jess locked eyes with me. "I see why you like him. I just brought it up because—"

"It's okay. I know what you meant. Maybe he *is* a little . . . vivid sometimes. Maybe we both are. It's just a mechanism, sweetie. It's how writers explain things to themselves."

"I know," he said, with only a trace of irony.

Jess, of course, had mechanisms of his own. A rough childhood and a decade of near-death experience had turned him into a hardcore skeptic. He distrusted most things until they were proven certainties, until they seemed incapable of disappointing or betraying him.

"Will you talk to him again?" I asked.

"If he wants to. I gave him my number. Don't these calls get expensive for them?"

"Donna doesn't seem to mind. It gives him something to do, I guess. And I call *him* sometimes."

Jess's eyes darted into the coffeehouse where his buddies were deep in conversation. "I should get back."

"I know."

"Are you okay?" he asked.

141

I nodded.

"Are you really writing?"

I rolled my eyes.

Jess smiled benevolently. "It'll come. Don't sweat it."

His face slipped into a scowl when he was jostled by a chubby guy in flannel headed for the terrace with a tray of cinnamon rolls.

"These fucking Bears," Jess muttered, and went back inside.

When I was about Pete's age I took a cross-country bus trip to New Mexico with the other boys in my Explorer post. We were heading for Philmont Scout Ranch, where most of us would experience the West for the first time. I remember our excitement when we learned there really *was* a Dodge City, and the rumble that ran through the bus when we heard we would stop there to buy cowboy hats. The other guys went for the ten-dollar model, a cheesy fake with wire in the rim, obviously intended for children. I spotted the word "Stetson" on an upper shelf and decided to go for the best: a mole-colored dome of genuine felt that screamed authenticity. It would take most of my spending money, but my souvenir would be one for the ages.

Alas, the hat was less suggestive of Steve McQueen (the person my mother said I most resembled) than of Tom Mix in one of those silly silent westerns. I learned this the hard way when I wore the bulbous monstrosity back to the bus, only to be greeted by a burst of rude laughter and a new nickname—Penishead—that would dog me for the rest of the trip. I told myself I'd be vindicated once the hat had been properly blocked in a mountain stream, but the taunts continued. I shed secret tears that night when we bunked at a nearby army base. And I considered thumbing into Dodge early the next morning, so I could throw myself on the mercy of the haberdasher and beg for my forty dollars back. But I knew there was no undoing the damage I'd already done.

I was never very happy at camp, and Philmont was no exception. I became the Designated Dork—an easy mark for the other boys—who, oddly, had never been that mean to me back in Charleston. This was the wilderness, though, and all rules were apparently off, so I kept to myself as much as possible and counted the days to my release. The only break in my misery came after a huge thunderstorm, a biblical downpour that loosened our tent pegs and drenched us to the bone. We were rescued by some Yankees at a neighboring campsite—New Jersey boys, as I recall—who shared their food and dry clothes with us. That night, as the rain pounded down, we joined them around their campfire. One of them put his arm across my shoulders so I could inhabit his poncho, and urged me to lean against him for warmth. The comfort I felt was a revelation. I can still conjure up the smell of that mildewy tarp, the toasty warmth of his chest against my back, those rough Yankee vowels forming so close to my Southern ear.

I had learned to jerk off earlier that year, but the experience had seemed more of a medical emergency than an act of lust. At Philmont I became an expert. I would jerk off in my sleeping bag after Taps, drawing on the images of the day: those olive-skinned Yankees in their wet underwear, the loinclothed braves of the Order of the Arrow, the time Bo Brandt dropped his shorts to prove to us how he could stick the tip of his little finger in his pee-hole. And when Taps was too far off, I would lock myself in the outhouse and pound away. It was there that Penishead (a limber lad in those days) made the useful discovery that he could suck his own dick—or at least, with some effort, lick the end of it. It wasn't exactly Nirvana, but it was a lot closer than he'd ever been to his heart's desire.

This came back to me last week when I rented a Cadinot porn movie called *Hot on the Trail,* in which a dozen French "scouts"—most of them at least twenty— tramped across the countryside and enjoyed each other's company. The film spent a lot of time on pre- liminaries: wrestling and swimming, tempting bulges in loose khaki shorts. It understood the essence of that youthful longing, the exquisite ache of anticipation and denial. And this, I have to say, is what *still* excites me, after all these years of license and exploration; this is why I liked it best when Jess left his Jockey shorts on.

It's hell to lust for your tormentors, to know from the beginning that your deepest need can only betray you, only expel you from the tribe. So when you grow up, you find a tribe of your own, with guys just like you, to keep from feeling that way ever again. Only you do sometimes, as I had done that morning at Pasqua, see- ing Jess among the leathermen, wondering what they could offer that I could not. That age-old pain came roaring out of nowhere to remind me that I'd never be strong enough, never be handsome enough, never be young enough, to really be a man among men.

Ten

The Monkey Wrench

I can pinpoint the day the bottom fell out. It was the day Matthew Shepard died, because that was the reason Donna Lomax called—"to hear a friendly voice," as she put it, to sort out her feelings about the latter-day crucifixion that had hit so close to home everywhere in America.

"What is it?" she asked. "Are people getting meaner?"

I told her this kind of cruelty had always existed, that only the circumstances around it had changed. Matthew Shepard had been openly gay, after all, and his parents had never been ashamed of him. For once there was no reason to hide the cause of his death, so the truth could be examined in full. And that was progress, I suggested, as grim as it might be.

"He was so *little*," she said, ignoring my political analysis. "I think that's what got to me. I know it's what

145

got to Pete. He hates bullies more than anything. He's been a mess about this for days."

I told her I knew that.

"Did he call you?"

"No. But Jess talked to him right after it happened."

"Really? You mean . . . *your* Jess?"

How I loved the sound of that possessive pronoun. "Yeah," I said, feeling warmer toward her than ever. "I thought it might be good for Pete. Jess has done so well with his own treatment."

"That was sweet of you."

"Actually, I thought they'd both enjoy it. And I wasn't wrong, as it turned out."

(Never mind Jess's talk about jewelling the elephant; he would just have to get over himself.)

"By the way," said Donna, "I hope I'm not out of line, but Pete said that you guys are . . . sort of . . ."

"Yeah. We're apart for a while."

"I'm sorry."

"Thanks. We're hanging in there."

"You guys are still talking, though. That's good."

I chuckled ruefully. "I don't know who else to talk to."

"Well," she said. "I'm here, if you need me. I know a thing or two about this stuff. My ex-husband was a couples therapist."

I laughed at the absurdity of that, then caught myself. "Sorry. I know that wasn't meant to be funny."

"Oh, yes it was," she said.

Now she was laughing with me.

"We learn this shit however we have to," she added.

And then the door buzzer sounded.

"What was that?" she asked.

"A visitor. Probably the gas man. Could you hold for a sec?"

"Sure."

I bounded downstairs to the intercom where I discovered that the visitor was Jess. I buzzed him up, thrilled about his serendipitous timing, then waited as he climbed the steps through the garden.

"I'm on the phone," I told him at the door. "With Donna Lomax."

"Who?"

"Pete's mother. Why don't you say hi?"

"I don't know . . ."

"C'mon. Just for a minute." I picked up the extension by the sofa. "Donna, there's someone who wants to meet you."

Jess gave me a frosty glance as he accepted the receiver. I sat down on the sofa and watched him with an expression of proud proprietorship.

"Hi," he began, turning his back to me. "This is Jess."

Their conversation must have lasted twenty minutes, but I was present for only the first five. They seemed to be getting on so well that I retreated to my office to allow for greater intimacy. The part I *did* hear began with a discussion of treatment options but soon relaxed into more folksy, personal stuff: movies they loved, politicians they hated, the limitations of small-town life. Jess grilled her about everything with obvious interest, like someone on a blind date that has turned out far better than expected.

I knew the call was over when the light on my office phone went off.

So I went back down to the living room. Jess was standing by the French doors, staring out at the city. He didn't turn around as I approached, or even speak to me. He just stood there, looking oddly distracted.

"How did it go?" I asked.

His silence lasted a moment longer. Then he turned and faced me. "You've never even noticed, have you?"

I felt uneasy without knowing why. "Noticed what?"

"It's the same voice, Gabriel."

"What is?"

"Pete and Donna have the same voice."

"Oh, I know. It's that flat Midwestern thing. Not very pretty."

"*No. I mean it's the same person.*"

Very slowly, my jaw went slack. "What in the world are you talking about?"

"How much plainer do I have to make it? His voice is exactly the same as hers. It's just a higher-pitched, more childish version. The rhythms are the same and the . . . intonation or whatever you call it. It's really obvious once you listen for it. That's why I stayed on the phone so long. To make absolutely sure. Somebody's been jerking your chain, sweetie."

I tried to absorb this, but I couldn't wrap my head around it. I couldn't even reconstruct Pete's voice—or Donna's, for that matter—as recently as I'd heard them both. "This is absurd," I said feebly.

"You haven't noticed it, then? The similarity?"

I shook my head absently. "No. Not particularly. Except the accent, of course, which must be what you're—"

"Have you ever heard them talking at the same time?"

Had I? I couldn't remember. I remembered that Donna had woken Pete once, so he could talk to me. I remembered her calling his name, and the sound of that tiny Bart Simpson voice, struggling out of sleep . . .

148

"Look," I said. "There are dozens of people who know them both."

"Name some."

"Well, his doctors, for one thing. And everybody at the hospital."

"You don't know that. You've just been told it."

"All right, then. What about Ashe Findlay?"

"Who?"

"Pete's editor. From Argus House. You met him at the ABA in Las Vegas."

"That old preppie guy with the dandruff?"

"Yes. He's publishing his book, for God's sake. Nobody does that without knowing—"

"Did he ever go out to Wisconsin?"

"I don't know. I'm sure he must have. Jesus, Jess, what possible reason could anybody have to do something like this?"

"I haven't gotten that far," he said.

No, I thought, you haven't. You just want to deny the reality of this heroic child. For some reason, it's too much for you to handle. Could Jess be *jealous*, I wondered, resentful of someone else with AIDS who had won my admiration? Had Pete simply stolen his thunder?

"How much are they getting paid for this thing?" he asked.

"What thing?"

"His book."

I could feel the blood rising in my face. "Oh, buckets," I said. "Six or seven figures at least. There's a lucrative market out there for abused-kids-with-AIDS books. It's a real publishing bonanza!"

Sarcasm was never a wise thing with Jess. He snatched his briefcase off the coffee table and headed

149

for the door. "Fine," he said, "I was planning to do some work in the office, but fuck it!"

"Wait a minute. Just hang on, please."

"I don't need this shit."

"Look, Jess, you can't just throw out some crazy conspiracy theory and expect me not to—"

"Why can't I? If that's what I'm thinking. Why can't you respect that? Why can't you just deal with things as they arise?"

"All right, okay. I'm dealing." I gestured toward the sofa. "Sit down. I'll get us some coffee. Let's talk about it."

He hesitated a moment, then sat down. I sighed audibly, relieved to have averted a fight at such a dangerous time.

Everything in my life seemed so perishable now.

When I returned with the coffee, Jess was cooing softly to Hugo, who had come down from the bedroom at the sound of his other master's voice. The old cur was on his back, his mouth open, his tongue lolling blissfully to one side, while Jess rubbed his stomach. The sight of them together again overwhelmed me. It was Jess's compulsive sweetness toward animals that had helped me fall in love with him, once upon a time.

He looked up as I set down his coffee mug. "He's getting really decrepit, isn't he?"

I nodded.

"Aren't you, beastlet? You're a decrepit old thing." He picked a speck of crud out of the dog's cloudy eye, then gave me a weary smile. He had shed the force field of anger that had surrounded him minutes earlier.

"I could be wrong," he said, shrugging.

I tried to be generous. "Their voices *are* similar. I can see how you might think that if . . ."

"How did this all get started, anyway?"

I explained how Ashe Findlay had sent me Pete's galleys.

"Did they *ask* for them to be sent to you?"

"Who?"

"Pete and Donna."

"Well, yes, actually. And Pete talks about listening to my show in the book, so Findlay must have thought it was a natural choice."

"How did you end up talking to Pete?"

"I asked Findlay if I could do it."

"It was *your* idea, then?"

"Yes. Completely."

He seemed to ponder that as he stroked the dog's chin. "So how did Findlay get the manuscript?"

"Umm . . ." I thought hard. "Somebody at Argus House knows Pete's HIV counselor. A guy named Warren."

"Have you ever talked to him?"

"No. But he's reachable, I'm sure." I sat on the sofa and began to scratch Hugo's matted rump while Jess continued rhythmically with the dog's chin. It was something of a surrogate experience, but it was wonderful how this broken-down old creature could pull us into a circle of familial affection. "And we could always call Findlay," I said.

Jess looked up at me.

"Right now," I said, "if you'd like."

"It's late in New York."

"He works late."

"Do you want to?"

"I wouldn't mind," I said. "If it puts your mind at ease."

I went up to the office and brought back the phone book. I dialled the number in front of Jess, then waited while it rang repeatedly. Finally, a peevish female voice answered—the kind you get so often in New York. Ashe Findlay had been at a sales conference, she said, and wouldn't be back that day. I left my name and asked her to have him call me tomorrow.

When I hung up, Jess said: "What about that Warren guy?"

"I don't know how to reach him. I don't even know his last name."

"Oh, well." Jess went back to massaging Hugo's stomach. "So much for putting my mind at ease. Huh, beastlet?"

His flip tone annoyed me, and I could feel a headache coming on. I was suddenly tired of catering to his chronic distrust. "I think I'll take him for a walk," I said, indicating the dog. "Let you have your time in the office."

The walk lasted an hour and a half. Hugo and I went all the way to Tank Hill and back while I tried to make sense of the monkey wrench Jess had just thrown into my life. I was mostly embarrassed for him, I think, since his wild speculation had only shown how far he'd go to sabotage something that didn't fit his skeptical vision of the world. Or was it just the fact that this miracle had happened to *me*? It would have been different, I decided, if Pete had first made friends with Jess, if Jess had been the one gathering the facts and telling the story, the one in control. But this was just broken-hearted, bejewelling me, far too needy and vulnerable right now to know a hoax when it stared me in the face.

When I got home, Jess was gone. He had tidied up the office, prioritized my correspondence, and posted a list of Things to Do on the bulletin board. That would have given me a sense of well-being, I suppose, had I not also seen that he'd acted on our earlier discussion.

Both the computer and the computer table were gone, leaving a hole in the room that might as well have been in my heart.

Eleven

A Little Like God

It's hard to say now what I expected from Ashe Findlay when he called back the next morning. Mild amusement would probably have topped the list, followed by bewilderment, then righteous indignation. I was ready for anything, given the lunatic nature of my inquiry. I spent a minute or two issuing disclaimers and covering my tracks—or ensuring that they *would* be covered—once the whole silly thing had been laid to rest.

"I'm hesitant even to ask," I told the editor. "If anyone were to hear about this . . . especially Pete . . ."

"Please," he said quietly. "You have my word. This is strictly between us."

"Okay, then. Do you know anyone who's actually met Pete Lomax?"

The line was so quiet I thought we'd been cut off.

"Ashe?"

More silence and then: "Hang on a minute. I have to close the door."

What can I tell you about that moment? It was beyond unsettling; it shook me to my very core, then left me standing on quicksand, holding my breath. It must have done the same to Findlay, because he was gone much longer than it would have taken to close a door.

"Gabriel?"

"I'm here," I said.

"First of all, let me say I know exactly what you're going through, because I went through it myself three months ago."

Don't say a word, I thought. Just let him talk.

"It's important to remember how dedicated Donna is to the protection of this child. Pete went through things that aren't even hinted at in his manuscript. Terrible things. Donna's a total professional, but she's also a mother, and that makes her a tigress when it comes to shielding Pete from strangers. And the poor kid has such low immunity right now that even the mildest flu bug is potentially threatening to his—"

"Ashe?"

"Yes?"

"I'd really like an answer to my question."

He waited a moment, then said, "No," in the most subdued tone imaginable.

"You don't know *anybody* who's ever met him?"

"No. Except her, of course."

"What about his AIDS counselor? Warren something."

"Warren Bloch."

"Yeah. What about him?"

"Well . . . he's a nice fellow. Dropped by the office last month."

"Then you *do* know someone!" The relief I felt was

155

so profound that I almost laughed. "Warren and Pete used to listen to my show together all the time! One of them must've mentioned that to you."

"Actually . . . they both did. But you're making an assumption, Gabriel. As natural as it is."

He had lost me.

"They listened to your show on the phone."

"What do you mean?"

"They listened to it at the same time. While they were on the phone with each other."

"Surely, at some point, they must've . . ."

"No. Warren did all his counseling on the phone."

"But . . . *why*?"

"As I was saying, Donna has been very circumspect about who meets the boy at this stage of his recovery."

"But surely a *therapist* . . ."

"It's just another person, Gabriel. Pete trusts voices more than he can ever trust a face. That's why your show was so humanizing for him. He could invent faces that didn't threaten him."

I remembered reading as much in Pete's galleys. I just hadn't guessed how thoroughly the concept had invaded his life. With a sudden shiver I recalled how I'd once remarked to Pete that life wasn't radio. In his case, it seemed, that was pretty much *all* it had been.

"Tell me something," said Findlay. "How did . . . these issues . . . arise for you?"

I told him that Jess had been skeptical about the high melodrama of Pete's life, and that he'd later noticed similarities between Pete's voice and Donna's. Once he'd passed these thoughts to me, a tiny, troubling doubt had begun to inhabit me like a virus.

The editor sighed. "I've been down the same road, my friend."

"You've noticed it, then? Their voices?"

"Oh, yes."

"And you didn't think . . ."

"No. It's just that Wisconsin thing. There's a sort of hokey music to it that's quite distinctive."

"That's what I told Jess!"

"You betcha!"

I laughed at his impersonation of Marge Gunderson in *Fargo*, though Pete and Donna sounded nothing like her. I laughed because I desperately needed the release, and because I wanted to regain the purity of my relationship with Pete. I laughed because I wanted my son back.

"Look," said Findlay. "It's easy enough to build a case for a hoax until you have to provide a motive. There's simply no reason for her to do this. To invent a child and impersonate him for well over a year and write a book in his name. They're getting a minuscule advance, I can assure you. And we both know that this little memoir will never reach a huge audience. Not to mention the fact that Donna is a decent woman who is thoroughly dedicated to her profession."

I said that she certainly seemed that way.

"You'll feel that even more so when you meet her."

"You've met her?"

"Oh, yes." The editor chuckled to himself. "Stupid of me. I should've mentioned that first. She came to New York for some sort of psychological conference last summer. We had a long and very pleasant lunch together. No horns or fangs visible anywhere."

I laughed, feeling better already.

"I must say, she was . . . extremely helpful."

"How so?"

"Well, it's a little personal, so I won't go into detail,

but . . . my wife and I were having . . . difficulties at the time and Donna had some very useful insights to offer."

Free professional advice, I thought. Hardly a reason to trust a virtual stranger.

"I know how that must sound," said Findlay, reading my mind, "but I had a good feeling about her, and I'm fairly adept at reading people."

And who doesn't think *that*? I thought.

"It all comes down to trust," he added. "Or faith, I suppose, to be perfectly accurate. I ended up telling myself that Pete is a little like God. No visible proof to speak of, but more than enough circumstantial evidence."

This was no comfort to me, and I told him so.

"Not the religious sort, eh?"

"Not when it comes to voices on the phone."

A pause and then: "May I ask what you're planning to do?"

"What do you mean?"

"Do you intend to go public with . . . this theory?"

This had never occurred to me, and I was shocked at the suggestion. "God, no," I said. "I just wanted some sort of resolution, and I thought you could help. Pete is very important to me, Ashe."

"Well . . . I know, but . . . I remembered how you feel about that outing business. You obviously have a *penchant* for full disclosure."

Perhaps because Findlay had pronounced penchant the French way, his tone suddenly struck me as irritatingly prissy. He was referring to an incident the previous year when I'd publicly criticized a famous actress for narrating a film on homophobia while refusing to talk to the press about her own sexuality.

158

Old-line liberals like Findlay had dismissed my be-havior as just plain bad manners. "Everyone" knew this woman was gay, so why should she have to pro-claim it to the world? Didn't I know that well-placed closet cases could accomplish a lot of good behind the scenes?

"It's not the same thing," I said flatly.

"Well, I don't understand these distinctions."

"It's not that difficult, Ashe. If there's major hypocrisy involved, I get peevish. If an established movie star is playing both ends against the middle and acting ashamed of something that I regard as perfectly normal, I might have something to say about it. I tend to be a little more lenient with dying children. I'm funny that way."

This outburst surprised us both. "I'm sorry," said Findlay. "It wasn't my intention to offend you."

"No," I replied in a milder tone. "Of course not."

"But I'm sure you can see my concern, Gabriel."

"I can. Yes."

"I could lose my job over this. There's no plainer way to put it."

"I understand. But . . . you're convinced that . . . he exists?" How very peculiar it sounded to put the basic issue into words.

"Yes. I am. I am convinced. I wouldn't risk so much if I weren't."

"Okay, then."

"So you won't . . ."

"Look, Ashe. If there's even the slightest chance he exists, I wouldn't dream of creating doubts about him. He's suffered too much already. He had a hard enough time just finding his voice."

"That's exactly right."

"I just wanted to be . . . completely comfortable with him. The way I have been."

"I think you can do that," said Findlay. "I've done it for almost a year. Warren has done it. A lot of people have."

"Is Pete on the phone a lot?" I had felt a little jolt of jealousy, I realized. Who were these other people, anyway—these *total strangers*—who were calling Henzke Street and sharing confidences with my son?

"Not a lot," said Findlay. "He doesn't open up to many people. He can be quite distrustful, in fact. Dismissive even. A girl here in the office read his stuff and asked me if she could speak to him. I'm afraid she laid on the sympathy far too thick."

"Oh, God," I said. "He would hate that."

"Mmm. He asked me not to let her call back."

"He doesn't appreciate pity," I said. "And neither does Donna."

"No. They're both quite refreshing that way."

We were talking about two different people again, so it seemed the natural place to sign off. "I have to go," I said, "but thanks for listening."

"Of course. I'm sorry I couldn't give you the resolution you wanted."

"Don't worry about it."

"If you'd like me to pull your blurb, by the way . . ."

"Oh, no. Leave it."

"You're sure?"

"Absolutely."

And that was the truth, largely.

That afternoon Anna left a message on the machine about collecting my latest receipts. I picked up the phone as soon as I realized who it was.

"Sure," I said. "Drop by anytime."

"Oh . . . Jess . . . I didn't think you'd be there."

"This is Gabriel," I told her.

"Oh . . . sorry. Wow, you guys sound just alike on the phone."

I laughed.

"You've never been told that?"

"Oh, yes. Many times. But it's especially funny right now."

Why hadn't I thought of that earlier? People who live together, who rely on each other for emotional support, often grow to sound alike. It had happened with me and Jess, and it had even happened to Anna, I learned.

"My brother and I are like that," she told me. "Drives people nuts. We're twins, of course, so that helps, but you'd think it wouldn't work that way when one's a boy and one's a girl."

And with those words she handily validated my thesis.

"Boy, have I got a story for you," I told her.

I had coffee ready when Anna arrived, so she could sit and listen without interruption. I have to say I relished the telling of the tale. There were aspects of it that still disturbed me, even as I put it to bed, but it helped to study someone else's reaction, to counter the chaos of real life with the symmetry of a neat little mystery, neatly resolved.

"It makes so much sense," I told her, "when you think about it. She gave Pete a whole new existence, a whole new family. She even gave him his name back. And after all those hours on the couch he must have . . . absorbed some of the qualities of her speech.

There's a name for it, isn't there? Imprinting or something?"

Anna gaped at me. "This was that kid on the machine? The one who called you Dicksmoker?"

I chuckled. "Yeah."

"You thought that was a woman?"

"I thought it *could* have been," I said. "For a little while." I was already beginning to be embarrassed. Talk about imprinting. Jess had implanted the idea of an elaborate hoax with barely any effort at all.

"And you don't think that anymore?"

I shook my head. "It's just too far-fetched."

"But if nobody's ever seen him . . ."

"Nobody I *know* has ever seen him. There's a big difference."

"So why don't you just call the hospital and ask if he's a patient there?"

It was such a no-nonsense Anna-like suggestion, but it instantly made me shudder. "I can't do that," I said.

"Why not?"

"I don't know the hospital, for one thing. And they probably register him under an alias, anyway."

"You'll never know until you ask."

"No. It might get back to him."

"What would be terrible about that?"

"I'm way too close to him, Anna. He trusts me. And I want him to know I trust him. I don't want to sneak around behind his back."

She gave me an off-kilter smile. "This person who might not exist."

"Yes."

"Do you even know what he looks like?"

I was ready for that one. I pulled out my wallet and produced the snapshot with the startling green eyes, handing it to her with a prideful smile. She studied it for a moment in silence.

"He sent you this?"

I nodded. "Well . . . Donna did."

She gave it back to me. "Sweet-looking kid."

She might as well have added: *Whoever he is.*

I returned the snap to my wallet, feeling awkward and a little foolish. Anna peered into her coffee cup intently, as if there were vital clues swimming just below the surface. "You know who he reminded me of on the machine?"

"Who?"

"Bart Simpson."

I smiled. "That actually occurred to me, too."

She took a sip of her coffee as she considered something for a while. Then she looked back at me and widened those Olivia Hussey eyes for greater dramatic effect. "Bart Simpson is a woman, you know."

"Pardon me?"

"On the cartoon. That's actually a woman's voice."

She had intended to rattle me, so I tried not to show how well she'd succeeded. "I guess I knew that," I said evenly. "Or read it. Now that you mention it."

Her gaze returned to her coffee.

"And you know who *you* remind *me* of?" I asked.

"Who?"

"Jess. He loves to tantalize me with that kind of shit, then see where I'll run in my imagination."

"So where did you run?"

"Nowhere. Except straight into a wall."

"Oh, well."

"This is a great parlor game, Anna, but it makes no sense at all, if you look at it logically."

"Why not?"

"Because no one on earth would go to all that trouble."

Anna shrugged. "Maybe it's no trouble. Maybe it comes to her naturally. Maybe she doesn't even know she's doing it."

This had not occurred to me, I must admit.

"That's it," she said, warming to her theme. "Maybe she's like a *multiple* or something!"

"Anna . . ."

"No, listen. This is totally logical. She had a kid once like Pete, who was abused and everything, and she was the one who saved him. So all of that is true. Only he didn't live, he died of AIDS or whatever. And she loved him so much she just couldn't accept his death. So she brought him back to life the only way she could . . . *by becoming him*."

"Stop it."

"Well, tell me that's not logical."

"This woman is a *psychologist*, Anna."

"So? They can be wacko, too."

"Okay, but I seriously . . ."

"She could even have him *embalmed* or something. Like a doll she keeps around for company. Or a *puppet* that she can operate by—"

"Would you stop it, please?" I winced at her in horror and annoyance.

"Sorry."

"These are real people, Anna. With real problems. It's not an episode of *The X-Files*."

"Sorry," she repeated. "You just got me so . . . interested."

She was right about that; I had no one to blame but myself. I already knew the curious power of this riddle. All Anna had done, in her youthful morbidity, was provide one far-too-vivid answer.

"Are you gonna talk to him again?" she asked.

"I don't see why not."

"It's so weird."

"No it isn't," I said firmly. "Not if you don't let it be. Not if you refuse to play this destructive game."

And who was I talking to now?

I had a feeling he would call that night.

You might assume that all this recurring doubt would disconnect us telepathically, or at least loosen our bond. But it didn't work that way. Pete had become more three-dimensional than ever. The longer I thought about him the more I grew convinced that he could sense not only my distress but the reason behind it as well.

The machine came on as I was rinsing Hugo in the bathtub. I paused and cocked an ear to identify the caller, giving the dog a fine opportunity for a good drenching shake. I muttered at him, then sprinted to the office. Pete was already gabbing away.

". . . so if you're *not* there, you'd better be out buying me another *Playboy*, because I've already dumped Miss November and I—"

"Pete!"

"Well, holy fuck, you *are* there."

I sat down breathlessly. "I was washing the dog."

"Is that like spanking the monkey?"

"Speak for yourself, Mr. Playboy."

He chortled. "You are one evil influence."

"We aim to please."

"The T-shirt is really cool, too. I'm wearing it right now. All the gay orderlies are jealous."

I laughed. "You're still at the hospital, then?"

"Yeah, but just for the morning. We go home this afternoon."

"Great."

"I'll say."

"You sound so much better," I told him. "You sound like yourself again."

Jesus, I thought. Of all the ways I could have put it . . .

Twelve

Laura

When I was Pete's age people often mistook me for my mother on the phone. Ladies from the Colonial Dames or St. Michael's Church would call the house on Meeting Street and chirp "Good morning, Laura" as soon as they heard my boyish soprano. But I was only mildly offended, since my mother was a celebrity of sorts, the moderator of a weekly panel discussion on WUTF Radio, whose call letters stood for We Uphold The Family.

Mummie's show was called *Time for Teens* and her four panelists were all of high school age: big, worldly kids with big, worldly problems to discuss, like the treatment of acne and whether necking would inevitably lead to more serious things, like petting. While it was just a public-affairs project for the Junior League, the show was so well received that older kids sometimes asked me if I had a sister named Laura. And once Mummie even posed for a picture that appeared on the front page of the *News and Courier*. She and her panelists were caught sipping soda in a booth at Hoffman's Pharmacy, their straws thrust rakishly into the same glass.

My mother's parents were British immigrants, and she clung to her roots with a vengeance, as if to remind snobby little Charleston that she'd come from a far more cultivated milieu. (This was why her children were instructed to call her Mummie, though I rarely used the name in public after the age of eight; it made me sound too much like Little Lord Fauntleroy, and my mother like an Egyptian artifact.)

This flaunting of all things English reached its fullest flower when Mummie was chosen to play Eliza Doolittle in the Dock Street Theatre's 1954 production of *Pygmalion*. She spent hours at home running lines with me and practicing her cockney, which, I've since come to realize, consisted of little more than dropping her H's. But I was so impressed that I studied her technique carefully and inflicted my own strangled cockney upon friends, as if it were some new form of pig Latin. And I remember what it was like at home on rehearsal nights when Mummie would leave a casserole in the fridge, or pay our maid, Lottie, to stay after work and fix us her fried chicken. My father would sulk in his den, his face buried in the latest tome on the Civil War. "Your mother's off at the theater," he would mutter, "with the fairies." He was desolate without her, an orphaned wretch—even with three children in the house.

If you'd known my mother, you'd understand. She was lovely, to begin with, in a creamy-skinned, hazel-eyed, Deborah Kerr kind of way. And she was such a light, such a beam of pure compassion, that darkness of

168

any sort—even my father's stubborn variety—didn't stand a chance in her presence. Drawn to strays of any kind, she was a pillar of the SPCA, but she rescued a number of humans, as well—or attempted to—over the years. I came to refer to them as the Refugees, since, for some reason, they were usually European, perhaps because it offered Mummie the illusion of a larger world. The Refugees were divorcées, or in the process of becoming: vaguely scarlet women who had met their American husbands at military bases overseas. Lured to the Low Country by the promise of True Love and Tara-like plantations, they ended up in trailer parks and tract houses, married to some abusive Bible-spouting dickhead whose name seemed always to begin with O—an Orville or an Olin or an Otis.

It was my mother's mission, she believed, to pry these women from their personal hells, to offer comfort and conversation, to find them suitable mates among the well-bred bachelors of the Yacht Club. She rarely succeeded. More often than not she landed smack dab in the middle of some knock-down-drag-out marital fracas. "Your mother's lost her goddamned mind," my father once reported. "She's hiding in a phone booth at a motel in Ravenel, and she won't come home until Veronique comes out." Exactly *why* Mummie was hiding—or what her Refugee was doing inside—I was never told, but my father did volunteer that Veronique was "common as pigs' tracks," and that my mother would end up in a serious lawsuit if she didn't mind her own goddamned business. I waited for all hell to break loose, but Mummie returned that evening in time to take her pot roast out of the oven and settle in for *The Bob Cummings Show*. As she snuggled up to my father on the sofa, all that betrayed her busy afternoon of espionage (and the apparent accomplishment of her mission) was the cryptic little half-smile blooming on her face.

In later years Mummie's caretaking was more confined to home. My father's mother—the grandmother we called Dodie—had Parkinson's disease and the beginnings of Alzheimer's, though we thought of it then as garden-variety senility. Dodie was shaky and bent over, a human parenthesis with a hearing aid as big as a prayer book hitched to her bosom. She needed help getting out of chairs and going to the toilet and even walking—all of which services my mother provided with unending goodwill. As the two of them inched across a room together, Dodie, who had strived for gentility all her life, could sometimes be heard to emit a barrage of unladylike farts. "Oh, goodness me," she would murmur in mortification. And Mummie would squeeze Dodie's shoulder and say: "That's all right. We'll just hurry and get away from it." Then they would both dissolve in giggles, bowing in their mirth to the awful hopelessness of it all.

Dodie's failing mind sometimes fell prey to demons. When I was in my early teens she became convinced she was being investigated by St. Michael's Church— by the Ladies' Auxiliary, no less. "They think I'm an alcoholic," I heard her tell my parents one night, and even then I guessed that this delusional nonsense was really about my grandfather and the firestorm of speculation that Dodie must have endured after his suicide. I had come across a bundle of old letters in the attic several years earlier: proclamations from local civic organizations extolling the virtues of the first Gabriel Noone upon his untimely death. Though they all avoided the particulars, there was a tone of anxious overstatement to them that invited suspicion even before I knew how my grandfather had died. In its concerted effort to remove the shame, the town had merely made it official. And Dodie had borne it for almost a quarter of a century. I remember passing her room late one night and hearing a sound that rattled me to the core. At seventy-five she was whimpering in her sleep like a baby, curled up there in the big mahogany sleigh bed that her grandfather's slaves had built.

My mother took care of everyone, but her firstborn was especially blessed. When I was as young as eight, she would bring me breakfast in bed on Saturday mornings, so I could listen to *Big John and Sparky* in the alpine lair of my upper bunk. My father, who complained bitterly of her "mollycoddling," had contributed to this indulgence by building a shelf near the ceiling that could hold both my shortwave radio and my vast collection of Hardy Boys books. Later, when I discovered *The Big Show* and its host, Miss Tallulah Bankhead, I would climb to my aerie after supper and surrender to the smoky-warm, mannish voice of a woman I worshipped as a goddess but had never actually seen.

In Mummie's version of things I was simply her eccentric child. My brother, Billy, was the athletic, methodical one, the natural heir to my father's gift for finance, a lively, uncomplicated kid who spent hours moving marbles across the rug as if they were beads on an abacus. And Josie, by definition, was the Precious Little Girl, a role so exalted that no one could imagine a future for her beyond marriage and motherhood. Of the three children, I was the puzzlement: the one my mother dubbed Ferdinand, since, unlike the other little bulls, I preferred to sit alone in the pasture and smell the flowers. How could she not have known from the beginning? She must have suspected *something* when I saw *Singin' in the Rain* eight times at the age of ten, when I entered my homemade vegetable dyes in the junior high science fair, when I spent weeks designing a stained-glass window for my bedroom.

"Gabriel is just naturally creative," Mummie would tell her friends, when Pap wasn't there to hear it. "One day he'll write a scandalous book that will embarrass the whole family. Just the way Tom Wolfe did." My mother had grown up in Asheville when Wolfe was wreaking havoc there with *Look Homeward, Angel*. She recalled the way the author's family had dined out for years on their literary notoriety. Old Mrs. Wolfe had always been ready with a stock reply when asked how it felt to have her dirty laundry aired in public. Drawing herself up grandly, she would proclaim with a stoic sigh that "Caesar had Brutus, and Jesus had Judas, and we have our Tom." But Wolfe was permitted his indiscretion, Mummie said, because he was a genius and a true bohemian; he had run off to the North, you see, and moved in with a Jewess who was *much* older than he was. You couldn't *get* any more bohemian than that, she said with a knowing look, as if to suggest that there might be a Jewess or two in my own future.

Though she played by the rules of Charleston society, my mother herself nursed private dreams of bohemianism. Her own mother had been an ardent suffragist in England and was still known to read palms and cite the theosophy of Madame Blavatsky. So Mummie would often make reference to karma and rosy circles and past lives, without fully knowing what those things were, and certainly without abandoning her weekly Episcopal prayer group. But I wanted her to be Auntie Mame as much as she did, so I egged her on at every turn. We went flea marketing together and bought exotic Indian cotton bedspreads for the house. Once, in a rare display of physicality, I completely rearranged the living room to showcase more dramatically her fine collection of blue Pisgah Mountain Pottery.

There were, though, limits to my mother's nonconformism, and I discovered them when I made friends with Rusty Ellis. Rusty, to my mind, was a perfectly prosaic kid from Minneapolis whose father had recently been transferred to an insurance company in Charleston. True, the Ellises were somewhat disrespectful of the South, and their living-room furniture was all Danish Modern, but I really liked knowing someone who said *davenport* instead of *sofa*, and Rusty's love of the movies was easily the equal of mine. Also like me, he had successfully made it to fourteen without learning the rules of a single sport. We spent our time together after school discussing the deeper meaning of *Vertigo*, or searching for the tomb of the real-life Annabel Lee, a local girl the young Edgar Allan Poe had once courted out on Sullivan's Island.

I was already jerking off at that point, but I felt nothing like lust for Rusty; I was just extremely comfortable around him. I had stumbled by chance upon a member of my own tribe, and Mummie must have realized this long before I did. She liked Rusty just fine—for the very reasons she liked me—but two fey little fantasists was one too many for her comfort. She pulled me aside one day and suggested gently that

173

maybe I shouldn't see so much of my friend. When I asked her why, she said that Rusty was a little effeminate—through no fault of his own, of course, but it might cause people to "think things." And I realized then that my secret deficiency wasn't just happening in my pants; it was part and parcel of my very being, a blazing scarlet H that could easily betray me at any moment.

"So what did you do?" asked Pete.

"About what?"

"Rusty."

"Nothing, really. I mean, nothing dramatic. We were still friends for a while. I just didn't talk about him at home. And then we just sort of . . . drifted apart naturally as we got older."

"Why?"

"I don't know exactly. I guess he started to strike me as . . . kind of corny and Midwestern."

"Hey!"

I laughed. "Sorry. Wrong word."

"Are you gonna do that to me?"

"Do what?"

"Dump me when you're tired of me."

"C'mon. I didn't dump him. And you're not at all like him, anyway." I knew Pete was just teasing, but he had struck a nerve nonetheless. "Besides," I added defensively, "we had a really nice reunion back in the eighties. He and his lover came here for the Castro Street Fair, and we all went out to dinner. They'd been following my show for years."

"Was he still corny and Midwestern?"

"He was very nice," I said firmly, but in truth I had

felt superior to the one true soul mate of my adolescence. Rusty and his lover were both court reporters in Atlanta, pleasant guys with shiny faces and careful hair who seemed to have acquired their personal style from the Shocking Gray catalog. They wore freedom rings and rhinestone-studded AIDS ribbons, and Rusty, poor soul, had one of those T-shirts that said *Surrender, Dorothy*. I found them both so middle-class and predictable that I cut short our evening with an excuse about an imminent deadline. The irony of that wasn't lost on me when I later learned that they had both died within a year of their pilgrimage to San Francisco. Deadline, indeed. And I had not remembered to send them the autographed books they'd requested.

Pete was still miffed. "The Midwest isn't so bad, you know."

"Thought you said it was a suckhole."

"Well, yeah, but . . . *you're* not allowed to say it."

"There's only one way to settle this, you know."

"What?"

"If you invite me out to see for myself."

The silence that followed was not attributable to anything. It was merely a silence.

"Pete?"

"You don't mean that, do you?"

"Why would I say it, if I didn't mean it?"

"Would you come like . . . right away?"

"Absolutely. In a couple of days, if you'll let me. I can stay at your local Ramada and we'll just hang."

More silence.

"Pete?"

"Yeah, Dad, I'm here."

"What d'you say, then?"

"That would be the coolest thing in the world."

"Good, then. We'll do it."

"I gotta check with Mom, though."

"Tell her I won't be in the way, okay? I can make myself scarce whenever you need to be alone."

"I'm sure it's no sweat. She's pretty cool about things."

"I know, Pete. You're lucky in that regard."

There was a brief pause as he apparently read my mind. "You know," he said eventually. "Your mom was just trying to protect you."

"Yeah . . . I know. But she passed her fear on to me. And that was the last thing in the world I needed."

"But you would have gotten that anyway. From somebody else if not from her."

"I know. I'm not blaming her."

"You shouldn't. Things were a lot different back then."

It was a simple observation that could easily have been gleaned from almost any book or movie about the fifties. The mores of the midcentury are a well-established cliché in the culture, one that a clever boy of thirteen could certainly invoke without ever having lived through the era. But somehow the phrase seemed pregnant with personal experience. It stayed with me all afternoon and into the night, crowding out everything else, like some ghastly repetitive jingle you're trying too hard to forget:

Things were a lot different back then.

Thirteen

Room For Disillusionment

Pete called back excitedly the next morning to say that Donna had approved my visit, so I spent the next few days in preparation. There was very little to do, actually—or *un*do, for that matter, since my calendar had become a wasteland after Jess had left. This little odyssey to Henzke Street would be a healthy act in every regard: something that would not only lift my morale but promote my self-sufficiency. I splurged on a first-class ticket to Milwaukee, then splurged again, reserving a big boat of a Buick for the long drive to Wysong.

There was only the issue of Hugo. He had never been boarded in a kennel, and this was hardly the time to start, given his age and health. Jess and I had always relied on house-sitters, but the usual candidates were unreachable that day, and I didn't want to unsettle the dog with strangers. The logical choice was Jess. He would love spending time with Hugo, and I loved the idea of him being here, sleeping in our bed. So I called and asked if he might be available for a few days.

"Sure. I guess. What's up? Where are you going?"

Was that worry in his voice? Did it disturb him that I might have plans of my own?

"Pete has asked me to come visit," I explained.

A pause, and then: "When did this happen?"

"A few days ago." It felt awkward exploding Jess's hoax theory in such a casual manner, but I'd already resolved not to make an issue of it.

"Are you planning to stay with them?" he asked after a silence. There was a distinct note of reticence in his voice.

"No. Pete gave me the name of a motel."

"That's good."

"What do you mean?"

"You don't know these people, babe."

"You're right," I said grimly. "They might make me into a lampshade."

Jess didn't rise to my sarcasm. "Do what you want, then. I just think you'd better have an escape hatch if it turns out to be tedious. Don't forget those dykes in Hermosa Beach!"

His shorthand made me laugh. I remembered that nightmare all too well. At the bitter end of a thirty-city book tour we'd been virtually imprisoned by a women's collective: forced to nap in their "guest room," submit to a tedious tarot reading, sit in a bookstore for hours on end while a handful of women in pastel sweats straggled in from the beach. It drained every last ounce of charm from me, but even in my wretchedness I found comfort in the fact of Jess, that sharp, loving eye I could catch across the room.

"Please," I said. "Nothing could ever be *that* bad."

Jess chuckled at the memory with an affection that belied how apoplectic he'd been at the time. "Jesus, remember that huge one who rode on a mattress in the back of her lover's minivan?"

"Oh, hell. The channeller. She channelled a nineteenth-century slave!"

"And I asked her lover if she'd ever channelled in bed and she said, 'Oh, no, she doesn't do it unless you pay her.'"

Laughing, I dredged up the shamelessly un-PC catchphrase we'd invented for the occasion: "'Inside every fat white woman there's a fat black woman struggling to get out.'"

"Hey," Jess blurted. "Maybe that's what's happening on Henzke Street. Maybe she's channelling that kid."

This was just a comic variation on Anna's "multiple" theory, but I didn't say so. It was time for this game to be over, and I suggested as much as nicely as I could.

Jess was contrite. "I didn't mean to make light of it. I'm glad you're doing this, in fact. It'll be good for you."

"Thanks," I said. "I'm a little nervous, actually."

"Why?"

"Oh, I just wonder what he'll look like. How far gone he is. He sounds so cute and energetic on the phone, but he must be in pretty bad shape, considering all he's been through."

"But he sent you a picture, right?"

"Yeah, but that could be fairly old. Even a month or two can make a difference."

"You can handle it. You handled it with Wayne. He was beautiful at the end, remember?"

"Yeah . . . he was."

"Just look into his eyes," said Jess. "You'll be all right."

* * *

The next order of business was to arrange accommodations in Wysong, so I called the place Pete had suggested—the Lake-Vue Motor Lodge—and reserved a single room for two nights. This was not their busy season, the desk clerk said, so I could easily extend my stay should I choose to do so. She was so chatty and cooperative ("Do you know about our antique auto barn?") that she put me instantly at ease. I could almost see the place already, with its greasy-antlered snack bar and knotty pine office, the stack of old jigsaw puzzles they probably kept behind the desk. And all of it less than a mile from Pete's house.

It was snowing in Wysong, the desk clerk said, so I should keep that in mind when I packed for my stay. This shouldn't have surprised me, but it did, a little, since Pete had never talked about the weather, presumably because he took it for granted; only Californians and Southerners see snow as something to make a fuss over. I readjusted my mental image, adding frost to the double-paned windows, a cornice of snow to the long row of rooms. As for that fabled Vue of the Lake, it was now enlivened by a random deer or two, or maybe even elk or moose, scribbling their signatures across the blue-white landscape. This was virgin territory for me, a place so unfamiliar that it was still susceptible to my imagination.

I consulted the elegant little leather-bound atlas my friend James in New York had bought me at Barneys just after Jess took off. (This had been James's way of saying that there was still a world out there.) Only a page was devoted to all the Midwestern states, so Wysong was nowhere to be found. I saw some wonderful names in Wisconsin, like Fond du Lac and Rhinelander and Chippewa Falls, but Pete's hometown would have to wait for a much more inclusive map. I knew I could find one downtown, and the thought of an expedition for that purpose was curiously exhilarating.

I was searching for my keys when the phone rang. Miffed that my mission had been delayed, I answered with a tart "Hello."

"Gabriel?"

My ill will vanished on the spot. "Pete! Sweetie! Guess where I'm heading!"

"No," came the voice at the other end. "It's Donna."

"Oh . . . of course . . . sorry." Thank God she couldn't see my face, which was traitorously aflame.

"No problem," she said. "We're used to it. Pete hates it when it happens, but that's boys for you. They don't wanna sound like some dorky girl. So it's better you did it with me."

Calming myself, I told Donna about my own mother and the way we'd sometimes been mistaken for each other on the phone.

"Did you both grow up in the same neighborhood?" she asked.

"Not really. Her parents were English, but she was born in western North Carolina. I grew up in Charleston."

"West Virginia?"

"No. The one in South Carolina."

There, I thought. There's your proof. Donna wouldn't have asked that so casually if she and Pete were the same person. She would have known *exactly* which Charleston I meant, since I'd already talked to Pete about it at length . . . unless, of course, she had deliberately played dumb to throw me off track. She might have decided that such a ruse was necessary, since I'd just mistaken her voice for Pete's. Then again, if she was a true multiple, she wouldn't even *know* what I had told her other personality, so it was still possible that one person could be . . .

Stop it, I ordered myself.

"Oh, I love *that* Charleston," Donna purred. "So pretty. I went there once for a conference on child abuse . . . Look, I'd love to shoot the breeze, but I'm afraid I'm the bearer of bad tidings."

Did I suspect then what was coming next? I didn't, as I recall. But I knew that *something* was seriously out of whack.

"I'm so sorry to do this, but we have to withdraw our invitation. I'm afraid it's just not the right time."

"Oh . . . sure . . . other visitors or something?"

"God, no. We're bored silly out here. A little stimulation would be wonderful. Especially from you. But Pete's immunity is zilch right now, and I just can't take the risk of outside contamination. I hope you can understand. I'm as disappointed as Pete is."

Disturbed as I was, I didn't put up a fight. I did let her know that my health was excellent, just in case it mattered.

"That's just the problem," she said. "Your system can easily live with things that would kill Pete. You could pick up a simple flu bug on the plane that he wouldn't be able to shake. One more strain on his system right now would be . . . all she wrote."

"It's that bad?"

She answered with a sigh. "I try to downplay it around him, so he doesn't feel like a china doll. But it's really precarious at the moment."

I didn't know *what* to feel: renewed concern for Pete's health or frustration over a clever excuse I could never refute. I certainly didn't want to infect Pete, but, until now, he hadn't exactly sounded like a boy in a bubble. And what about all those trips to the hospital? He must have encountered new people all the time. Why would one more be so threatening?

"Even his buddies from the hospital have to keep their distance," Donna went on. "They have to wear masks and wave at him from across the room. It cramps his style something awful. He loves being around people. Thank God he's got the telephone."

Fine, I thought. But why did you even invite me in the first place?

"I don't expect this to be permanent," she added, as if in response to my silent rebuttal. "I'd love for you to visit soon. But we got some new tests back yesterday that were pretty disappointing, and I would never forgive myself if he were to . . ."

"I understand, Donna. Really."

"Oh, I hope so, Gabe. I really do."

There was something about the inflection of that phrase that sounded disturbingly like Pete.

But Pete, of course, would have known not to call me Gabe.

I called Jess to cancel his house-sitting duties, but there was no answer, so I left a message. He came by the house early that evening, obviously still uninformed, having spent the day on the run. I tried to ease into the news, but somehow he sniffed it out and jumped ahead of me:

"She bailed on you, didn't she?"

"Well, I wouldn't put it that way, but—"

"I *knew* this would happen!" He wore a look of fiery triumph, as if some risky, far-flung investment was finally showing big dividends.

"Of course you knew," I said darkly. "You always do."

He regarded me through half-lidded eyes. "Meaning?"

"You predict calamity, and calamity happens. It's not that hard to do, you know. If you're always suspecting the worst, every now and then you're bound to be right."

He studied me, assessing my emotional state, and apparently decided that another raving madman would be more than the moment could safely support. "So what did she say?" he asked with uncommon calm.

"Does it matter?"

"I would be interested, yes. If you don't mind."

I hesitated. "He got some tests back yesterday. She worried about him picking something up."

"What sort of tests?"

"I don't know, Jess. The usual, I guess. I didn't ask."

"Why not?"

"Because I didn't want to sound like I was interrogating her. I didn't want her to think I was suspicious."

"*Are* you suspicious?"

"I don't know *what* I am."

"But you think she thinks you're suspicious?"

"I don't know. Probably not. I'm being way too paranoid, I guess."

"Why should you be paranoid at all? You haven't done anything."

"I know. But I'm still . . . I dunno . . . afraid."

"Of what? That she'll figure out you're on to her and won't let you talk to him anymore?"

I shrugged. He'd come excruciatingly close to the truth.

"Do you know how strange that sounds?"

"Yes," I said quietly. "I believe I do."

"You're never gonna meet him, you know."

"Jess . . ."

"You know what else, sweetie? Someday soon she's gonna call you and tell you that he died the night before, and that's how she'll end it. And you'll just have to live with that, because you'll never be able to prove it one way or the other."

"Well, thank you so much for that. That helps a whole fucking lot."

"No, listen to me. If you want to keep on talking to him, fine; enjoy it for what it is. But leave some room for disillusionment. And stop expecting to meet him, because it's not gonna happen. Not in this lifetime. I don't know what's going on . . . if it's a hoax or some sort of pathological thing, or just an overprotective mother. But whatever it is . . ."

"Why are you so determined to destroy this?"

"Because I see where you're heading and it worries the fuck out of me. He's not your son, sweetie. No matter how much you want him to be."

I felt so exposed, so mortified, that all I could do was feign ignorance. "My *son*? Where the hell did you get that?"

"It doesn't matter."

Had Pete told him? Or Donna? I couldn't imagine either of them doing that. "Now you're just making things up," I said feebly.

"Why would I do that?"

"You tell me. Because someone else has my attention for once? Because I have a relationship that you didn't actually approve?"

Jess stared at me as if I'd just announced my Martian origins.

"Okay . . . it's not exactly an ordinary relationship. But it's the first thing that's made me feel human in months. I don't know what's happening any more than you do, but whoever that is on the phone has made a difference in my life, and I would think you'd be happy for me. Would that be so hard? Just to be happy for me?"

Jess regarded me soberly. "I asked myself the same thing last month."

"When?"

"When I told you I had a chance to live."

My heart caved in. I'd hoped that Jess hadn't clocked my shameful turmoil that day, the conflict I'd felt between his improving health and the fact that he was leaving me. As usual, he had read me like a large-type book. And, as usual, I couldn't come clean. "I *was* happy for you," I insisted. "I was happy for both of us. I *am* happy."

Jess shook his head with a thin smile. "You couldn't even fake it."

"You don't know what it's like," I told him. "Loving someone for ten years, loving them more and more all the time, but expecting to lose them at any minute. Talk about room for disillusionment! I'm an expert at that! All I ever did was that. I couldn't allow myself the luxury of thinking we would be forever. You had that luxury every single day. You *knew* you would have me until the end of your life, no matter what. How do you think it felt when you just . . . got better and changed your mind?"

"We *never* agreed to monogamy . . ."

"I'm not talking about monogamy! I'm talking about two people together, taking on the world together. We had that, Jess, more completely than anybody I've ever known. A lot of people never find it at all. I waited half of my life to find it, and I was so sure of it that I just . . . relaxed." Angry tears flooded my face. "I had never allowed myself to give in to that dream, but I did with you. I put total faith in something for the first time in my life. And you just threw it away, so you could stomp around in jackboots and have your fucking New Life Crisis or whatever it is. We had something much stronger than sex, and it takes years to build that, and a lot of work. I'm fifty-four years old, Jess. This was it for me. For better or worse. I was ready for you to die in my arms."

Jess's face had turned to stone. "Well, I'm sorry to spoil your plans."

That was a low blow, but it stung because there was truth to it. I *had* been planning his death, romanticizing it even, in a frenzied effort to contain the horror of losing him. It was impossible *not* to embrace his death before the fact, when there were so many living corpses walking the streets.

"That isn't fair," I said. "Nobody ever dreamed—"

"*I* dreamed. I dreamed all the time. I wanted to live and I worked like hell to do it. And sometimes I felt so alone, Gabriel. Because you just left it all up to me. You just made speeches about loving a dying man and forgot about the details. I was the one who took care of you."

"Now wait a fucking minute—"

"No, I wanna say this. Last week Frank came over and we were lying there after some really great sex, and

187

he turned and said to me: 'I would take care of you if you'd let me,' and I thought to myself how nice that would be for once. I've spent my whole life taking care of people. That's what you and I were about from the beginning. You cried in my arms the day after we met. You sensed that you could do that with me. You were so sad and lost that I thought: here's somebody I can really take care of . . ."

"Jesus, Jess, how can you say that? All I ever wanted was to take care of you. You wouldn't even let me half the time. You hated to be fussed over when you had the slightest little cold. You'd get all moody and withdrawn because you weren't in control anymore. I used to worry what it would be like, in fact, when you really got sick, if all the tenderness would just disappear and . . . goddammit, Jess, I took care of you all the time. In every way. I loved you. I made it so you didn't have to work in an office. I shared my income with you."

Jess gave me a pointed look. "*Your* income."

"All right, ours. Whatever."

"No, that means something, Gabriel. It's always been *your* income. That's the way you see it, isn't it?"

At that moment I couldn't see anything but the "really great sex" with Frank that Jess had felt so driven to remark upon. "Well, I'm sorry," I told him, "but I did write the goddamned books."

"And I did nothing? Somebody else set up your IRA and organized your tours and your fucking publicity and held your hand at every taping and brainstormed with you every time you had something new to write? You established credit because of me, Gabriel. You bought this house. It's even in your name, because I wanted to make things easier for you when I died. I

188

spent a quarter of my life getting your life in order, and I've got nothing to show for it."

"You had everything," I told him bleakly. (And you threw it away, I thought, for the nearest swarthy man who would tie you to a cross and let you call him sir, someone, in other words, who would impersonate the father who had terrorized you.) "Am I supposed to feel sorry for you?" I asked. "You're the one who's leaving me, Jess. This has been your choice all the way. I was completely blindsided."

"That is such bullshit."

"Don't tell me how I feel, please."

"If you were blindsided, Gabriel, it's because you chose to be. You don't confront things at all. You live in your own little fantasy world. You act like the tough stuff will just go away if you don't acknowledge it. I dropped lots of hints about our sex life over the years, but you refused to pick up on them. So I avoided anything that made you uncomfortable. You think of me as a bull in a china shop, but I'm not—not all the time. I learned to be very careful about the stuff that you can't handle."

Like what? I wondered, my guts twisting with the fear that he might actually tell me. What intrinsic flaw in my being had made me so impossible to live with? Was I just too old for him now, or too self-absorbed to be in a real partnership? My fame had once been a consolation in times of distress, but now it just made me feel worse. For if Jess could walk out on the myth he'd helped create, the real me must be someone truly unlovable.

"This isn't just about S/M," he added with his customary clairvoyance. "There are things I have to figure out on my own."

He had omitted the ampersand, I noted, thereby reminding me that they call it S/M these days, not S & M.

I couldn't even *say* it the right way.

I don't remember how that conversation ended, only that I wanted out of it as quickly as possible. I do recall that Jess broached the subject of money and that I wrote him a check to cover his expenses for the next two months. It was agonizing for both of us. We had vowed in the past never to make an issue of money, which had always been easy enough for me, since Jess had been so conscientious in that regard; *I* was the one inclined toward overspending. Money, however, was the monster that loomed over us that afternoon, because I'd started to believe that Jess was as desperate as I was, but in a different way. Would he even be here at all, I wondered, trying to be civil with me, if he had any other means of staying alive?

That night, as I lay on the sofa hoping that Pete would call, I remembered the time Jess first came down from Oregon to visit me. I had a tiny cottage on Noe Hill then, and it was riddled with mice, since I didn't have the heart (or the stomach) to set traps. As we cuddled in bed that first night Jess was aghast at the chorus of squeaks that greeted us as soon as the lights went out. The next morning he went down to Cliff's Hardware and bought several dozen mousetraps, all of which did their job within a matter of nights. I would lie in Jess's arms, wincing and laughing at the horror, as the traps snapped away in the darkness, sometimes two at a time. How had I let it get so bad? And who was this sweet, volatile man who had come out of nowhere to slay my dragons? He'd taken care of me all right, and I'd loved every minute of it.

Fourteen

Stranger And Stranger

Ashe Findlay, poor soul, could never have guessed how bad his timing would be when he called the next morning to update me on the progress of *The Blacking Factory*. I think he must have wanted some reassurance that my doubts had subsided, so he could proceed with Pete's book without further anxiety. What he got, thanks to the state of my heart, was a cranky antagonist, desperate for a resolution of any kind.

I guess I was provoked by his blithe description of the book's cover design. They were featuring a photo of Pete, he said—"an utterly charming shot"—but they were altering his face, naturally, to protect the boy's privacy.

"Is he wearing a sweatshirt?" I asked, wondering if this was the same shot Donna had sent me.

"Yes. I believe so."

That seemed evasive, as if I couldn't be trusted with

such ticklish information. My response was glacial. "You *believe* so?"

"Well, it's back with the art department now. I only had a quick glance at it."

"Were his eyes green? An unusual shade?"

"Not that I remember, but of course they'd altered it by then."

"But you must've seen the original?"

"Yes. I did. I think they *were* green, yes. Now that you mention it. Very striking." His well-bred voice was positively writhing in discomfort.

"I must tell you," I said. "This whole thing is sounding stranger and stranger. And a little unprofessional on your part."

"I'm sorry to hear that," the editor replied soberly. "You seemed fine about it last time. Would you like to reconsider your blurb?"

"This isn't about my blurb, Ashe. I need some answers here. You got me into this, and you're gonna have to get me out. I'm tired of being jerked around." This sounded a lot like a threat, I realized, and a not-so-veiled one at that. I started to soften it but changed my mind. A threat might be what it would take to get some action.

"Has something else happened?" the editor asked.

Has it ever, I thought. My life, I realized, had been reduced to a loose confederation of uncertainties, and I was sick to death of it. I wasn't inclined to unload on this constipated Yankee, so I offered him only the hard facts: my invitation to visit Pete and its unceremonious withdrawal.

"I believe I warned you," Findlay said. "She's extremely wary of him meeting people."

"So why didn't she just say that to begin with? Why

would she give me all that crap about her chili and let me make plans for several days, if she never intended for it to happen?"

"I couldn't tell you that."

"Well, I can. She did it because she wanted me to think it was possible. She wanted me to believe there was actually someone there I could visit."

"Gabriel, my friend, you'll only make yourself crazy if you continue to dwell—"

"Please don't call me crazy, Ashe. I don't think I'm the one who's being crazy here. I think I'm being very sane, in fact. And very reasonable, under the circumstances."

Another silence, even longer. "What would you like me to do?" he said at last.

"I don't know. Poke around, at least. Be a little more aggressive about authenticating it. You're in a position to do that. I'm not."

"Do you want me to say that you're having—"

"No! God, no! Leave me out of this. This is between you and one of your writers. If there's anything left to salvage between me and Pete, I'd like to be able to do it."

"I understand."

"And get back to me, please. As soon as you can."

I spent the rest of the day in bed, inert and powerless. My only visual was Jess's apartment building, suspended in the bedroom window. Its edges were blurred by swirling fog, and there were times when it disappeared completely, then magically rematerialized, as the moon can do. Unlike me, Jess dreaded the fog. It depressed him when it lasted too long, closing him in with his demons. He was up there right now, I imagined, staring out at this infinite grayness, feeling the sad fallout of our fight. I wanted so badly to call him, but I knew there was nothing more to be said, nothing that would fix us.

I drifted into troubled sleep, only to be roused by Pete's voice on the machine. And this time I was sure it was him.

". . . just had this funny feeling. So if you don't feel like talking, I'll try you again when—"

"Pete?"

"Oh, good, Dad. You're there."

"Yeah."

"What's going on?"

"What do you mean?"

"I've been getting these signals all day. Something's been bothering you big time."

Even in that groggy state I was completely unnerved, so I tried to jest my way out. "What is this? The Psychic Friends Network?"

"I'm serious. What's going on?"

"Nothing . . . well . . . I'm disappointed, of course, that I won't be seeing you."

"Me, too. But Mom says we can do it in a month, if you still want to. They've put me on a new protocol."

"Well, that's good," I said vaguely.

"But that's not it, is it?"

"Not what?"

"What's bothering you. Have you had a fight with Jess?"

Astonished, I wondered for a moment if Jess had told Pete as much, but that didn't seem likely given his skepticism about the boy. "I did, actually," I said at last. "Yesterday."

"I knew it."

How could everyone around me be so rife with intuition when I felt like a blind man stumbling through a minefield?

"We had a talk," I admitted. "And we said some things we've never said before."

Pete took that in for a moment. "Well, that's not necessarily a bad thing. Sometimes it's bad to leave too much unsaid."

Tell me about it, I thought, wondering if this was the wisdom of a therapist or just of a kid who'd been seeing a therapist. And did it matter, really, when I still had so much to get off my chest?

"So what did you fight about?" asked Pete.

"Oh, lots of stuff. He says I never confront things. That I don't communicate what I'm really thinking."

"Is that true?"

"Oh, yeah. I'm a big scaredy-cat."

"What were you afraid of with him?"

"The usual. That he wouldn't love me anymore if he knew what was really on my mind." I could have been talking about Pete, I realized, and maybe I was, on some unconscious level—getting as close to the truth as I could get without tipping my hand. "You learn to camouflage when you're a baby homo. You learn to tiptoe around things. At least I did. And it's a hard habit to break, even when you're grownup and out of the closet."

"What about yesterday? Did you tell him everything that was on your mind?"

"Some of it. I said how hard it was to love someone who might be dying. To feel closer and closer to them but know you can't count on them being there in your old age."

"Well, that was the truth, wasn't it?"

"Yeah, but just part of it. Actually, I think it was easier for me to commit to Jess because I knew it wouldn't have to last forever. And I could even feel a little noble in the process. I gave him hell yesterday for throwing away what we had, but you know what? When things got too depressing, I used to tell myself I'd have another shot at loving someone. I'd see myself back at the baths again, chasing my dick around one more time before it got too late to do it. And I would imagine this guy I'd meet someday, who wouldn't carry the virus and wouldn't be as angry as Jess, and we would get it right finally. I was disloyal, Pete. I accused *him* of that, but I did the same thing, really. I thought about a future he would never be part of. I dreaded his death, but I knew it would give me an out. I knew it would give me another shot at things."

"C'mon, Dad, that's just a protective thing. It's natural to—"

"So why can't I do it now? Why can't I take this golden opportunity to spread my wings and meet new people?"

"You will."

I didn't want to hear that. I wanted him to tell me that Jess would be coming back.

Him, not her. Wanted *him* to tell me that.

At dusk I walked Hugo up to the edge of the forest in an effort to clear my head. And something troubling occurred to me: that my relationship with Pete bore a distinct resemblance to the one I'd had with Jess. In both instances I had split myself into two person-alities, one of whom was capable of fearless, unconditional love, while the other, braced against the prospect of imminent loss, warned me not to surrender completely.

So who was the multiple now?

Fifteen

Room Tone

The next five or six days—the ones that mattered, ironically enough—have dropped from memory. Nothing so grand as amnesia, just a run-of-the mill blank spot in the life of a writer unable to write. I've checked my appointment book for clues as to my state of mind but found only the usual evidence of an ordered but uneventful journey to sleep:

Gym.
Eileen—2 P.M.—teeth cleaning.
Laundry ready.
Screening at Castro?

I'm pretty sure I never made it to that screening, whatever the movie was, since Jess and I still weren't talking, and I would have dreaded the thought of sitting alone in that theater, of all those inquisitive queens whispering behind their hands about the solitary state of Gabriel Noone.

I'm pretty sure, too, that Pete didn't call, though I must've wondered why he didn't. Maybe I thought I'd finally overloaded him with my shitty life. That's entirely possible. And maybe that's why I didn't call *him*: to give him a break from all that rampant self-indulgence.

It's strange to think that I might have altered the course of everything had we spoken even briefly during that time.

It was Donna who answered when I did call. Her voice was so colorless that I knew in my gut something terrible had happened.

"It's Gabriel, Donna."

"Oh . . . hi."

"Are you okay?"

"Not really. No."

"What's wrong?"

"Those bastards at Argus have cancelled Pete's book."

"*What?*" My response was only partially phony. I was shocked to hear the news all right, but in no way confused about what had precipitated it. Every nerve end in my body was already screaming with guilt.

"They've cancelled his goddamn book," she repeated. "He worked on it for two years and they've just changed their minds."

"Was this Findlay?"

"Who else?"

"Do you know why?"

"Sort of. It doesn't make any sense, but . . . oh

200

dammit, Gabriel, they are *such* slimy bastards. I should have known not to trust . . ."

"Tell me what happened, okay?"

She paused to catch her breath. "Sorry. I'm really wired right now. Things are pretty awful around here. Pete is barely talking to me."

"Oh, Jesus . . ."

"Poor little dude. If there were any way in hell . . ."

"What did Findlay say? Did he give you an explanation?" Oh, please, God, no, I thought. Don't make me answerable for this.

"He wanted to send some PR guy out here."

"For what?"

"Background material! Is that a crock or what? He gave them a four-hundred-page manuscript that's nothing but background material. What more could they possibly need?"

I tried my best to sound annoyed but, at the same time, reasonable about the requirements of publishing. "Oh, hell. You know what that is, Donna? That's just their tired old way of doing things. Publishers are nothing but factories these days, and they don't turn off the machinery even when they've got a special case like Pete. It's just a matter of routine, really. I'm sure if you—"

"Fuck their routine. I'm not jeopardizing Pete's health for their routine. Not to mention dredging up all that hurtful shit again. Pete's put his pain down on paper and he's not gonna do it again. He's not gonna be their trained monkey, no matter what they say. It's taken too long to get him as far as he is. I can't do that to him. I just can't!"

I had never heard her so impassioned—or so out of control. "Did you tell Findlay that?"

201

"Damn right. He said he'd have to get back to me. Then he called back yesterday and said the whole thing was off. Just like that. Without a word of discussion. Can you fucking believe it?"

I murmured my outrage, my heart racing faster by the second.

"Of course I've got it figured out," she added darkly.

Now my heart seemed to stop altogether as I held my breath.

"Somebody upstairs has just realized that they won't get to send this one off to Maury Povich or Jenny Jones or whoever the fuck they were planning on selling him to. They can't milk him for publicity, so he just isn't worth their precious time and money. It's as simple as that, and it's so callous it makes me want to . . . Jesus, I still can't believe it."

I thought for a minute she was going to cry, but all I heard was the sound of her breathing. I chose my words with care, knowing there was still a chance for compromise if I could just angle her into the right frame of mind. "So . . . you didn't plan for Pete to do . . . any publicity whatsoever?"

"God, Gabe, name me a reason why we should! The last time he was in front of cameras it was because a lot of sick grownups wanted to get off. Do you think I'd put him through that again? Make him sing for his supper? Turn him into some poor little pederast poster boy, just so they can—"

"But if you let that guy come out . . ."

"What guy?"

"The PR person. Whoever. Maybe that person would . . . you know, obviate the need for any other publicity. Maybe one interview would take care of it. And you could control it completely, make it as short and easy as you want. There wouldn't even have to be cameras there."

"That's what Findlay said."

"Well, don't you think maybe . . ."

"Look, Gabe. There are times when I wonder if Pete is gonna make it another day. He's weak as hell and very fragile emotionally and *very* self-conscious about the way he looks. I just can't let some stranger in here to pump him about the gory details. It's too risky in every way."

"Did you tell Findlay that?"

"Of course!"

"And?"

"He was completely unbending. He just kept saying, 'I'm terribly sorry, but these are our requirements.' He was a total asshole about it. It was like he was a different person. Like he'd already made up his mind."

"I'm sure he's just . . ." I didn't know how to finish this, so I didn't try.

"Just what?"

"Who the hell knows? He's one of those repressed Yankee types. I'll talk to him, though. Maybe there's something I can say."

"What could you possibly—"

"I don't know. But I'll try, okay? I'll do my damnedest. This isn't a bit fair."

"Tell me about it."

"Is Pete there now?"

"In the other room. He hasn't even eaten since we heard."

"Fuck."

"He won't even talk to me. He's being as stubborn as Findlay. He just rolled up in a little ball and faced the wall."

This image so haunted me that it took a while to form words. "Do you . . . uh . . . think he would talk to me?"

"Oh, God, Gabe, I don't know."

"Would you ask him?"

"You won't be hurt if he doesn't . . ."

"No. Just ask him, though, would you?"

A loaded pause, and then: "Hang on."

There's a term we use in radio called *room tone* that came to mind in the anxious moments that followed. Room tone, put simply, is the sound of ordinary silence. When you're recording, say, a radio play, this sound is required in the editing process to make the background into a seamless whole. That's because a silent room is never the same as the total absence of sound, and no two silent rooms are ever exactly alike. There are subtleties that are almost undetectable to the ear: atmospheric oddities, the exhalation of a heating duct, the distant drone of traffic or plumbing. The sound of nothing can be cacophonous, in fact, when weighed against the cold polished chrome of Absolutely Nothing.

What I heard while I waited for Pete was the teeming silence of room tone. A void that said more than any sound, a living entity that could mold itself into shapes and colors and flesh itself, speeding me across a continent to a room I might never see, a boy I might never hold.

"Dad?"

"Yeah, Pete. I'm here."

"She told you, huh?"

"Yeah. She did."

"This is so fucked, man."

"Yeah, it is. It *is* fucked."

More room tone, then a tiny squeak that told me he was crying.

"Oh, Pete . . ."

"It's okay."

"No. It's not. I'm gonna talk to Findlay. See what we can do."

"Won't do any good."

"Don't be so sure. Findlay listens to me when he has to."

Does he ever, I thought. The squirrelly bastard.

"Forget about it," said Pete.

"Why?"

"Because it won't do any good."

"Look, Pete, this is just about their silly publicity requirements. I think we can offer them a compromise that would give them what they want and still . . . protect your privacy. Don't give up hope yet. You're gonna be an author if it's the last thing I—"

"You don't think this is about publicity, do you?"

I felt a tightening in my chest. "Well . . . yeah . . . sure."

"They would cancel a whole book just because of that?"

"Maybe. It's all about sales these days."

"What about those guys that never do publicity at all? Like . . . you know, Thomas Pynchon or somebody?"

"Well . . . there are always exceptions, I'm afraid. Especially if you're that famous. You can demand anything you want." (Could a thirteen-year-old—even one this bright—know about Thomas Pynchon?)

205

"You know what I think?" Pete said.

"What?"

"You have to promise me you won't tell Mom."

Bewildered and extremely wary, I considered the ramifications of such a pact. If there was even a remote chance I was dealing with a multiple, was it wise to start taking sides, to conspire with one personality over the other? "Are you sure you want to do that?" I asked him finally. "Secrets are not very healthy things, you know. Especially in families."

"Yeah, but this would really upset her. She's way too worried about me already, and I don't wanna make it worse. I know how she is, Dad. She takes things too hard. She's not as strong as she looks."

But I don't even *know* how she looks, I thought. I could walk right past her in broad daylight and never know she was there. She would just be one more of those strangers who smile at me oddly at stoplights and on elevators, recognizing my face from a book jacket. Should I be keeping secrets from someone who had that kind of advantage over me?

On the other hand, what choice did I have?

"Okay," I told Pete. "This is between you and me. Tell me what you think."

I heard him take a breath, as if to steel himself for the moment. "I know why they wanna send out that PR guy. It's to prove that I exist!"

I had not expected this somehow, but there it was— so unadorned and unaddressable that I was the one who turned into the fraud. "Oh, c'mon, sweetie. That's crazy. What are you talking about?"

"Don't you get it? They've never seen me or anything, so they want proof before they publish the book. That's the only reason they're doing this! The fuckers

206

don't even believe me!" He began to sob now, a terrible animal wail unlike any I'd ever heard from him. "I knew this would happen! I knew they would never believe me if I told the truth!"

"Oh, sweetie."

"Hold me, Dad, will you?"

"I am holding you. I'm doing that right now."

The sobbing continued, then trailed off into sniffles. I could feel his wet cheek against my shoulder, the hothouse warmth of his breath.

"This is too hard, Dad. I can't do it anymore."

"Do what?"

A pause, and then: "Any of it."

"Oh, c'mon now," I said softly, unable to manage anything else.

"I mean it, Dad. It hurts too much."

"You mean . . . physically?"

"Every way. I'm really tired all the time. I got shingles now and I ache all over and I can't even breathe half the time. We just keep going to the hospital . . . and I just wonder . . . what's the point? Even the doctors think that. They start sighing real loud as soon as they see me coming."

"To hell with 'em. Tell 'em to do their job."

"They are, Dad. It's just not working."

"It *is* working. You're alive and . . . you're creating and . . . there are people who love you, Pete . . ."

He began to sob again.

"Oh, sweetie, I am so sorry . . ."

"It's not *your* fault. You're the only good thing that's ever happened to me."

"No, I'm not. Don't say that. You have lots of good things. You have Donna and your friends and . . . lots of things."

"My book was the only part of *me* that I liked."

"Oh, Pete, you don't mean that."

"I do, Dad. Before my book I was so ashamed of myself I wanted to die."

"Ashamed? What do you have to be ashamed of?" I caught a quick flash of that grisly shed where Pete's father had fucked him while his mother had wielded the video camera. Then I saw those other monsters, faceless and numberless—unaccountable—who had ordered this child off the Internet, like a cheap ring or a Beanie Baby. "You were just a little kid, Pete. There was nothing you could do. It wasn't under your control at all. C'mon, I know you know that. I'm sure Donna's told you that a thousand times."

"Yeah. But I didn't believe it until I wrote it down."

"And it's *still* written down. I have it right here on my desk. The whole thing. Nothing has changed, Pete."

"But they don't believe me."

"We don't know that for sure."

"I do. I can feel it. They think I made it all up."

"Well . . . look . . . I'm gonna talk to Findlay and—"

"You never doubted me, did you?"

And with that the boy in my arms twisted his head to gaze up at me, those beach-glass eyes growing wider with urgency and need. He blinked at me several times, still holding tight, bracing himself for my answer.

"Of course not," I said.

"Never?"

"Oh, Pete, why would I doubt you? What reason could I possibly have? I'm a writer myself, remember? I know how hard it is to tell the truth in print. Don't you think I would respect that?"

"I guess," he said softly.

My face was afire now, my stomach queasy with deceit. I knew I couldn't sustain this sanctimonious charade a moment longer.

"Okay," I said briskly, "here's the plan. First, I'm gonna talk to Donna about how we can—"

"No!"

"Why not? I'm just gonna propose a plan."

"What kind of plan?"

"Just a way we can . . . satisfy their requirements at Argus."

He was silent for a moment. "You won't tell her what I said, will you? About them thinking I'm a phony?"

"No," I said guardedly. "Not if you don't want me to."

"You can't. She'll totally flip out. She hates it when people don't believe kids. It sets her off more than anything."

Which *could* be useful, I thought. An irate mother on the rampage might put Findlay on the spot in a way that I would never be able to do. Then again, what if things got so hot that the editor felt compelled to defend himself, to say who had planted his doubts in the first place? Or at least reinforced them. Findlay had left me out of it so far—as far as I knew—but I would certainly be pushing my luck if I provoked Donna.

"Okay," I said. "I'll just talk to Findlay. And if he goes for it I'll talk to your mom."

"If?"

"Well, I think he will. I'm pretty sure, anyway."

"You're not gonna tell me what it is, huh?"

"Sure. In a day or so. Just let me do my stuff, okay?"

"Okay, Dad."

He's counting on me, I thought. His old feral terrors are back again, no longer contained by his writing, free to prowl and maim at will.

And he needs his old man to make it all better.

Sixteen

The Sandbar

The terrors of my own childhood were petty next to Pete's, but they're really the only measure I have:

I would get hysterical in department stores whenever I heard the sound of those old-fashioned pneumatic tubes—the ones that once carried money and paperwork from place to place. To me there was something deeply disturbing about them: the way they would scream and swoop overhead like the Wicked Witch of the West. And when those canisters finally dropped in front of me with a creepy thud, my panic was not negotiable; the only remedy was retreat into my mother's arms and her solemn promise—tearfully extorted—that we would never return again.

I was almost as sissy about merry-go-rounds. I could handle the animals that just went around, but the ones that went up and down were the stuff of nightmares, and no amount of gentle persuasion could ever get me onto them. An even greater fear was of our cemetery;

not of corpses or ghosts or the like, since it was just family history, after all, but of being locked in there after dark. I knew the place closed at five o'clock, that the big iron gates were chained shut then, so I kept an eye on the mausoleum clock when my father pulled the weeds off our ancestors after church. I was certain that without my diligence we'd be trapped in there all night, forced to eat worms and drink rainwater until the caretaker came in the morning.

Our cottage on Sullivan's Island was a disheveled, gray-shingled thing that tiptoed above the tide on barnacled pilings. I loved it there. I liked to get up early, when the sand was still cool under the house, and crack the crust of it with my toes. Sometimes, all by myself, I'd head down to the place we called the Point, where there were dozens of odd little beach-bound pools, warm as piss and very shallow, where fickle tides were known to dump a treasure trove of flotsam and shells. My cousin Lucy, who was my age and lived two cottages away, would join me there after breakfast, and we would spend the morning digging for coquinas—brightly hued little clams no bigger than a black-eyed pea. In the belief that these poor creatures were lonely for their own kind, we would build them orphanages in the sand, lodging them according to color, as God had surely intended.

But I rarely ventured into the surf. The horror I felt under the dead weight of the waves was something primal and undeniable. My father once tried to break me of this by tempting me with the offshore sandbar. It might be scary near the beach, he said, but if you went out far enough, there was a place where the water was less than a foot deep, where you could stroll along as easy as could be, like Jesus on the Sea of Galilee. And I didn't even have to be able to swim, since he was tall enough to walk us there, if I would just ride on his shoulders like the tough little roughneck he knew me to be.

I didn't like the sound of that at all. But the old man promised we'd come back whenever I wanted, so I rode him like a trusted steed into the foam, anxiously awaiting the sandbar. I could see the waves forming in the distance, brittle as broken glass and grimly dark green on their undersides. Most of them petered out after a while, but one, I could tell, was building with evil intention. As I sank closer to water level I yelled at my father to stop, to turn around and go back, or let me down, but he just tightened his grip on my legs and headed toward that emerald menace like a madman.

"Hang on, son," he bellowed above the roar of the surf. "We're gonna jump that sorry son-of-a-bitch." When I screamed again in protest, realizing his betrayal, he told me not to be such a crybaby, not to be such a goddamn girl, and this hellish green wall exploded over us, ripping me from his shoulders and spinning me backward and downward, like a palmetto bug caught in a storm drain. When I washed up in the shallows, coughing and sobbing, my father clapped me manfully on the back. "Goddamn," he said, "that was a son-of-a-bitch, wasn't it?" But I knew who the son-of-a-bitch was, and I wouldn't speak to him until suppertime. The next morning, as Lucy and I were busily segregating coquinas, I told her what I'd learned from this: that when I got old and had kids of my own I would never lie to them, never promise them a sandbar I couldn't deliver.

* * *

When I reached Ashe Findlay, he came on the line like a coroner confirming the death of a loved one: "I assume you've heard."

"Yeah. Last night."

"Did she call you?"

"No. I called them. I talked to them both."

"It's a shame, really. I wish there were another way."

"Well . . . there is, I think."

"It's a little too late for that, I'm afraid."

"No. Please. Don't say that. I can't do this to him."

A silence, then a sigh. "You're not the one who's doing it, Gabriel."

"But you would never have killed it, if I hadn't—"

"No. That's not true at all. I had my own misgivings even before we talked. I told you that. You asked me to leave you out of it and I did. This was strictly our decision. You have no reason to be troubled."

"I have every reason! This boy matters to me, Ashe! Haven't I been clear about that? I'm not some big heartless publishing house. I haven't got ice water in my veins. If there's even the slightest chance that Pete is what he says he is . . ." I suddenly heard myself and stopped, realizing I was about to damage my case beyond repair. "Look," I said in a more reasonable tone, "I've got an idea . . . a good one, I think . . . and I'd like to run it by you."

"I'm afraid we're beyond that."

"Would you just listen to it, goddammit!"

"All right."

"I'm sorry, Ashe. I don't mean to be difficult, but . . . I'm just so worried that . . ."

"That's okay. Go ahead."

"Well . . . what if *I* were the one to interview Pete?"

The editor's silence was so dramatic that I knew I

had a chance. If you sell this very carefully, I told myself, you might still be Pete's hero. *Just hang on, son. We're gonna jump that sorry son-of-a-bitch.*

"I want to do a special edition of my show," I said. "With Pete and me just talking and . . . you know, having fun together. He could read from his book, and I could explain how he used to listen to me in the hospital. It would be great stuff, and wonderful publicity for his book. He's comfortable with me, and we wouldn't even have to get into the gory details. We could talk about the writing process and that sort of thing. And that would sort of make me his sponsor. You know, help legitimize him."

"You would do that?" he said.

"In a heartbeat."

"But you seemed so certain that—"

"Look, I know how I sounded before, but . . . I've had a lot on my mind lately, and I wasn't thinking clearly. I'm past that now. I believe in this child. I've never believed in *anything* so much."

"Yeah, but will Donna go for it?"

"Why not? She's heartsick about this, Ashe. And it's not that threatening. It's just another phone call, really, when you get right down to it."

Another long silence, but this one was imposing, a huge green wall curling above me. "A phone call?"

"Sure. It's radio, remember."

"You mean you wouldn't go out to Wisconsin?"

"Well, no. The idea was not to be invasive, and this seems like the perfect way to do that."

Another sigh. "That rather misses the point, doesn't it?"

"Well, I don't see why it wouldn't accomplish . . ."

"It was *proof* we needed, Gabriel. Not an interview. That can't have been lost on you."

"Look . . . If I'm willing to make him part of my show . . . to go out on a limb like that and virtually endorse him . . . doesn't that take some of the ethical burden off Argus?"

"Would that it could, my friend."

This reply, with its archaic wording and unctuous delivery, was so typically Findlay it infuriated me. I realized he wasn't listening at all. He was merely biding his time until the whole nasty business was behind him.

"This is not right," I told him. "You can't grant this boy a voice, then just take it away from him."

"I'm afraid we can, Gabriel. And must. There are too many questions still unanswered. I'm not willing to risk my reputation and the reputation of this house on a sentimental whim. There are too many risks, frankly. Too many people who know about this thing."

By which he means me, I thought. For Findlay had been perfectly willing to publish Pete's book when he had only his own doubts to contend with. It was *my* doubts that had queered the deal. Without me around he might have lied or pleaded ignorance if Pete's book—or Pete himself—had proven a hoax. Two people in the know constituted a conspiracy, and that made the whole thing too dangerous. And Findlay knew that I knew this.

"You know," I said quietly. "I wouldn't say anything if it turned out that . . . Pete wasn't what we thought."

"What do you mean?"

"Just that . . . you could count on me in that regard. I would never point a finger at anyone. I'd have nothing to gain by—"

"Please, Gabriel. Don't dishonor us both."

"I'm just saying—"

"I know what you're saying, and I know why you're saying it. I like him, too, and I'm sure I'll miss him terribly. And Donna as well. Especially Donna. She despises me now, but I know what a special person she is. I'm just as heartsick as anyone, Gabriel. Make no mistake about that."

Sensing finality, I scrambled for an alternate plan. "Well, then . . . okay . . . what if I talked to Donna again? Really laid it on the line with her. Maybe she *would* let me come visit if I told her—"

"Didn't she refuse you just last week?"

"Well, yeah, but—"

"And I've already laid it on the line with her, Gabriel. It didn't do a bit of good."

"But if she knew it would save Pete's book . . ."

"Nothing will save it. That's what I'm telling you. I've already met with the publisher. We've had a long, agonizing talk, and . . . we've come to the end. You've done your best, Gabriel. We both have."

"No, Ashe. You have *not* done your best. You've just taken the coward's way out. And now you've got the nerve to try and make it acceptable. So don't include me in this, please. You've deserted this child in the most heartless way, and I plan to say so. To the world, if necessary."

A long pause. "I'm sure you'll do what you have to do."

I slammed down the phone.

I didn't tell anyone anything for hours. I hated the thought of setting this calamity in stone, of making my fuckup official. Again and again, I retraced my steps, looking for the place where I'd taken the wrong turn. And for a while I even shifted the blame to Donna. She had been much too stubborn, I told myself, when even the smallest amount of compromise would have allowed Pete his self-expression as well as his privacy. Then I remembered that Donna knew Pete better than anyone, what his limits were and what it would take to unleash his demons. Who was I to judge that? And what did I *really* know about the nature of Pete's abuse? Hadn't Findlay suggested darkly that there were aspects of it too ghastly to include in the book?

Then I began to ponder the editor's odd remark about Donna: how "special" she was to him and how much he would miss her. He had sounded almost like a spurned lover, as if Donna might have offered more than marital advice when they met for that lunch in New York. Had their last heated exchange on the phone been complicated by something else? Had Findlay been denying his doubts because of feelings for Donna? And, if so, had he and I been seduced by two sides of the same person?

I wanted to kick this around with Jess, but we had left so much unresolved after our fight. And I was afraid he'd tell me to stop obsessing and get a life— something I knew in my heart I was no longer able to do.

Anna arrived late that afternoon to find me on the sofa in a pathetic state. She set down her briefcase as soon as she saw me.

"What happened?"

I outlined the catastrophe as succinctly as I could.

It sounded even worse when reduced to its essence.

"Well," she said with a shrug. "It's not like you didn't try."

"Right."

"Have you talked to him since it happened?"

"Once. But I told him I would try to fix things." I could see Pete lying there as I spoke, probably in his oxygen tent, gasping for breath as he waited for me to come through.

"Are you gonna talk to him again?"

"Well . . . yeah. But I can't handle it right now." Anna's dark, intelligent eyes were fixed on me so intently that her question seemed more than idle curiosity. "Why do you ask?"

She sat down on the edge of the couch next to my feet. "I hope you don't mind but . . . I talked to Edgar about this."

I drew a blank.

"My brother?"

"Oh, yeah. Your twin."

She nodded. "He works as an intern out at Skywalker Ranch. Sort of a glorified flunky."

"Cool job, though." I could picture a male version of Anna bustling through that fantasy factory in the Marin hills, a blueprint for the new *Star Wars* prequel tucked under his arm. Doing some quick arithmetic, I realized that those twins had barely been born when the first *Star Wars* was filmed. I would have killed for such a glamorous job at Edgar's age.

"One of Lucas's producers eats at my mom's restaurant, so Edgar made a pitch to him one day. *Anyway* . . . I told Edgar about this kid of yours and his mom and all, and he said there's a real simple way to figure out if they're the same person."

I groaned and pulled a sofa pillow over my face.

"Shouldn't have blabbed, huh?" Anna said.

"No, not that. I'm just burned out. And disgusted with myself. I don't wanna creep around anymore, Anna. It makes me feel too guilty. I would never have raised the issue in the first place if I'd known that Findlay was such a worm. In fact, I'd be blasting him in public right now, if I had any way in the world to—" I cut myself off.

"To what?"

"Nothing. Forget it."

"To prove that the kid exists, right? At least to yourself. To prove that he and his mom are two separate people. That's all you need, right?"

I nodded glumly.

"Well, there's a simple way to do that. You just get a voiceprint made. You know, those things the cops use."

"I know what they are, but . . ."

"Well, they're just as good as fingerprints, Edgar says. Even if somebody's trying to disguise his voice. Or *hers*."

"Maybe so. But it would just humiliate him further. There's no way you could keep it secret. It would be all over the place in no time."

"Why? I don't get it."

"Anna, look. Whenever the cops get involved . . ."

"You don't *need* cops. That's what I'm saying! Edgar could have it done out at Skywalker! They've got the best sound equipment around. And nobody would have to know."

I sat up on one elbow. "I thought you said he was a flunky."

"Well, yeah, but . . . he knows this girl who's a sound

220

person." She widened her eyes in a meaningful way.

"A girlfriend, huh?"

"Probably. Who knows? He's such a private little squirt."

I smiled at her. "I thought twins were supposed to share everything."

"That's a big misconception. It's not that way with us at all."

"Really?"

"When somebody knows you really well, you just have to hide things even more."

Had I been doing that with Jess? I wondered. Had he been doing that with me?

"Let's go check your machine," said Anna, already assuming I'd approved her voiceprint scheme. "I bet there's something on there we could use. You never erase your messages." She headed for the stairs, then stopped abruptly, beckoning me like a siren. "C'mon."

"Look, Anna. This is not really . . ."

"C'mon. It'll be fun."

I followed her up to the office, where, as predicted, there were no less than seventeen messages stored in the machine. "This is so cool," said Anna, rubbing her hands together. "I feel like Inspector Tennison. Where should I look?"

"I don't know if they're even on there," I said. "I've mostly been calling *them* lately."

"So I'll start at the beginning, okay?"

"Fine. Whatever."

She skipped past three messages—one from my agent in New York, one from Jess, one from a nearby Thai restaurant confirming my order—before arriving at Pete's distinctively chirpy voice. I had picked up the phone immediately, so all you could hear was a sassy fragment: "Hey, Dicksmoker, I was wondering if you were . . ."

Anna turned and frowned at me. "That's it?"

I nodded. "Piece o' cake, huh? All we have to do is get his mother to say 'dicksmoker.'"

Anna frowned, still poking the forward button. "It doesn't have to be the exact same word."

"You're sure about that?"

"That's what Edgar said."

"There's nothing else on there," I told her, indicating the machine. "At least not from her. I know she hasn't called in the last ten days."

"But you said you talked to her."

"Yeah. But I called *her*."

"Okay, then . . . call her now and tape your conversation."

"I can't do that."

"Why not?"

"For starters I don't have a tape recorder."

"You can do it off the machine, dummy. The tape recorder's built right in."

For someone in radio, I'm unusually technophobic, but I had never been more so than at that moment. As soon as I located its record button, that machine became something lethal to me, a nuclear device that would detonate with the slightest mishandling. "I still can't do it," I told Anna. "Not now. It would feel too weird and cold-blooded."

"Why?"

"They're waiting for an answer about Pete's book. They're expecting me to fix things."

"So? It doesn't matter what you talk about."

"It does to me, Anna. I can't break their heart and record it."

"*Their* heart?"

"His heart. Her heart. Whoever's."

My bookkeeper gave me a long, soulful look. "You need help," she said sweetly.

Later, when Anna was gone, I took Hugo on his walk. It was already dark. I would have to call Henzke Street as soon as I got home; I knew I'd never sleep knowing that Pete might still be awake, still expecting that sandbar. But I mustn't get tense about the call, or let myself feel guilty in the least. It was Ashe Findlay, after all, who had rejected Pete, and the greater part of the damage had already been done. My sad little report would just be a postscript at worst, an unpleasant aftertaste.

But I would try to make it easier for him. I'd be funny and warm and sympathetic and pissed off as hell at those bastards in New York. I'd tell him that having a book published was not really *that* big a deal, not the transcendent chest-thumping thrill it's often cracked up to be. The real reward, I'd say, sounding as if I meant it, was in the writing itself, in the truthful setting down of things. Whether your words had an audience of one or one million, their merit lay only in their artful placement on the page.

And after we'd talked for a while, I'd ask to speak to Donna.

Unless, of course, it was Donna who answered the phone.

In either case I would *not* be nervous about the machine. I would simply push the record button as soon as I got a dial tone and leave it on for the duration of the call. Even for me, that was foolproof enough.

Unless it made a noise of some sort. Like an intermittent beep, or one of those disembodied voices— God forbid—that would bark out the word *recording* and betray me on the spot.

I consulted the owner's manual when I got home to ensure that there were no telltale sounds when the recorder was on. Then I took a long shower and headed for the office. I would have preferred the bedroom, where I could stretch out on the bed and feel less formal, but the phone there was only an extension and lacked the necessary equipment.

I sat at Jess's desk and took a deep breath, then dialled the number I knew by heart. After one ring I pushed the record button, but what I heard shortly thereafter was so bewildering I was sure I had made a mistake.

So I dialled again.

And heard the same thing: "We're sorry. The number you have called has been disconnected or is no longer in service. If you feel you have reached this recording in error, please hang up and try your call again, or dial zero for an operator . . ."

Seventeen

Just Turn The Page

Jess and I added the lych-gate several months after moving in. I had grown up with one in Charleston and had loved the cozy enchantment of it: the shadows under its eaves, the way the honeysuckle would pile up on its roof in a fragrant yellow avalanche. It wasn't very grand—my father had built it over a weekend out of two-by-fours and asphalt shingles—but I remember being intensely proud of it. It was exotic to me, a fragment of Old Europe, like the porcelain fixture that sprouted mysteriously in my parents' bathroom after their first trip to Paris. "You pronounce it bee-day," my mother told me demurely, though she declined to explain its purpose.

I knew the purpose of lych-gates. My English grandmother had told me that *lych* meant *corpse*, and these gates had been designed to keep coffins dry in rainy churchyards. Jess and I found another use for ours: repelling invaders. Before we built the gate visitors

225

would zigzag all the way up through the garden to ring the doorbell. And since the front of the house is just a series of French doors, the living room was utterly exposed. It would only be a matter of time, we believed, before one of us would look up from a blow job on the sofa to find himself eye to eye with a volunteer from the Haight-Ashbury Free Clinic.

Or, with any luck at all, a Jehovah's Witness.

There was also the issue of my celebrity. From the second-floor bedroom we could already see discreet little groups of *Noone at Nighters* (identifiable by the books in their hands) casing the house from the sidewalk across the street. If we didn't do something soon, Jess argued, I'd be signing autographs at the door in my nightshirt—whether I wanted to or not.

So we found a craftsman who could design us something sturdy but graceful—more Japanese than English, really—that would accommodate a buzzer and an automatic lock. Once the lych-gate was installed, the garden became just another room of the house, affording a whole new level of peace and security. Now, when we heard a noise at night, the gate at least assured us that it couldn't be anything human; had to be just another skunk squeezing under the fence, or a bird sideswiping the house, or the black bamboo tapping softly against the window in the wind.

Which was why, on this particular night, I leaped up from the sofa as if I'd just heard a scream:

There was someone on the steps.

Someone I hadn't buzzed in.

Someone I could barely make out through the

226

filigree of the tree ferns, a shadowy figure in black, climbing swiftly to the porch.

"Jesus!" I said. "You scared the fuck out of me."

"Sorry," Jess said contritely, peering in through the French doors. "I wondered if I should buzz first."

In his leather jacket and bike helmet he looked like the Creature from the Black Lagoon. Despite my shattered nerves I was glad that he'd used his key. It seemed to suggest that he hadn't gone for good, still considered this place his home. "No, it's okay," I said. "I'm just jumpy."

He came into the living room holding a plastic bag, and set it down on the coffee table. Then he pulled off his helmet and placed it next to the bag, very delicately, as if it were a fragile heirloom. His face was a little blotchy from his ride, and he suddenly seemed older to me, more angular and careworn, closer to middle age than to the soft-featured boy I'd fallen in love with. I was unexpectedly touched by this, touched to be reminded how long we'd been fellow travellers, whatever our troubles were now.

He pecked me on the lips. "Who did you think it was, anyway?"

I rolled my eyes. "Nobody. Anybody. You don't wanna know." Meaning that I didn't want to tell him; that I was too embarrassed to admit the depth of my paranoia. For the past five days my guilty mind had been conjuring up things that weren't even faintly rational, much less possible.

"I brought dinner," said Jess, indicating the bag on the table, "in case you haven't eaten."

I wanted to cry, or at least to hold him for a while, but I was wary of his rigid body language. What had prompted this visit, anyway? Was he feeling the remorse that I'd been feeling about our last conversation? Or was there something else altogether, some terrible news he had yet to break?

"Smells great," I said. "Straits Café?"

He nodded. "Spring rolls and okra. And I got us some of those barbecued oysters."

Savoring the sound of *us*, I took the bag into the kitchen and began to arrange the food on plates. Jess followed and stood in the doorway, surveying the room. It was littered with dirty dishes and empty takeout boxes, completely betraying my state of mind.

"Are you okay?" he asked.

I shook my head. "Something awful's happened."

He gazed at me solemnly. "I know."

For a moment I felt a flicker of hope. "Did Pete call you?"

"No. Anna told me. She's worried about you."

"That's nice."

"Have you heard from him at all?"

"No. Nothing. They seem to be out of my life."

"Did you talk to Findlay about it?"

"Oh sure."

"What did he think?"

"He wasn't very forthcoming, but . . . I'm sure he thinks this proves he was right all along."

"That it was a hoax, you mean?"

"Or something." I looked him directly in the eyes. "Is that what you still think?"

He hesitated. "Does it matter?"

"Oh, yeah, Jess. Absolutely."

"Well . . . the main thing is: it's not your fault."

I went back to arranging the oysters.

"You know," said Jess, "for someone with such a

228

healthy ego you always manage to think the worst of yourself. Why is that?"

"Look . . . analysis is the last thing I need right now."

Jess shrugged. "Maybe it's the first thing."

I tried to stay calm. I didn't want another fight, but I didn't want to be told how to fix myself either. Not by the man who'd left me.

"Where shall we eat?" I asked.

We ate where we always had—on the floor next to the coffee table—and our silence was long and agonizing. It was Jess who broke it: "I'm really sorry," he said. "About last time."

"Oh, sweetie, I am too."

"You're all I've really got, you know. Nobody knows me like you do."

With no fanfare at all, tears began to spill down my face. I didn't move though. I was afraid of taking this where it might not be leading.

"And I'm sorry about Pete," Jess added, "but I hated having to hear it from Anna."

"I know. I wanted to call. I just didn't know whether you'd—" I cut myself off.

"What? Say I told you so?"

"Yeah. Or tell me to stop feeling guilty."

Jess smiled faintly. "Like I just did."

"But you understand, don't you?"

"A little, I guess, but I think you might be—"

"I took away his voice, Jess. That's no small thing."

"Well . . . yeah . . . if he ever existed in the—"

"All right, *if*. *If* he existed, I took away his voice. He spent two years shaping that atrocity of a life into something he could understand. And I took that away from him overnight. Or caused it to be."

Jess shrugged. "So give it back to him."

"What?"

"You still have that power."

"C'mon. I have no power at all. I did everything but rim Findlay, and he wouldn't even—"

"You don't *need* Findlay. Forget him. You've got your own editor."

"So? He'll be no more inclined to publish it than Findlay was. Especially when he hears that Argus has—"

"I'm not talking about Pete's book, I'm talking about *yours*—the one you could write from all this. It's better than any novel, babe. Just start at the beginning and tell the whole thing. How you read his galleys and talked to him on the phone and got really close to him and . . . everything. It's an amazing story, Gabriel. You couldn't make this shit up."

I just sat there blinking at him.

"Don't you think?" he asked, blinking back.

"I could never do that."

"Why not?"

"Because, for one thing, I don't know how it would end."

"So get off your butt and go find out." Jess widened his eyes in a playful, challenging way.

"Go where, for God's sake?"

"Where else? You've got their address, don't you?"

"Oh, no. Forget it. I could never do that."

"Why not? You were all set to go last week."

"I was invited then."

"Oh, don't be so damn well bred." This was one of Jess's pet themes: while he himself was poor white trash, brash as hell with nothing to lose, I was a timid little country-clubber who tried way too hard not to misbehave. "You don't even have to write this book," he said. "You're living it. Every bit of it is there, if you'll just turn the page."

The prospect of taking action, *any* action, after so many days of frustration was undeniably appealing. But I didn't trust the fire Jess was trying to light in me, or the peculiar tingle I felt when I thought about shaping this story for my own purposes. It seemed too much like fun, and therefore totally inappropriate for the subject matter. "This isn't some Hardy Boys mystery, you know. We're talking about a sick kid who could be dead in a month."

"Exactly! So why are you just sitting here? You'll never get any answers if you don't go out and find them. Look . . . if Donna called tomorrow to say that Pete had died, would you even know what to think? You wouldn't, babe. You wouldn't know whether to feel heartbroken or totally fucked over. You wouldn't have a clue. You'd be in limbo for the rest of your life."

He was right, of course, and such a ghastly moment was not at all beyond the realm of possibility.

I sighed. "I keep hoping it's temporary."

"What?"

"This . . . silence. Maybe they went unlisted because they needed a breather. That wouldn't be unreasonable. Pete's really weak right now and depressed about the cancellation. Maybe they just needed some quiet time."

"Why wouldn't they call and tell you that?"

Good question. Was Donna pissed off at me? Had Findlay really left me out of it as promised, or had he revealed my doubts to Donna as a way of lending support to the cancellation? That would certainly explain my sudden exile. Or maybe Pete himself had finally told Donna of his own suspicions about the cancellation, and they had concluded that I was part of it. But Pete had been so trusting the last time we talked. Wouldn't he want to hear the truth from me first, before shutting me out of his life forever?

I gave Jess a desolate look. "I can't handle this much longer."

He took my hand in his. "I don't mind watching Hugo."

Eighteen

A Convenient Pseudonym

The woman across the aisle from me had been casting exploratory glances since we'd passed the Rockies, though she didn't strike me as a fan. Seventyish and plump, relentlessly permed and pantsuited, she seemed more like a member of Oprah's audience than of mine. Which is not to say that such people don't listen to my show; I just don't expect them to recognize me on airplanes. This woman, I figured, was just lonely and cruising for a little conversation, so I tried to oblige her: "Comfy, isn't it?"

"Oh, yes," she said, flashing a row of way-too-perfect teeth. "These seats are just wonderful. I've never flown first class before."

"Same here," I said. "I'm usually crammed back there in steerage, eating my eight peanuts." This wasn't true—at least not lately—but I wanted her to feel at ease with me. I was already trying to charm her, I realized, a knee-jerk reaction I'd learned from my father.

Despite his vast catalog of prejudices the old man could be lovely with strangers, and no less gracious to a cleaning lady than he was to a visiting banker. It was his duty to be nice to people he didn't know; it was how he proved his goodness to himself.

"My daughter sent me this ticket," said the lady. "I always come out for Christmas, but this year they wanted to do something special for me."

"How nice."

"Mmm. Even got me my own suite at the Pfister Hotel."

A consolation prize, I thought. Up until now she's stayed at her daughter's house, but her son-in-law has finally put his foot down, paying dearly for the privilege. I imagined the lady knew this on some level, and therefore sorely needed me to confirm her great good fortune.

"The Pfister is marvelous," I told her. "Huge high-ceilinged rooms and hallways. Very pretty." I stopped short of saying that I'd stayed there once on a book tour, since I knew where that would lead, and I didn't feel like trotting out my dog-and-pony show. This trip had already been a sort of out-of-life experience, and I wanted to keep it that way. Someone else could be Gabriel Noone for a while. I would be anyone this woman imagined.

"Do you live in Milwaukee?" she asked.

I shook my head. "Here. I mean, there." I pointed behind the plane with a smile. "The Bay Area."

"Same here. Walnut Creek."

"Ah."

"Nice and warm there."

"Yes, it is."

"So you have family in Wisconsin?"

234

"Yes," I said, after a moment's hesitation. "My son lives there. With his mother."

She bit her lower lip and frowned with concern, nodding slowly.

"I get to see him on holidays," I told her.

"Well, that's nice."

"It is, yes. I can hardly wait."

"How old is he?"

"Thirteen."

"Oh . . . nice age."

The hell it is, I thought. It's a terrible age. It's the worst fucking age of all.

"Do you have any pictures of him?"

I couldn't help grinning. It's hard to say which I found more preposterous—her June Cleaverish question or the *Father Knows Best* answer I was able to provide: "As a matter of fact, I do." I reached for my wallet like any overproud parent who's been given such an easy opening.

She studied the snapshot soberly for a moment, pursing her lips. "Oh, my goodness," she said. "Just look at those eyes."

"Yes. They're something, aren't they?"

"He has your nose and chin, though."

"Does he?"

"Oh, yes. I'm sure you've been told that."

"Well . . ." I shrugged modestly and looked away. A passing flight attendant—male and cute in his brisk, bubble-butted way—locked eyes with me for the briefest of moments. This time the look was unmistakable.

"What's his name?" asked the woman.

"What?" I turned back to my interrogator with a start.

"Your son. What's his name?"

"Oh . . . Pete. Pete Lomax."

She looked at the snap again, as if to link the name with the face, then handed it back across the aisle. "Well, he's very handsome, Mr. Lomax."

"Thanks." I returned the snap to my wallet, blushing furiously, amazed at how rapidly I'd become such a fraud.

"My name is Vera, by the way." The lady held out her chubby, ring-encrusted hand.

"Oh . . . hi . . . I'm Peter."

"Aha," she said, beaming. "He's named after you, then. That's sweet."

I summoned a sickly smile.

"I have a granddaughter who's named after me. They don't call her that, it's just her middle name, but still . . . it's nice to have another little version of you out there in the world."

I was on the verge of changing the subject when that bubble-butted flight attendant did it for me.

"Excuse me," he said, kneeling in the aisle between me and Vera but addressing only me. "I saw your name on the passenger list, and I hope this isn't too pushy, but . . . well, I just want to say that I really appreciate everything you've done . . . you know . . . for us."

"Thanks," I said, as sincerely as I could. "That's really nice. It's been my pleasure, really."

He regarded me a moment longer with great solemnity, then patted me on the shoulder and hurried off.

Vera was watching me, slack-mouthed. "You've done something for flight attendants?" she asked.

*　*　*

I ended up telling her I was "kind of a labor negoti-ator," though I preferred not to discuss it, since I was travelling incognito. I was horrified at my ready-made mendacity and how quickly it had gotten out of hand. I imagined that any moment the flight attendant would come scurrying back with one of my paperback editions, earnestly requesting an autograph, and I'd be compelled to tell Vera that I sometimes wrote when I wasn't busy negotiating, and that Gabriel Noone was just a convenient pseudonym. But the flight attendant kept a respectful distance for most of the flight, approaching only for official duties and a brief, furtive offer of extra ice cream, an event which wasn't lost on the ever-more-fascinated Vera. Her sweet conspira-torial smile seemed to be saying: "Don't worry, Mr. Lomax. Your secret mission is safe with me."

This pointless little charade was closer than I'd come in years to impersonating a heterosexual, though I assured myself it had nothing to do with some lingering fear of public exposure. I had already proven that on an airplane, in fact, on a painfully long flight to Europe six or seven years earlier. Determined to beat jet lag, Jess and I had been following a program that required us to eat a carbo-heavy dinner at our normal time, then dress comfortably for bed and go immedi-ately to sleep, regardless of what the rest of the plane was doing. So we repaired to the head and reemerged minutes later in our black satin eyeshades and long cotton nightshirts—blue for him, pink for me—to be greeted by waves of laughter and a respectable smattering of applause. When someone shouted across the plane to ask admiringly where we'd bought the nightshirts, Jess yelled "San Francisco" back at him, and the place cracked up all over again.

I had basked in that moment, the joyful recklessness of it, the way all those strangers could see for themselves that we were a couple and didn't give a damn who knew it. When Jess conked out before I did, and his fuzzy blond head sank onto my shoulder, I wore it there for ages like an epaulet of honor, proud as a man could be as I waved off the flight attendant who had come to bring us supper. It was wonderful to have witnesses.

The Milwaukee airport was chaos itself: a slushy pileup of flatulent buses and angry people scrambling for home. I had packed lightly enough for a carry-on, so there hadn't been the usual delay at the carousel, but my rental car took almost an hour, thanks to a computer breakdown. While I waited, I had a cup of coffee in a snack bar, surrounded by more apple-cheeked white people than I'd seen in ages. Once removed from the mindless purgatory of the plane I felt slightly overwhelmed by the logistics of what lay ahead. Wysong was much farther north, and it was already late afternoon and getting dark. Should I crash here and get a fresh start in the morning or press on into the night?

I decided to press on. A map I'd been given at the rental counter made my route clear enough: north along the limp dick of Lake Michigan past Sheboygan and Green Bay, then west on Highway 29 toward Wausau. I probably wouldn't make it to Wysong that night, but I could stop anywhere I wanted: and anywhere would surely be preferable to the great bland nowhere of the airport. Besides, the longer I sat still, the more I began to question the wisdom of this pilgrimage. I was fearful of losing my nerve.

So I trudged across a snow-scabbed lot to the white Taurus I'd selected. (I'd decided against anything fancy, since I wanted to remain as neutral and invisible as possible.) The air was numbingly cold—a cold I'd all but forgotten—and the sky was the dingy off-white of an old T-shirt. My fingers felt brittle as I wiggled the key into the car door, and, once inside, I was greeted by the icy kiss of blue vinyl. I started the engine immediately and fidgeted with the heater controls, muttering "fuck, fuck fuck" as I waited for the blast of air to feel anything close to warm.

Moments later, I looked up to see a face that already seemed to belong to another world entirely. It was Vera, my fellow traveller, bundled up in a huge Christmas-red coat, crossing the lot with two other adults, presumably her daughter and disgruntled son-in-law. I was sure she wouldn't see me, but somehow she did, turning to twiddle her fingers merrily and mouth the words *Mr. Lomax* before disappearing behind a row of cars.

Vera is my welcoming committee, I thought with an odd little shiver, my very own white rabbit.

And now that she's led me down the hole I'm strictly on my own.

Nineteen

Man's Country

After an hour on the interstate, the snow began. It seemed to fall in all directions at once, gusting in sideways from the lake or spewing up like gravel from the wheels of hell-bent tractor-trailers. In this blinding blur even the signs on the overpasses became hopelessly hieroglyphic, blobs of green ectoplasm that lunged out of nowhere to set my nerves on edge.

I found a pop music station on the radio that calmed me for a while, but I was forced to abandon it when its bouncy songs proved to be invoking Jesus with disturbing regularity. I eventually settled on an all-polka station—just the right sound track for the territory, I thought—though it faded out after half an hour, casting me back into Top 40 hell. Then I remembered my proximity to Pete and searched in vain for Wisconsin Public Radio, combing the left end of the dial for the spot where the boy had first discovered me.

It was odd to think that my voice had preceded me

here, a place so frozen and desolate that a shopping mall at a cloverleaf could believably pass for an arctic weather station. There were folks here who knew me already—or thought they did—somewhere out there in the warmth of those stoic little houses. I had listeners here, for God's sake, so why should I feel like such an intruder, someone who had come to upset the natural order of things? If this story was happening to me, I had just as much right to live it as to tell it.

Even if I didn't have an ending.

Dinner happened at a truck stop outside Wausau. It was a mammoth warehouse of a restaurant: a sort of *Hofbrauhaus* on steroids, with Christmas lights twined around the rafters and huge suspended panels of colored Plexiglas meant to evoke stained-glass windows. I took a seat near the front and was promptly handed a menu—plastic-sheathed and profusely illustrated—by a tired redhead with a blinking snowman on her lapel. I was somehow seduced by all this. I couldn't remember the last time a uniformed waitress had served me, and there was something about this Teutonic shelter from the cold that compelled me to order a bacon double cheeseburger and get pleasantly shitfaced on old-fashioneds.

From where I sat I could see the parking lot and the trucks that idled there, snorting shafts of white breath like bulls in an icy corral. Across the highway in the distance, there was some sort of power plant, a Plutonian cityscape of domes and towers and cylinders, that stained the snow around it with a poisonous green light. The restaurant itself harbored a number of teenage boys that night, huddling in packs and full of scattershot menace. I avoided their eyes as usual, and it struck me that I'd been wary of these creatures all my life. As a small child I'd seen them as towering bullies, but even in my own adolescence I'd felt utterly removed from their stupid strutting ways, as if I was something less than them and better than them all at once. Forty years later I *still* felt that way, so that every time I passed a ball game or a clot of baggy-pantsed hip-hoppers waiting for a bus, I would brace myself instinctively for their casual abuse.

Pete, of course, had been the exception, my only ambassador to that alien world. It helped that he was an outsider himself, that he was largely a mixture of childlike need and grownup kindness. The two of us had filled in the blanks for each other, meeting in a place of our own invention to enjoy something rare for males of the species. Unless, of course . . .

Suddenly I was on my feet looking for a telephone. I knew this was an impulsive act—and probably fuelled by alcohol—but I didn't care. If that disconnected phone had just been temporary, it was only fair to let Pete know that I was on the way, that I would be there soon, tomorrow at the latest, asking his forgiveness and understanding. And he *would* understand, surely, if I kept my heart open and told him the unvarnished truth. No good could possibly come from creeping around like a spy.

I found a bank of phones next to the rest rooms and dialled his number. It was a local call now, thrillingly enough—or at least the same area code—but my hopes were dashed by the same recording: "We're sorry. The number you have called has been disconnected or is no longer in service . . ."

242

*　*　*

Back at my table, I ordered another drink and slid into a much darker place. What if the Lomaxes had moved away for good? That was possible, I realized. Pete might have been so depressed by the cancellation of his book that Donna had decided on a permanent change of scenery. On the other hand, what would I do if they *were* still on Henzke Street? Walk up and ring the doorbell? Leave a note? Ask the neighbors if a single woman lived there with her sick little boy? Wouldn't they find me suspicious? See me as one of Pete's former tormentors, come there to do him harm?

"There you go!"

My waitress was back with my drink, smiling down at me with tarty goodwill. I thanked her absently, barely forcing the words out.

"Can I get you some dessert? Some nice mincemeat pie?"

"No thanks . . . but . . . I was wondering . . ."

"Yeah?"

"Do you know a place called Wysong?"

"Sure. Up north a few hours."

"How many's a few?"

"Oh . . . two maybe . . . three. With the roads like this."

"Should I try to make it tonight?"

The waitress regarded me for a moment. "After three drinks, you mean?"

I hadn't meant that at all, in fact, so I wondered if I seemed more fucked up than I actually felt. She had a point, at any rate; bourbon didn't mix with a blizzard, especially after a draining day of travel. I asked her if there was a motel nearby.

"Oh, sure. Just around back there." She gestured out the window past the trucks. "It's not fancy, but it's clean. You better hurry and register, though. A lot of these guys are sleeping over tonight."

I won't pretend this didn't conjure up a certain image. It sounded, in fact, like the opening line of an old-fashioned porn novel, a less-than-subtle suggestion of orgies to come. And by the time I was crunching through the snow to the motel office, wishing I'd brought a scarf or a much more substantial coat, my mind had been so loosened by fatigue and whiskey that it was already making plans to move south.

The last sensible thing I did that night was call Wysong and reserve a room at the Lake-Vue Motor Lodge for the following day. I had hoped to reach the person I'd dealt with ten days earlier, the woman who had arranged, then unarranged, my first reservation. (Somehow it would have made me feel more welcome to hear her jolly voice.) But the desk clerk was young and male this time and deeply disinterested in my history with the motel. He took my credit card number and told me flatly that check-in time was twelve noon. That was fine with me; I could sleep late and take my time getting there, mapping out my strategy along the way.

My room at the truck stop was as basic as advertised but perfectly adequate: a second-floor niche off a common walkway that commanded a view of the whole complex. Once I'd brought in my bag and brushed my teeth, I put a sweater on under my coat and went outside to survey my surroundings. The snow had stopped, so the Oz-like minarets of the power plant had come into sharp relief against the horizon. I could smell the grease belching from the kitchen below and hear the frigid thunder of truck doors being slammed. Out toward the highway at the edge of a thicket I saw what had to be a public toilet: a small, square building with milky windows, toward which men were trudging, pilgrimlike, through the snow.

I was drawn there without a moment's thought. It was as if some younger, more reckless version of myself had taken over, emboldened by my solitude and the raw anonymity of the situation. I headed down the steps, then followed a newly beaten path across the parking lot, threading my way through the maze of trucks. Here and there I saw men stamping the snow off their boots or sprawled in the cabs of their rigs, their faces aglow in the phantom flare of a match. For all their big-buckled bravado, they seemed less threatening to me than those free-range teenagers back at the restaurant. The air was rife with the certainty of ritual and something else—a feeling I couldn't quite identify—a sort of gruff, unspoken understanding.

The toilet was nearly as cold as the parking lot and had the unmistakable ferny smell of fresh semen. As I entered, there was already action in one of the stalls. I stood at the urinal for a while, pretending to pee, wondering if I had spoiled the game for someone else, but there was only a brief shuffling sound before the sounds began again.

Then a man came in and stood at the trough next to me. He was thirty-five probably, burly and balding and unremarkable, except for a fat candy apple of a cock that he shook one too many times after peeing. Returning his semaphore, I shook back at him—two or three longs and a short—as I clocked his reaction from the corner of my eye. When it seemed we were speaking the same language, I sidled closer and reached for him.

I'd done nothing like this since the early eighties, but even then I hadn't done it for the danger, the threat of exposure that some men find so thrilling. For me, the thrilling part—beyond the sex, of course—was the tacit implication of brotherhood, the stripped-down humanity of connecting with a stranger and banking everything on his decency as he banked everything on mine. But I'd always wanted privacy once that leap of faith had been made.

"I have a room," I told the man. His cock was plumping in my hand, miraculously warm and silken.

He cast an anxious glance at the door, then back at the stalls, then reached down and weighed my balls soberly in his palm, as if they might help to make up his mind. "Where?" he asked finally.

"Here." I jerked my head toward the motel.

He stuffed his cock back into his trousers, which I realized (somewhat to my chagrin) were beltless and polyester. Taking his cue, I buttoned up my jeans and led the way out of that rank little room, grateful for the bite of fresh air in my nostrils. As we tramped down the path together without a word, I caught him gazing sideways at me. He's wondering if I'm a cop, I thought. Or a serial killer.

"I'm visiting," I offered. "From California."

He didn't react, just kept walking.

When we reached the parking lot, he stopped and turned. "I wanna go to my place, okay?"

"You mean . . . you live around here?"

"Up there." He cast his eyes skyward, as if I were about to be abducted on a UFO.

I looked up and saw the cab of a truck, a metallic red cubicle with someone's name—his, presumably—painted primly on the door in tiny silver letters. My first reaction was to smile, remembering a long-gone bathhouse in New York called Man's Country where—somehow—the management had installed the cab of an actual big rig on an upper floor, so that horny chorus boys and ribbon clerks from Bloomingdale's could enjoy in relative safety the vivid archetypal experience of being fucked in a truck.

"You're kidding," I murmured.

He looked right and left, checking for witnesses, then scrambled up and unlocked the door. "C'mon," he whispered, and I obeyed without a word, curiously flattered but sane enough to feel anxious. A headline formed in my head—GABRIEL NOONE FOUND DISMEMBERED IN WISCONSIN WOODS—as I reminded myself that this was the state that had given us Jeffrey Dahmer. Not to mention Ed Gein, the real-life inspiration for Norman Bates.

But once inside the cab I found comfort in the prosaic: a cardboard air freshener shaped like Santa Claus, a dog-eared copy of *Field and Stream*, a photo of a woman and several children tucked into the visor. It was almost cozy up there, pristine and well padded and lofty enough to be private. Behind the seat lay a rectangle of foam rubber onto which we spilled in a ridiculous jumble of limbs.

We kissed longer than I'd expected, sparring with our tongues as we lapped the warmth from each other. I reveled in everything: his flat little nipples (as inexpressive as his dick was eloquent), the musty pucker of his butt, the satiny slap of his meat against my face. We ended up side by side, jerking off together, and I

247

found myself laughing out loud as I came, a guttural volley from the back of my throat that shoved out my last ounce of breath. He smiled at me sleepily, then swiped at my come with his forefinger. "Daddy," he murmured, and slid the finger into his mouth.

I lost track of time. I was already in that place where just the heat of someone's leg across your own seems to contain everything extraordinary that came before. I was struck by the sense of relief I felt, the feeling of having come home again to my own body. I'd been sleeping alone for less than two months and would never have guessed how deeply I'd missed the sound of another heartbeat so near, this warm, entangled, animal reassurance. What I had here wasn't a disembodied voice on the phone or a distant building winking in the fog; this was the real goods, however casual or anonymous. Everything seemed possible again—or at least redeemable.

"Should I be going?" I asked.

"That's okay."

"To go or to stay?"

He chuckled quietly, lumbering to his knees, his tackle dangling clumsily between his legs. Then he pulled a paper bag from the corner and began—rather earnestly—to search for something. For one blood-chilling moment those headlines started up again, predicting a grisly end for our visitor from California. Then Mr. Dahmer-Gein exhumed a couple of family-sized Snickers bars and handed one to me.

"Hey," I said. "Dinner *and* a movie."

"No . . . sorry. I don't have a VCR."

I didn't bother to explain my flimsy metaphor, just

tore into the candy bar as he slid in next to me, warming my side again.

"Is that your family?" I asked, nodding toward the photo on the visor.

"Yeah."

"Nice-looking."

"Thanks."

One of the kids in the picture was in his early adolescence. His head was partially in the shadows and covered with a baseball cap, but there was something about the line of his cheekbone and the light in his eye, something about that crooked little Bart Simpson smile . . . It was impossible, of course, and utterly absurd, but the more I studied the picture the more I toyed with the creepiest idea: What if that actually *was* Pete up there? And what if somehow— through the wildest of flukes—I had stumbled across his real father, stumbled across him and sucked his cock in the back of a truck?

Oh, give it a break, I thought. You will *not* write an ironic end to this, no matter how much it might distance you from your emotions. Pete's father had been a foreman in a hosiery factory, and Pete had testified against him, for God's sake. The monster was in a prison somewhere, locked up for life, not cruising toilets in his tractor-trailer. I also knew that my imagination had a way of turning feral after sex, roaming the landscape like some ravenous snuffling beast. This had sometimes proved useful in my work, in fact, when the beast didn't get out of hand. When it didn't turn on me with a slobbery yellow grin and start to weird me out . . .

"Do you live around here?" I asked.

The man shook his head as he polished off his candy bar. "Florida."

I checked the photo again. There was even a ragged palm tree as proof. I let go of my nasty reverie with a sigh.

"What?" said the man.

"Nothing. Florida's nice."

"Lots nicer'n this." He rolled on his side and gripped my leg between his furry thighs like a bear shinnying up a tree. "Too goddamn cold here."

He's really nice, I thought. Just a regular guy who needs the comfort of other guys sometimes. I was certain he was a closet case—that eternal bane of my existence—but I forgave him everything for holding on to me, for needing my warmth that night as much as I needed his.

"My name's Gabriel," I ventured without offering my hand, which would have felt foolish, since I'd already offered everything else.

"Named after the angel?"

"No. My father. And my grandfather."

"Oh."

"They weren't angels. Still aren't."

"Your grandfather's still alive?"

"No. But the old man is."

"You get along?"

"We don't talk that much," I explained. "He's a banker, and . . . I'm not."

"What are you?"

I hesitated, fearful of forfeiting this peaceful anonymity. "I'm a writer," I said at last.

"What kinda writer?"

"Novels. Stories."

"Like what? John Grisham or something?"

"No. Not exactly." My postcoital confidence was slipping by the second. Why, I wondered in an ugly

250

spasm of self-betrayal, had I never written a novel like John Grisham? A novel that a regular guy like this might have read? Had I been preaching to the choir all my life? "My stuff is on the radio, too," I said, trying another angle. "Ever listen to NPR?"

The guy just frowned at me. "What's your last name?" he asked.

"Noone."

"Gabriel Noone?"

"Yeah."

The frown deepened as he shook his head. "No. Sorry."

"That's okay."

"I don't read much, I guess. And I mostly just play tapes in the . . ."

"So what does your wife think?"

The guy drew back. "About what?"

"You know . . . sucking dick in the back of your truck."

"Hey, man!" My partner in passion scrambled to his knees, his eyes narrowing in anger and alarm. "What the fuck is this?"

"Nothing. I was just wondering what—"

"If you're a cop or something, you was the one who grabbed *my* dick!"

"I know, I know. Stay cool."

He remained there on his knees, breathing heavily, distinctly Neanderthal in his panic.

"I'm not a cop," I said quietly. "Or anything like it." I offered him a faint, peacemaking smile. "I'm just another queer like you."

"Fuck you. I'm not a queer."

"Okay. Sorry. Whatever. It doesn't matter."

"It fuckin' matters to me. What was that shit about my wife?"

"Nothing, man. I was just curious. I didn't mean to give you grief. Really."

This was a lie, of course. I *had* meant to give him grief. I'd meant to make him squirm for a moment, to punish him in some small but palpable way for not recognizing my name. And here was the kicker: if he were to beat me to death with a tire iron and dump my body in a snowbank, I'd have only my vanity to blame.

He was still breathing heavily, still glowering at me. "My wife is a goddamn saint, all right?"

"I'm sure. I'm sure she is."

He picked up my jeans and flung them at me. "Get dressed and get the fuck outa here."

I accomplished that in record time, scrambling down the side of that gleaming red mountain without attempting another word. But I misjudged the distance and fell hard against the icy asphalt, skinning my palm in the process. I staggered to my feet, ignoring my new-found stigmata, and strode briskly away, pausing only once to look back at the truck. I remember finding irony—if not exactly amusement—in the sign I saw emblazoned on its bumper.

It said: WIDE LOAD.

Back in my room, I collected my wits as I dabbed at my bloody hand. My first instinct was to call Jess. Not because I'd had a scare and feared briefly for my life, but because I'd had a bona fide adventure.

Oh, Jess, I wanted to say, you would be so proud of me. I've braved the undiluted world of men again, where dicks are king and sex is everything and nothing. If you were here tonight, I'd tell you all about Mr. Wide Load. I'd lie in your arms and laugh about the postures of the closet and the sad, silly demands of my own unwieldy ego. I'd give you every last juicy moment, then tell you how little it had meant, how little it would always mean when weighed against the age-old certainty of Us.

But I didn't call him; I'd had enough of telephones.

Twenty

The Shock of Recognition

I slept solidly but not as long as usual. I awoke just after six and hauled my bag down to the car, noticing how radically the configuration of the parking lot had changed. Mr. Wide Load's love machine was gone, and the maze of trucks I had followed the night before was no longer the bustling village lane of memory. The gypsies had all but vanished, leaving only black rectangles on a white plain as proof of their encampment. Even that distant men's room seemed different now: lustless and one-dimensional, hammered flat by the sharp halogen light of dawn.

I ate some eggs and sausage at the restaurant and bought a local map from the cashier. It proved too cartoonish to be useful, but I found a certain comfort in the smiling cows and dancing cheeses, the legions of happy hunters and bikinied water-skiers that would lead me north to 511 Henzke Street and the apple of my eye. I felt good, despite my banged-up hand, so I plunged into the blazing blue day, already a gypsy myself.

Once on the road, I was filled with the kind of tingly anticipation I'd felt as a child on our summer drives to Canada, when there was breakfast in my stomach and the prospect of a thrilling roadside attraction just ahead. I'd loved the spooky ones most of all, the ones that asked the questions that were never answered: a place in New Brunswick called Magnetic Hill, where drivers could watch their cars roll inexplicably uphill; or any of those specially constructed Mystery Houses, where the proportions were so out-of-whack that plumb lines seemed to fall at an angle and little boys like me looked twice as tall as any grownup.

Once beyond the roiling vapors of that power plant, I found the landscape more to my liking. North of Wausau there were pleasant farmsteads and dark green forests and countless ponds winking through the birches like pocket mirrors. I was so close to a state of enchantment that I stopped impetuously at a pseudo-rustic convenience store because a sign out front promised hot chocolate. What I found was hot all right, and a distant cousin of chocolate, but it shot from a machine in a vile diarrheal blast that tasted as bad as it looked. I bought a soda instead, then considered the notion of calling Pete again; no, I decided, I didn't need the sucker punch of hearing that message one more time.

The towns on the way to Wysong were too basic to be as pretty as their setting: grungy little grids of auto-repair shops and video stores and pizza parlors with their windows steamed gray against the cold. The houses that straggled into the outskirts were small and shabby, their drafty places plastered with those asphalt shingles that are meant to look like bricks but never do. Everywhere there were satellite dishes aimed hungrily at the heavens, though they seemed so sad and junky in the snow, so unfuturistic, like a broken-down car on blocks or a bedspring left to rust in the woods.

Wysong announced itself with billboards. Or rather its main attraction did. SEE THE GODFATHER'S DEATH-MOBILE was the first indicator, followed by ELVIS'S FAVORITE CADDIE! and HISTORIC FUN FOR THE WHOLE FAMILY. Americans are pathetic, I thought, always suckers for a sideshow and so easily seduced by engines and icons. But the billboards proved useful, since they led me in a matter of minutes—sooner than I'd expected and maybe even sooner than I'd wanted—past the entrance of the Lake-Vue Motor Lodge.

It wasn't what I'd expected. I'd envisioned something from the fifties, from the hand-tinted memory bank of my own childhood. One of those plain white trains of a building with a painted iron swing set on its manicured lawn. I'd banked everything on the cutesy spelling of *Vue*, but here stood a pink brick monstrosity from the eighties, as bland and soulless as any industrial park. The lobby was blue and mauve with white plaster tables and curly white plaster floor lamps, the Reagan era's take on deco. And there was a Christmas tree in one corner—white, naturally, with blue ornaments.

I identified myself to the desk clerk, who was female but far too young to have been that folksy woman on the phone. She gave me a key—or rather my card—after consulting her computer, then pointed out the hallway that led to my room. I took off immediately, relieved that I didn't have an escort, didn't have to comment on the room or hear another spiel about a minibar.

The room was more of the same. I dumped my suitcase on a blue-and-mauve bedspread and sank into a chair with a sigh. What on earth was I doing here? How could I possibly *not* be disappointed by what I would find? Nothing had ever met my expectations, since nothing could compete with my doctoring imagination, my pathetic compulsion to make the world quainter, funnier, kinder, and more mysterious than it actually was.

I remembered a time before I'd met Jess when I'd tried anonymous phone sex. One of my partners had been so aurally appealing that I'd insisted upon meeting him and found myself—that very night—trekking across town to an apartment in the Mission. The guy wasn't a troll by any means, and he hadn't misadvertised himself, but he wasn't what I'd pictured, and I just couldn't complete the wiring, couldn't make the voice on the phone hook up with the actual person. It was like a Japanese monster movie where the dubbing was so bad that you couldn't believe it at all.

It will be like that with Pete, I thought. You'll find a child, all right, in the house on Henzke Street, a flesh-and-blood boy who is small and frail and close to death. But he won't be the Pete of your imagination. He'll be slightly off somehow, slightly out of sync with the son you've so painstakingly constructed. It won't be the euphoric moment of bonding you've dreamed about. It will be awkward and disruptive, maybe even disturbing, and certainly rife with embarrassment. You'll have to start over again, build a new relationship from the ground up.

257

If that's even possible.

If he even wants you, after he learns what you've done.

My spirits improved after a shower and a fresh change of clothes. I stood at the window, assembling my courage, placing myself in context before I ventured out. There wasn't a single Lake in Vue, at least not from this direction. I could see a piece of the snowy parking lot and a piece of the highway snaking into the trees and a corrugated-iron building that could only be the famous Neilson's Antique Auto Barn. And across the highway a clot of slushy gas stations and burger joints that probably led into Wysong itself.

There were clouds in the sky again, gray flannel bolsters that promised more snow and plenty of it, so I headed down to the lobby without further idling. The watch had apparently changed, for this time there was an Asian woman behind the desk. She was middle-aged and slender, pleasant-looking, with a hairdo that hugged her head like a scalloped bathing cap.

"I wonder if you could help me," I asked.

"Sure thing, hon. What is it?"

I recognized the voice immediately. This was the woman on the phone, the one who had taken my first reservation. The one I had already pictured in a knotty pine office: plump and rosy-cheeked and, yes, Caucasian. I smiled as another assumption collapsed on itself. I thought of Anna and how she would have teased me for regarding the world as white until proven otherwise. *Well, Gabriel, you can take the boy out of Charleston . . .*

"Is there lipstick on my teeth or something?" The lady had obviously noticed my reaction.

"No." I laughed. "I just realized . . . we've already met. I was the guy who called from San Francisco a few weeks back."

"The one who cancelled on me."

"Exactly."

"Jeez, what happened to your hand?"

"Oh . . ." I glanced down at my scabbing stigmata. "I fell off a truck."

"Ouch. Hope it wasn't a potato truck."

"What?"

"Nothing. Bad joke. That's what they used to say in Missouri. 'He looks like he just fell off a potato truck.' Don't ask me what it means. You want a Band-Aid for that? I've got some in the office."

"Thanks, but . . . I think it's better in the open air."

"Did you hitch here or something?"

"No. Why?"

"Well . . . if you fell off a truck . . ."

"Oh, no . . . it wasn't moving or anything. I was just . . . visiting the truck."

The woman nodded slowly, taking that in. Or trying to, at least, bless her heart. "So what can I do for you?"

"I'm looking for Henzke Street," I told her.

"That's easy. Across the highway and into town. There's a Denny's just past the first stoplight. You take a left there and go three blocks and turn right. That's Henzke Street. It's one of the main streets. You can't miss it."

I headed for the door, then stopped. "Left at Denny's, three blocks, turn right."

"Right."

"Thanks."

"Don't forget the Auto Barn now."

"How could I?" I said.

I had a gut feeling well before I got there, well before I saw the tatty commerce of Henzke Street and realized how unlikely a setting it would be for the bungalow I'd built in my brain. I'd seen this address only once, after all—on the back of an envelope that Donna had sent—and I had never questioned it since. Stupid mistake. Why would a woman so ferociously protective of her child surrender his location that readily?

I parked against a snowbank and trudged around the corner to the door. There was a Laundromat on one side, a pink-and-chrome beauty parlor on the other. 511 Henzke Street was just what it should have been, just what I would have guessed, had I thought about it longer: one of those private post offices with a precious name—in this case, Mail 'n' More. I entered without hesitation, but I felt scriptless now and markedly criminal.

The room had a red-white-and-blue motif in homage to its federal ancestor. There were two men behind the counter, one of whom was funnelling Styrofoam popcorn into a large cardboard box. The other was wrangling with a cranky geezer at the head of the line who wanted some guarantee that his package would make it to an army base in Italy in time for Christmas. The other customers—half a dozen at least and all of them burdened with boxes—had begun to sigh and shuffle histrionically. I joined the end of the line, grateful for the delay, the chance to collect myself.

It's a small town, I thought; they're bound to know Donna. She must come here all the time if she doesn't

260

get mail at home. She could even be here now, in this very room, one of these yule-weary women waiting in front of me. At any moment she could turn and confront me. Or would she just remain silent—and invisible—in the face of my suspect behavior?

You have not been invited, I reminded myself.

When my time came with the clerk, I went for partial confession in the hope that my candor would be disarming. I tried to be as breezy as possible, but the words came out sounding forced and overhearty. "The good news," I began, "is that I don't have a package."

"And the bad?" The guy was about thirty and actually had a cigarette dangling from his lips, a display that seemed—to a Californian eye, at least—only slightly less brazen than a penis dangling from a fly.

"Well," I said. "It's not bad really, but I need your help finding a friend of mine. She lives here in Wysong, and we've been talking on the phone for a while, and . . . well, I've sent her stuff here and everything, and she's written to me . . . I've always assumed . . . really stupidly, I know . . . that 511 Henzke Street was her actual address."

The clerk squinted at me like a suspicious horned toad. Then his lips twisted into a leer, making the cigarette bob obscenely. "You meet her on-line or something?"

I laughed nervously. "No. Nothing like that." Fuck, I thought. I'd deliberately left Pete out of my explanation so this guy wouldn't think I was some creep who stalks kids he's never met. So now, apparently, he thought I was stalking Donna—or at least determined to nail her. "She's just an old friend. We've known each other for years . . . I've just never been to Wysong before and I always assumed . . . I'm sure she thinks I already have her address . . . that's the frustrating part."

"Right."

"She must come here a lot, actually. Donna Lomax?"

The clerk took the cigarette from his mouth and ground it into a stray Snapple cap. "Know what she looks like?"

I tried my best to reconstruct Pete's description in *The Blacking Factory.* "Oh . . . brown eyes, lanky . . . attractive. She's a psychologist. Has a kid she's adopted."

He seemed to absorb that for a moment. "And you want her address?"

"If . . . you know . . . it's cool with you." *Cool with you?* Why was I talking like a VJ from MTV? And why had I taken this idiotic approach? It sounded much too desperate and wormy.

I was debating whether to reveal my benign homosexuality when I realized that the clerk was smirking at me. "You know why most people pay us, don't you?"

"Sorry, I . . ."

"They pay us so they don't *hafta* use their real address. That's the whole point of this place."

"Well, of course, I understand that completely, but . . . Donna's an old friend, and I've come a long way, and I'm sure she'd . . ."

"I can't make that judgment, pal."

"Not even if—"

"Nope. Not even."

"Right." I gave him an insipid smile. Now the people behind me had started to shuffle, fully aware that I had no valid business here.

"You can use the phone," the clerk offered, "if you wanna call her or something."

"You know her, then?"

"Who?"

"Donna Lomax? You recognize the name? She has a box here?"

"Look, man, you're gonna hafta . . ."

"Okay. Fine. Sorry."

I slunk out without argument, my face as scarlet as the countertop, while the other customers witnessed my humiliation. I could feel their eyes on me as I left, hear their little grunts of disdain. And I knew what fine camaraderie they would share at my expense, once I was out the door.

Dazed, I wandered without purpose or thought for at least ten minutes, finally seeking refuge in one of those Italian restaurants where Christmas decorations are all but lost amid the raging year-round gaudiness. There, over a cup of coffee, I faced the question of the hour:

What, if anything, did I know for sure?

I could see that house so clearly in my mind's eye: a single-story bungalow with its scaffolded bed and its shelves full of Tom Clancy and *The X-Files* and me. I could see rooms that Pete had never described: a blue kitchen with a neat row of cereal boxes, and the bedroom across from Pete's, where Donna probably slept. I could even see into the yard sometimes, especially at night, when the light from Pete's window would cast a golden Rembrandt glow on the snow. There were trees in that yard, I imagined, evergreens and sturdy sentinel oaks that baffled the sound of the cars out on Henzke Street.

No. Not Henzke Street. Somewhere else entirely. And who could say where that might be? It had to be here, though, somewhere, maybe only blocks away. Maybe I could find it. Wysong wasn't huge, after all; I could walk around for a while, ring a few doorbells until someone recognized Donna's name or knew of Pete's predicament.

Uh-huh. They'd call the cops the minute I left, tell them about this strange man from California who'd been asking about that poor little boy. I could explain myself, of course, but only after a great deal of trouble and public embarrassment. Should I care about that? Yes, I decided, I should. Donna and Pete might well be angry with me already, knowing more than I thought they knew. This was hardly the time to make a spectacle of myself.

What about her car, then? People actually parked in front of their houses here, and Donna's car could be the tip-off. But what did it look like? Pete had bitched about it, I remembered, annoyed by those long drives to the hospital in some totally uncool machine. Had he ever mentioned its make or color? And was it Donna's car or someone else's—like that friend across the street who rode with them sometimes: Margaret Something. No, *Marsha*. Marsha might help me, assuming she was listed in the phone book, assuming I could remember the rest of her name.

I couldn't, of course; I wasn't even sure if Pete had ever told me. My memory of our conversations was anecdotal at best, too crowded with jewelled elephants to be useful now. And even those precious images felt perishable, shimmering and fading beyond recognition, like a photograph in a darkroom when the door is opened suddenly without warning.

* * *

A boy came into the restaurant, stopped at the counter, asked something of the cashier.

About thirteen, I figured. Dark-haired and handsome, but decidedly healthy-looking.

I watched him from the corner of my eye, lifting my cup to my mouth as camouflage. His face was angled away from me, so I waited for his profile to appear in relief against the faux-grotto wall. My mind began to fidget with a troubling new possibility, until someone snapped me out of it: a man of forty or so, obviously the kid's father, signalling to him from a table in the back.

I looked away, ashamed of my ridiculous need, then slapped money on the table and left.

It was snowing now, really hard, and the flakes were gross and misshapen, not at all the miracles of symmetry they're supposed to be. The air was suddenly much colder, so I turned up my collar and hurried back to the car—or where I thought it should be—but the snowbank I'd parked against had disappeared. For a moment, I admit, it all seemed part of a theme, as if some giant celestial eraser was rubbing out everything familiar to me. Panicking a little, I picked up my pace and changed directions on Henzke Street, then studied the storefronts carefully until I found the Mail 'n' More. I sighed with relief when I spotted that anonymous white vehicle around the corner, just where I had parked it. This is my base camp, I thought, my only true constant in this shifting wilderness.

I started the engine and turned on the heater full blast, rubbing my hands together furiously. The windshield had been whited out by the snow, so I reached for the wiper knob, only to stop when I noticed something strange: a pattern of sorts, like a runic inscription, etched on the glass. A passerby—some kid, no doubt—had written something there that was disappearing rapidly in the latest flurry. The letters were cursive and impossible to decipher in reverse, so I climbed out of the car and studied the thing head-on. It was a short word—no more than five or six letters—but its meaning wasn't readily apparent. The second letter was probably an O, the last a D or a T, though I couldn't tell anything for sure.

What was wrong with me anyway? Why was I looking for clues in such a random and offhanded act? Worried for my sanity, I climbed into the car again and turned on the wipers without a second look.

What now?

I drove around for almost an hour, longing for the shock of recognition in a place I'd never seen. There were several streets with the kind of bungalows I'd envisioned, but many more were lined with new brick condos and town houses, any one of which could easily have harbored Pete. Meanwhile, the light was beginning to fade and the snow was becoming a serious threat. It led me into a ditch, in fact, when I could no longer distinguish the line between street and sidewalk. I escaped after a brief spinning of wheels, but the message had been delivered just the same:

You don't know where you are or where you're going

or even how to drive in this mess. Why don't you go home, pilgrim?

Home for the moment was the Lake-Vue. I took a hot shower, changed into sweats, and dug out a joint I had stashed in my shaving kit. I smoked it on the bed as I considered my options, wishing Jess were there to egg me on, to curb my unending cautiousness. Jess would have a plan, even now, some risky renegade scheme that would scare the shit out of me but end up, as usual, working very nicely.

Why not call him? I needed to touch base again, if only to tell him he'd been on my mind in the midst of this frustrating quest.

I picked up the phone and dialled. It was mid-afternoon in San Francisco, a good time to reach him usually, and I figured he'd be at his place then. He answered after three rings, laughing uncontrollably. At least I assumed it was him.

"Jess? What's so funny?"

"Who's calling?" asked a man whose voice I didn't recognize. He was laughing even harder, as if somebody there was goosing him repeatedly. Could this actually be Frank, the motorcycle buddy?

My blood turned to ice water. "This is Gabriel . . . Noone."

"Oh . . . hang on."

A muffled moment or two, and then: "Hi. Where are you?"

"Is this a bad time?" I asked coldly.

"No . . . no . . . not at all."

"Sounds like it is."

"Oh, that's just Tom from down the hall. Being silly."

Jess knew what I was thinking, and was trying hard to sound matter-of-fact, either because my fears were unfounded or because they weren't. "He came over to watch a documentary on Jung," Jess added. "He doesn't have a TV."

And you do? I thought. When did you get a TV? You're not even supposed to *like* TV. You gave me hell about it constantly, called it a drug and a depressant, a brain-rotting waste of time. And why would you lay out that kind of money, if you have any intention of coming home?

"Have you found him?" asked Jess.

"Who?"

"Pete."

"Oh." My mind was no longer working, at least not on our conversation. The heartfelt reunion I'd wanted had a witness now: some creep in the background called Tom from Down the Hall. And who was to say he wasn't that guy I'd seen in Jess's lobby, the cocky little leather number with the Shetland pony build?

"What's the matter?" asked Jess.

"Nothing. This isn't the time, that's all."

"Oh, c'mon . . ." His voice was gentle. He knew how much I was hurting and he hated it, but he seemed incapable of comforting me.

Just tell me you love me, I thought. Tell me you've made an awful mistake. Tell me that no one on earth has ever known you the way I have. Tell me that now in front of Tom from Down the Hall.

"I hope you're okay," said Jess.

"I'm fine," I said. "I haven't found him yet, but . . ." My voice trailed off, too weakened by my green-eyed demons.

"He's not there, you mean?"

268

"I have to go, babe. I can't do this."

"Fine. All right. Whatever."

"Take care," I said.

"Right," he said and hung up.

I had needed a good cry, and I got one, curled up there on my blue-and-mauve bedspread. I had run out of people to call. There was no one beyond Pete and Jess that I could trust with my pathetic disfigured self. I lay there for almost an hour while the tears scalded their way out. When there were none left, I got up and went to the bathroom, threw water on my swollen eyes and returned. The room was dark now, so I snapped on the lamp by the bed, then went to the window to shut out the blackness.

My hands were on the curtain cord when I saw it. It was fairly far away, almost overpowered by the lights of the gas station in the foreground, but I could make out its shape against the trees, hovering there above the town.

I left the room, forgetting I had a telephone, and raced down three corridors to the lobby, where the pleasant Asian desk clerk was still on duty. She gazed up from a magazine with a concerned frown.

"Is everything all right?" she asked.

"That star," I said. "Where is it?"

"What star?"

"The electric one. The one I can see from my window."

"Oh, the Christmas star."

"Right."

"That's on the old water tank."

"But where is it?"

"Oh, lord, lemme think. It's a coupla blocks behind the high school, which means it would be on Curtis, or maybe McIntosh. No, here's what you do: Go down to Henzke Street, just like I told you before, then take a left on Maple just past the BP station, and go four or five blocks to Simmons, no not Simmons at all, Regent Street, and head straight out until . . ."

There's no point in recreating this labored litany; I wasn't even listening at the time. My mind was elsewhere entirely, wrestling with a fragment of memory that was trying hard not to reveal itself. But when it did come, it came with such sudden clarity that I spoke the words out loud:

"Roberta Blows!"

"Excuse me?" said the desk clerk.

Twenty-one

Family Things

The star I'd seen had been as literal as a star could be: five evenly spaced points pricked out with blue light-bulbs. We had a smaller version of this on our tree in Charleston that Pap extracted annually from the Gordian tangle of Christmas lights he kept stored in the attic. The installation of that star was the season's first ordeal, a ritual so fraught with tension that it made me cringe before it began. The old man would perch on a step stool, cursing and grunting like a field hand as he teetered into the tree and tried to ram its apex into the tiny orifice of the star. Mummie would wait below, nervously cooing her appreciation but unable to refrain from asking if the tree might be a tiny bit crooked. And hearing another "Jesus H. Christ" from my father—a serious warning sign—we children would stay unnaturally still on the sofa, holding our breath until stellar penetration had been achieved.

Christmases were like that: edgy and absurd, full of

empty ritual. Even the presents under the tree were a false conceit, since Mummie bought most of them, certainly the ones that we children exchanged, and the ones that came from my father, and, for that matter, the ones we gave to him. The presents from distant relatives meant even less—socks and scarves and puzzles—and they stymied our orgy of greed, because my mother had to record all of them in a book, so she could write thank-you notes later. She carried Christmas on her back, Laura Noone, much as she carried our secrets.

She carried mine long before I knew that she knew. Her early suspicions were confirmed by a girlfriend of mine—a friend, really, nothing more—who had flown out to San Francisco in the preposterous belief that I had seen the light and was ready to propose. All I'd wanted, in fact, was a generous listener, someone from home to witness my fledgling joy, to hear about this handsome doctor I'd met, this stalwart professional that even Pap would find acceptable. Becky Ravenel listened all right, her mouth slightly agape, pausing only to slip a Valium from her purse and gobble it dry like an after-dinner mint. The next day, when I was off at the radio station writing ads for waterbeds and singles bars, she phoned Charleston to break the news to the mother-in-law she would never have.

Mummie, mind you, never told me this. She harbored the knowledge for three or four years as that malignancy grew in her breast. She wasn't shocked, she told Josie later, but she was worried about the way the world would treat me, and the life I'd lead later. Maybe it seemed all right now, when I was young and reckless, but what would it be like when I was older, when I was fifty, say, and lonely and childless? She was just as worried about my father, resolving to keep the news from him at any cost, knowing how it would destroy him. But she did her best to educate herself, spending hours in the stacks of the Charleston library furtively reading books she was too ashamed to check out.

The following summer my folks came to visit. I wanted them to see, if not the whole truth of my life, at least the effects of that truth: my charming little house on a rooftop, my circle of presentable friends, my blazingly evident happiness. I wanted them to feel what I'd been feeling in the hope that it might transform them, force them to see the rightness—the staggering simplicity—of this thing that I'd feared so foolishly for most of my life.

So we took a drive up the coast, winding our way up Highway 1, where the golden hills and sparkling bays were certain to make my father a mellower man. Just outside Bolinas I spotted a teepee in the middle of a meadow. I had been to this place the month before, had met its occupants, in fact, and thought they would make the perfect field trip for my parents' first visit to Lotusland. Explaining nothing, I led them across the meadow—Pap in a business suit, Mummie in her black wet-look trench coat—and yelled out a greeting to the teepee. Within seconds, a lion-haired kid of twenty had emerged, soon to be flanked by his tentmates, tawny girls in stretched-out T-shirts—two of them—braless as the day they were born. When I asked if they'd mind visitors, they invited us in for chamomile tea.

My folks handled it beautifully at first. Pap surveyed the teepee in silence, chuckling to himself, then finally declared it the damnedest thing he'd ever seen—his highest accolade. He asked questions about their water supply and what they used to protect their food from predators, and even made a sly joke about the utterly benign herbs drying above him on strings. Mummie exclaimed over the tea and the loveliness of the lagoon shimmering in the distance. And our hosts were so gracious, so courtly in their sweet hippie way, that I believed I'd pulled off something wonderful: a meeting of polar opposites that had somehow altered everyone for the better.

Once we were back in the car, heading north to the Russian River, I could sense the sea change. Pap was quiet at first, then began to mutter about draft dodgers and degenerates, worthless little freeloading bastards who had never learned the value of hard work. I'd been trained not to argue with him, but it incensed me that he could be so charming and tolerant one moment and so bitterly condemning the next. I said as much, questioning his right to judge people he didn't know, just because they were different, just because they weren't like him. He called me a damn fool idiot, and his face turned dangerously red, and it just escalated from there.

I stood my ground as never before; at thirty I was sick of his tantrums, tired of playing my mother's old game of placation and retreat. This wasn't about hippies, after all, at least not for me; it was about becoming my own version of Gabriel Noone, though I'd never actually suggested what that might be. On my father's part, there may have been something else at play, something to do with being married and sixty. Maybe it had struck him— out there in the warmth of that sunlit meadow—that he would never again be young enough to live in a teepee with a couple of braless girls.

Mummie may well have sensed all this, but she was helpless to prevent our collision. She watched her men do battle with a look of mounting horror, as if we were about to brandish pistols. She was used to my father raising his voice, but the sight of her eldest yelling back must have rattled her to the core. When Pap wasn't looking, she would catch my eye tenderly and mouth the word *don't*, as if to say that I alone had the power to stop this madness, that I was the one who knew how to be reasonable. But I didn't *want* to be reasonable; I wanted to be the loose cannon for once, to bluster and bully like my old man. And I was doing this for her, I felt, for all the times she had bitten her lip to preserve the peace.

It was no one's victory, of course, but I knew it was over when Pap invoked his imminent death—his personal version of "You won't have Nixon to kick around anymore." I cut short the trip after that, heading back to the city by way of the freeway. There was a fatal silence in the car that my mother tried valiantly to break by gushing about the scenery or reading aloud from billboards. Something collapsed that day, and I knew we'd never be the same again, though by the time we'd reached the bridge we were hungry enough to discuss dinner. I proposed a place on the waterfront, a sailing ship outfitted as a restaurant. The old man just grunted, but once we'd arrived and our gin-and-tonics were firmly in hand, we found it easy as always to retreat to our mutual amnesia. Pap looked out at the rusty freighters and the little red tugboats and the gulls making loops above the darkening bay and pronounced them the damnedest thing he'd ever seen.

* * *

I didn't tell them until three years later—and didn't really tell them then; I had one of my characters do it. Will Devereaux wrote a letter to his parents that was plainly intended for mine. My radio stories weren't broadcast nationally then, but I was mailing tapes to my folks every week, so even a blind man could read the semaphore. And Will was as forthcoming as I'd always wanted to be. He wrote of the relief he felt upon finally being himself. He wrote of his love for his parents and how he refused to dishonor it with secrets. He told them not to worry who had "made him this way" because it was what he was meant to be, and because, above all, he was happy.

Such declarations weren't commonplace on the radio a quarter of a century ago, so the letter attracted attention. *Newsweek* did its first piece on *Noone at Night*, identifying me as a "gay storyteller" in the process. Passive as ever, I waited for the mushroom cloud to appear over Charleston—or at least an anxious phone call from my mother when the old man was at work—but there was nothing for almost a month. Then a letter arrived, a single paragraph scribbled on a sheet of bank stationery:

Dear Gabriel,
As you know, your mother is very ill. Any additional stress can only cause her condition to deteriorate. Please try to remember that and act accordingly.
Pap

For all its stiffness, the message was clear enough: I was killing my mother with my selfish exhibitionism. I could only guess about the scene at home, the ranting and raving my mother must have endured, i.e., the "additional stress" for which I alone was responsible. Had I known then how long she had protected me I would have gone home and faced the consequences. I should have done that anyway, I know, but I just didn't have the strength. And I told myself that my father, beneath all that sound and fury, wasn't strong enough to handle it either.

So I turned my attention elsewhere. It was fun, after all, to be young and randy with only a reputation for outrageousness to uphold. I could swing from the radio station to the glory holes and back again on my lunch hour, sharing my exploits with flabbergasted co-workers—and feel righteously political in the process. There was nothing I wouldn't tell the truth about; I am faggot, hear me roar. If my family didn't want me, I would build a family of my friends and lovers, and to hell with anyone who couldn't cope. I puffed myself up the way I'd seen my father do when railing against the communist menace or the scourge of integration. And though I meant every word of it, my zealotry served as a convenient distraction, a shield against the unthinkable loss that lay ahead.

For a while it was easy to believe that Mummie would survive. I wasn't there, after all, for most of it. I didn't watch the slow draining of her spirit, the daily indignities that would add up to death. Even in catastrophe she was her usual selfless self, down-playing her pain for others, and turning sassy when her options dwindled. After her mastectomy, she granted an interview with the *News and Courier* in which she talked breezily about having "the Big C," an homage to John Wayne that pleased my father no end. Privately she was fond of telling her lady friends (in her bravest impersonation of Auntie Mame) that the only adequate compensation for having a breast removed was having the other one tattooed.

Meanwhile, she got her house in order. She called me one night to say that she wanted me to have Dodie's bed, that big mahogany sleigh bed built by her grandfather's slaves. Billy and Josie had already received family things as wedding presents, she said, so it was only fair that I get something nice, since I would never be married. That her blessing came in the shape of a bed wasn't lost on me. I cried the day it arrived, seeing its familiar dents and the little sack of hand-wrought bolts that my father had labeled with a felt-tip pen. And I cried when I first shared that bed with someone else, lying against him in its curvy embrace, knowing that my mother, with her signal sense of theater, had imagined such a scene.

When the time came, it was Josie who told me to come home. As the female nearest Mummie, she had been entrusted with the grunt work of dying, the messy specifics from which the men, myself included, had been unfailingly protected. Arriving at the hospital on a scented spring night, I found my father pacing the corridor in a state of hearty denial, assuring anyone who'd listen that Laura was going to be fine, that the doctors were just overreacting as usual. He looked so tired and terrified that I wanted to put my arms around him, but I knew it would be too much for us both.

My mother's ashen face surprised me in a way I hadn't expected. Maybe because of the morphine—or maybe not—she wore an air of serene authority that made her seem like someone else. She held audiences with us all afternoon, individually at first, then with groups, though she asked me to repel several of our relatives; she had endured them for too long, she told me, and she felt no call to do so on this day that was completely hers.

Her instructions were as precise as a shopping list. She wanted to look pretty, she said, so she asked my sister to paint her fingernails and specified which of the ladies at her beauty salon should do her hair for the big day. Josie was also to find "a nice travelling companion" for my father, though my mother was adamant that Sookie Newton, a local widow with a sharkish glint in her eye, be kept away at any cost. And she told Josie to stay closer to me than ever, since I would need her support in the years to come.

When my turn came, Mummie greeted me with a parlor trick. Seeing me in the doorway, she poked a foot out from under the sheets and splayed her toes in a most unladylike fashion, wriggling them as freely as if they were fingers. She had always been able to do that, she claimed, with a note of pride in her voice. She had done it the day I was born, in fact, to the amusement of the nurses on the maternity ward. I'd never known about this talent, and it stunned me to think that she'd saved something for the very end that could draw us back to the very beginning, when we were first alone together in a hospital room. I laughed and grabbed her foot, ostensibly to stop her wiggling toes, but really to embrace her. And I held on to her foot the whole time we talked, feeling it curl naturally into my hand, as smooth and cool as a seashell.

And her instructions? This is what I remember: She told me to write "a sweet book" someday, by which she meant one that wasn't dirty, something like *The Snow Goose*, she said, that would lift people's hearts. She told me to go easy on Pap, since, given time, he would see the light. Just as I was leaving and Billy and

Susan were arriving she told me to come back early in the morning, because there was someone she wanted me to meet. She had a very nice orderly, she said, a man who liked Hitchcock movies and old houses, and she thought we might enjoy each other.

Pap and I slept on her floor that night. At least I think we did. I've told this story so often that there may have been some bejewelling over the decades. Maybe I just meant it metaphorically back then—it's hard to imagine what we would have used for bedding—but I do know that we stayed until dawn, camped out like Gypsies in defiance of the nurses' orders. My mother wasn't expected to die that night, so Billy and Josie had gone home to their kids, and the old man and I were left alone—on the floor or in chairs or somewhere— talking quietly while the patient slept.

And there, against the sound track of my mother's labored breathing, my father said something unexpected: that he'd known I was gay—or sensed it, at least—since I was a child, and that he was sorry he hadn't brought it up earlier and made life easier for me. I didn't know what to say except to thank him. Pap had never even used the word *gay* before, and this was closer than he'd ever come to addressing my needs. This must be how it feels, I thought, to be close to your father, to receive his love without the burden of conditions. It didn't occur to me until later, when the funeral was over and I was back in San Francisco, that this sweetest of paternal moments may have been orchestrated by the woman sleeping next to us. And sometimes I wonder if she was even asleep.

All this was on my mind that snowy night in Wysong, not because I had some prescient sense of what was already happening in Charleston—I didn't—

but because I was thinking about the bond between mothers and sons. Some mothers would do anything for their boys; mine would have, certainly, and did. And had I confessed that I was a serial killer, say, instead of a run-of-the-mill homosexual, Laura Noone would have dealt with that too, sooner or later. She would have found a way in her boundless heart to make me the sweetest, most misunderstood serial killer in the world.

Donna and Pete had a bond like that, I knew, a love so strong that it lay well beyond the strictures of ordinary morality. And that scared me a little as I set off into the night, following a star to a child I'd never met.

Twenty-two

Snow Blindness

A wise man would have waited until morning. It was pitch-black outside, and I already knew how hard it was to find my way around town in the snow. But I remembered Pete's description of that derelict water tank, and how you couldn't see the star from his bedroom, and how the light spilled over to accentuate the graffiti, and I knew that most of those things would be difficult—if not impossible—to determine in daylight.

No one could argue that I was acting rationally that night. Somehow I'd lost my perennial sense of authorship. What had begun as a simple mind game, a troubling diversion, had become the only universe I knew, as if I'd been reduced to a mere character in the story.

As if someone else was controlling the plot.

* * *

Finding the water tank was the easy part. The desk clerk's directions—and the star itself—led me there in a matter of minutes. A gross brown onion on rusty legs, it was just as lethal-looking as Pete had described, with a Cyclone fence and an ugly coil of concertina wire to keep off the inmates of the junior high school. The neighborhood itself was residential and early twentieth century—close to what I'd imagined— though my heart sank when I realized how many of these little houses commanded at least a partial view of the water tank. I climbed from the car and turned up my collar against the snow. Then, gazing up at the pulsing blue ember of the star, I circumnavigated the tank until only the faintest haze could be seen creeping around its side. All the while I murmured this mantra under my breath: *Roberta Blows, Roberta Blows, Roberta Blows.*

I could make out a few indefinite scribblings, the sort of fat-lettered tagging you find all over the world. Seeing them I pictured Pete in his oxygen tent, peering up dolefully at the terrible proof that other kids could fly. I sighed at the thought, even as I realized that Roberta was nowhere to be seen. Maybe, then, I'd find her on the other side; the light, after all, had to spill in both directions. So I walked back to the star and kept walking until it was once again eclipsed by the tank. There was much more graffiti on this side, the side that could be seen from the school. I saw WOODSMEN RULE and BRENT AND MEGAN and, largest of all, a boldly lettered CLASS OF 2001. That number seemed downright jarring in such a traditional setting, like the climax of an old *Twilight Zone* episode in which the hero discovers that his time machine has landed in the wrong century. That will be me, I thought, all too soon: adrift

283

and alone in a new millennium when I hadn't yet found my footing in the old one.

Abandoning Roberta, I turned my attention to the neighborhood itself, concentrating on the houses on the dark side of the tank. The street was deserted, the cars all tucked into their driveways, having long since morphed into giant white tortoises. It was past ten o'clock, and most of the houses were already dark, though here and there, through filmy curtains, I could see figures bathed in the blue aquarium glow of television. I couldn't tell you now what I'd hoped to find on this haphazard prowl: a mailbox labeled LOMAX, perhaps, or a quick glint of steel from Pete's bed, or Pete himself, green-eyed and haunted, peering out into the dense albino darkness.

But I soon began to notice the cold. My toes were turning brittle in my soft-sided California shoes, and every breath I took felt more glacial and invasive than the last. I was on the verge of making some decisive move—ringing a doorbell, maybe—when I realized I had company. Someone in a bungalow across the street was watching me from the shadows of her living room. My first thought, of course, was Donna, though I ruled that out as soon as I saw the woman duck behind a curtain. Her body language suggested someone in her seventies at least, possibly even older, nothing like the person Pete had described. This was just a nervous old lady, I reckoned, understandably wary of a stranger stalking her street after dark.

Then again, I knew so little about Donna. After all, I had never even seen a picture of her. And voices could be deceptive on the phone, especially when it came to determining age. If I doubted any part of Pete's story, why not the part about Donna being young and vigorous? For that matter, where was the proof that she existed at all? I'd been worrying for weeks that Donna had invented Pete, but I'd never once considered the reverse. Maybe Pete was the real one, in fact, and he'd created this loving, compassionate, perfect mother to aid in his search for a father, to give a man he'd never met permission to love a thirteen-year-old boy.

If, after all, their voices were uncannily similar, who could say who was impersonating whom? It could just as easily have been Pete who mailed me that photo from Henzke Street, Pete who told me that Pete was near death and needed my love more than ever, Pete who invited me here for Donna's chili, only to back out when he realized he could never pull it off. And—perhaps most disturbing of all—it could have been Pete who flew into that terrible rage when *The Blacking Factory* was cancelled.

All right, could have. *Could have.* Even supposing that was true, where the hell would he live? And with whom? A kid that age didn't occupy a house on his own, didn't occupy anything on his own. Unless he was homeless, of course, operating out of soup kitchens and private post offices, escaping his tormentors the only way he could. But how would he survive in this unrelenting cold? In Manhattan he could have slept in an abandoned subway tunnel; in San Francisco, in a cardboard box in the park. Here the options for shelter would be severely limited. Abandoned structures wouldn't stay that way for long.

Unless . . .

I jerked around suddenly and stared at the water tank. Pete had told me that it was no longer in use, so there had to be an empty chamber inside. It wouldn't be warm in there, of course, but it would probably be dry enough—and private as anyone could want. A clever kid like Pete could have slipped through that fence the way those taggers had. He could have found his way around with a flashlight and built a nest with a pile of rags, a hideout that no one could find. And he could have brought along a portable radio to keep himself company . . .

Right, dipshit. Could have, *could have.*

Feeling slightly hysterical, I turned back to the bungalow again. The old lady had moved from the window and was standing in an alcove near the back, reaching for a telephone on the wall. It didn't take me long to decide she was calling the police. I'd been there for over a minute, after all, staring at nothing and everything, the very model of a rapist or a madman, and there was no easy way to alter that impression. So I walked away—slowly at first, casually—trying to suggest that I was just a harmless neighbor out on an evening ramble. Once past the old lady's window I thought about the police again and broke into a run. I ran for at least three blocks, leaping and stumbling and gulping the icy air, then resumed my studied stroll, in case someone else was watching.

Where had all this guilt come from? I wondered. Why had I spent so much of my life feeling intrinsically culpable? I couldn't see a cop car in my rearview mirror without twisting my guts into a knot—or walk into a store without worrying that a clerk would suspect me of shoplifting. Even my dreams were populated with storm troopers, righteous protectors of decency who broke down my door in the dead of night and dragged me off to justice.

* * *

A coffee shop materialized, a place on a corner that marked the edge of a commercial district. It was open, amazingly enough, so I ducked inside, grateful for its aromatic warmth and the comforting drone of other humans. It was a coffee shop of the old school, the kind that still serves one kind of coffee from a Pyrex pot along with the chicken salad sandwiches. To one side lay a hive of red plastic booths, so I took a seat there and ordered a cup of tea and a cherry cobbler while my shoes puddled extravagantly on the floor.

I would have to find the car again, I realized, but that would be easy enough, since I'd parked it next to the water tank. I would head there as soon as I'd thawed out, then drive back to the motel for a good night's sleep. It was time to be rational again. I could make a few calls in the morning, check in with Ashe Findlay maybe. He might even have a home address for the Lomaxes, since he had once been close to Donna and had even . . .

I slapped the table as it came to me. Of course. Donna Lomax *had* to be a real person, because Ashe Findlay had met her. He had met her when she came to New York for some psychiatric convention. He had sung her praises so much, in fact, that I'd wondered about the nature of their relationship. How I'd forgotten this important detail I couldn't tell you. Write it off to snow blindness, I guess, or my deeply preoccupied imagination. Or maybe I'd just been looking too hard for answers, forcing an exotic resolution when a simple one failed to present itself naturally.

My stigmata had begun to throb again, since I'd stupidly whacked the table with my damaged hand. I looked down at the scab and smiled at my own madness. I'd been slightly out of control ever since I'd left

287

the airport in Milwaukee. I needed to be gentle with myself, tread more carefully in this hour of confusion. For if Pete had ever loved me, that surely hadn't changed in the past two days; he still loved me, wherever he was and whatever he was thinking. And that should be enough for now.

My back was to the door, so I didn't see her when she came in, but it must have happened some time after my cobbler arrived. She wasn't visible behind the high walls of the neighboring booth, but I recognized her voice immediately, that fusion of smoke and silk that had charmed me from the beginning. This time, though, the sound of it made me freeze like a cornered animal, as if *she* had been the one who'd been looking for *me*.

"There now," she said. "Don't you feel better?"

For one macabre moment I thought she meant me. That she had been there all along and had recognized my voice when I placed my order with the waitress.

But the next time she spoke, it was clearly to someone nearby. Someone in her own booth: "You're hungry, aren't you? I'll fix you something good when we get home."

I turned my head and cocked an ear, shutting out the room tone as best I could. But there was no reply— nothing at all.

"I know," she continued. "You love those burgers, don't you? But they're awful on your stomach."

My mind was racing just as wildly as my heart. This is the moment, I thought, the one I always knew would come. He's right there with her, less than five feet away: my pride and joy, the offspring of my heart. But why isn't he speaking?

288

"Don't look at me that way," she said.

He's been traumatized, I thought. The ordeal of the last few weeks has been too much for him. The cancellation of his book has thrown him into such a deep depression that it's taken his voice. Unless, of course, he was born that way. Unless Donna had been his voice all along, telling his story on the phone because he wasn't able to do it himself. Or maybe it was something more gruesome, something that happened later, something to do with the people who'd abused him. Maybe they had forced him into silence. Maybe they had cut out his tongue when they were done with him.

I closed my eyes against the force of my own imagination. When I opened them again, I made an unnerving discovery: the mirror behind the cash register reflected another mirror that caught the face of Donna Lomax. She was looking down, so I risked a quick assessment: late thirties, long brown hair, strong jaw, handsome fleshy features. Not far from the image I'd already constructed. That might have reassured me somewhat had I not also noticed that she was completely alone in the booth.

She'd been talking to herself.

At that point all I wanted was to get out without being discovered, to avoid a showdown at any cost. But I knew my voice would betray me if I asked for my check, and there was no way to leave without passing Donna's booth. So I just sat there and sipped my tea and waited for the problem to resolve itself. If I stayed long enough, she might just go on her way. She had probably come in here for the same reason I had: to thaw out before heading home, wherever that might be.

All I had to do was keep quiet and bide my time and hope that she didn't spot me in the mirror.

But keeping quiet wasn't easy. The waitress returned seconds later with a big solicitous grin on her face.

"How's that cobbler?"

I smiled back, nodding appreciatively but not making a sound.

"You need another tea bag?"

I shook my head, desperately afraid that the next question would require something more than a yes-or-no. But my interrogator just yawned noisily and moved to the next booth. The one with Donna in it.

"Oh," I heard the waitress say pleasantly. "You're back."

"Mmm. Does twice in one day make me a cocoa junkie?"

The waitress chuckled. "Not in *this* weather. That's what you want, then?"

"Please."

"What about him?" asked the waitress.

Him? I thought. Had I heard that right? My eyes dared another glance at the mirror, but there was still no one but Donna in the booth.

"No, thanks," said Donna. "We shouldn't make a habit of it. He'll expect it every time we come in."

What the fuck?

"It's just those eyes," said the waitress. "They get to me every time. You mind if I . . ."

"Of course not," said Donna. "He needs all the lovin' he can get. Don't you, Janus?"

Janus? *Janus!*

Another glance at the mirror revealed that the waitress had already squatted to stroke the Lomaxes' beloved family pet. I couldn't see the dog—a yellow

Lab, wasn't it?—but I could hear its murmurs of gratitude. It was all I could do to keep from laughing out loud.

"Okay," said the waitress, rising to her feet again. "We've had our fix. One cocoa coming up."

I looked down at my cobbler, still wary of being nailed as a spy. But the mere sound of that dog had erased my misgivings. Pete had played with this very animal, I remembered; he had laughed with me about its hatred of vacuum cleaners; I'd even heard Janus barking in the background.

It was such a relief to be in the presence of sanity again.

More time passed. Most of it I spent composing my remarks, rehearsing the breezy, unthreatening tone I would use when I approached her table. I would admit to almost everything, I decided. I would tell her that I'd flown to Wysong to surprise them, having made a stupid assumption about their address. I would leave out the part about the water tank, which might sound desperate or even a little unhinged. I wouldn't mention my role in the book cancellation until I could prove my good intentions. And maybe, if Donna invited me home to meet Pete, I wouldn't have to tell her at all. I could call Ashe Findlay in the morning and say that I'd seen the boy with my own two eyes and demand that he proceed with The *Blacking Factory*. Everything would be back to normal again.

Had I thought a little less about my salvation and a little more about that unseen dog in the next booth, it might have occurred to me why Janus was such a familiar sight to the waitress, and why, for that matter,

291

he was even allowed in a restaurant in the first place. As it was, I didn't wise up until Donna murmured "Let's go" and rose—earlier than I'd expected—to make her exit. She and the yellow Lab left the restaurant as a unit, her companion guiding the way as her left hand held tight to his harness.

Twenty-three

The Eleventh Hour

Why does a sane man track a blind woman through the snow? Moments before I'd been full of good intentions, but now I was thinking like a felon again. I could have approached her before she left the restaurant. I could have come clean on the spot. But the very predicament that made her such a "special" person—to use Ashe Findlay's carefully chosen word—might have made my sudden appearance seem threatening. I was much too close to finding Pete—or finding *something*—to risk the chance that Donna would refuse me access to the boy. So I gave her enough time to get down the block, then headed out the door after her.

Why does a sane man track a blind woman through the snow?

Because he can.

She and the dog were about twenty yards away,

standing beneath a streetlight that wore a furry nimbus in the snow. They were waiting to cross an empty street, and the sight was so poignant it was all I could do to keep from shouting "All clear!" I wondered if blindness was a new experience for her or if the dog was just more cautious in this weather. Then I heard Donna say "Forward" and Janus trotted smartly across the street. I waited until they had reached the other side before following them.

Half a block along, they turned left down a side street bordered by a hedge with a thick cap of snow. Then another left past an open field and a cluster of low-slung brick buildings, and I realized we were skirting the junior high school. Both Janus and his mistress moved more confidently here, settling into a steady rhythm, as if the world was finally behind them and home was almost at hand. I looked around for the star, and sure enough, there it was: a burst of blue behind the dark tracery of the trees.

It made sense now, all of it. No wonder this woman had been so paranoid about motherhood. She'd been entrusted with a boy whose grisly history demanded constant vigilance, but her resources were severely limited. She had no way of identifying Pete's enemies, no way of knowing when alien eyes were upon him. *Of course* she kept Pete's friends and counselors confined to the telephone. A world comprised solely of voices put her vulnerable family on an equal footing with everyone else.

Was that why Ashe Findlay never told me she was blind? Had Donna demanded his silence as part of the deal? And was that why this crucial detail was nowhere to be found in *The Blacking Factory*? Findlay had told me there were things I didn't know, valid reasons to trust Donna's motives and respect her wishes. This was obviously what he'd meant. When I'd pressed the issue, he'd cancelled Pete's book rather than reveal the omission that made it something less than the whole truth.

Were blind people allowed to adopt children? Why not? Especially a psychiatrist, someone equipped to deal with the boy's emotional health. She wouldn't be able to drive him anywhere, but that could easily be done by a social worker or a friend. Someone like . . . Marsha from across the street! Marsha who rode with them on those long, boring trips into Milwaukee, Marsha who'd been so very helpful, by Donna's own account.

Beyond the junior high school the street became more residential and wooded. It was snowing harder now, so I expected Donna and Janus to pick up speed, but instead, without warning, they stopped dead in their tracks. Some forty feet behind them, I found myself doing the same—an odd sight indeed for anyone watching from a window.

"C'mon," said Donna. "I thought we took care of that."

Janus mumbled something in his own language.

"Okay," replied his mistress. "Do it, then."

The dog squatted in the gutter and shat, the steam from it curling in the air like smoke from a genie's lamp. Janus, meanwhile, looked around with the mortified expression that canines wear on such occasions. For a moment, his eyes seemed to settle on me, though I was almost a block away. In my consternation I couldn't decide whether it was better not to move or move in a way that might be interpreted as natural.

Mercifully, the dog looked back at Donna when she spoke to him again. "Yeah, that's a good one, I can tell." She was talking about his shit, I realized, and it gave me a twinge of remorse to have invaded her privacy so completely. I myself had paid similar compliments to Hugo—and unashamedly—but I would not have looked kindly upon eavesdroppers.

"Okay," said Donna. "Let's go." With that they were off again, moving faster than before. The blocks were shorter here and the streets more mazelike, so I knew I would have to keep pace or lose them completely. I decided to trail her from the other side of the street, where I would look a little less like a stalker. I made myself promise not to lose my nerve.

Then I heard a voice coming from a house.

"Hey," it called. "You're gonna miss him."

It was a woman's voice—one that Donna obviously recognized. "Oh, hi." She brought the dog to a halt. "Miss who?"

"C'mon now. Who would you miss at eleven o'clock?"

"Really? Is it that late?"

I stopped behind a tree and pretended to kick snow off my shoes, an unconvincing charade intended only for this unseen woman. I was fairly sure she hadn't spotted me, but I wanted to look innocuous in case she had. There was no quicker way to forfeit my invisibility.

"What are you doing in this mess?" said the woman.

Donna sighed. "I just had to get out for a while. I like this, anyway. It's so peaceful without the traffic. Is it really eleven o'clock?"

"'Fraid so. You wanna come in and listen? I could make us some cocoa." There was something about her tone that seemed unusually tender and solicitous— even for someone speaking to a blind lady in a snowstorm.

"That's sweet, Pat. But I'm beat."

"You sure?" coaxed the woman. "Should be a good one. Jamie's eccentric uncle gets back from his hunting trip tonight."

"I've heard that one already," said Donna. "These are all reruns, you know. He hasn't done anything new for ages."

Then it hit me: they were talking about me. Or at least about *Noone at Night*. Donna's voice, while remaining civil, seemed to have a dismissive ring to it, as if she wanted no part of this woman's fandom.

"Well, go home, then," said the woman. "Tuck yourself in."

"I hear you," said Donna, putting a fresh spin on that late-twentieth-century cliché. She had heard me for years, after all. She had *only* heard me. Like other sightless radio listeners, she had built a teeming three-dimensional world from the sound of my voice alone. Judging from the letters I received, that intimate aural connection could be far more potent than anything the eyes could contain. But if Donna had once known that experience—and shared it with her son—she seemed to have lost it now.

I heard a door close solidly as the woman went back inside. Then Donna and the dog went on their way, and the knot in my chest loosened a little. I waited until they had rounded the corner before continuing my bogus stroll. At that moment, a clock began to toll gravely in the distance, offering proof of the eleventh hour. I half expected to hear my own voice coming from one of those houses, intoning the intro to my show: "I'm Gabriel Noone and this is *Noone at Night* . . ." But there was only the clock, and the sound of a faraway train as it screamed through the frozen night.

At the end of the next block I heard the jingle of keys and realized that Donna was almost home. Still watching from across the street, I kept my distance as she stopped in front of her house. The place was nearly—though not exactly—what I'd imagined. It was set back on the lot, but there were no trees to speak of, just a huddle of overgrown shrubbery against the windows. And the house, while compact, wasn't a bungalow at all but an L-shaped brick ranch from the sixties with a cluttered carport to one side. The aluminum-framed windows afforded a partial glimpse of a still-lighted Christmas tree. Still lighted, no doubt, for the benefit of the neighbors.

Or the benefit of *someone* other than Donna.

The implications were both heartening and terrifying. After all my reckless sleuthing, I was suddenly paralyzed with indecision. This was clearly not the time to confront this woman, much less force a meeting with an ailing boy. It would be better to return in the morning when Donna wouldn't feel so cornered and I could pretend that I'd found their address through legitimate means. I could bring them some flowers, perhaps, or a nice Christmas present, something to soften the blow of my rude invasion. And I would feel more rested then, ready to face whatever it was that awaited me.

I turned and walked away briskly, heading back the

way I'd come. The relief I felt was enormous, but only temporary, since I couldn't resist the temptation to look back at Donna one more time. She had stopped halfway down her front walk and was facing toward me with a new expression on her face. Had she been sighted, I would have known right away that the game was over. As it was, I had to wait for the sound of her voice:

"Come now, Gabriel, aren't you going to say hello?"

Twenty-four

The Idea of Him

My first thought, irrational as it sounds, was that she wasn't really blind; that the guide dog and the harness and the careful mannerisms were just a clever ruse to flush out the people who might be tempted to exploit such limiting circumstances. People like me, for instance.

But when I got closer and caught the dull pewter sheen of her eyes, the reality was undeniable. I was so lost for a response that I heard myself affecting a tone of jovial astonishment, as if we were old friends from college who'd just bumped into each other in a crowded European airport:

"*Donna?*"

Her reaction was laughter, deservedly enough, a throaty chuckle that might have reassured me if it had not raised the hairs on the back of my neck. "Save us both the trouble," she said. "Hank told me you were here."

Hank? Who was that?

She read my confusion and explained: "The clerk at the Mail 'n' More. He called me as soon as you left. Said some guy from California was asking about me. I figured you'd turn up eventually."

"I'm so sorry, Donna." My effort to sound sincere was undermined by the distracting thought that guide dogs might also be trained to attack. Janus seemed friendly enough, but he had a sort of wait-and-see gleam in his eyes that worried me. "I know how this looks," I went on. "I tried to reach you by phone, but you were disconnected and . . . I really didn't mean to . . ."

"Right."

"I heard you up the block here. Talking to the dog. But I wasn't sure if it was you or just somebody who . . ."

"Oh, please," she said wearily. "You heard me at Plato's."

"Where?"

"The restaurant. You were in the next booth. And you've been following me ever since." The corner of her mouth flickered in private amusement. "I took the scenic route just for you."

I managed a feeble laugh.

"Never knew you had such fans, huh? Way up here in the frozen north." I assumed that she meant her neighbor, which suggested that her own remark about my productivity had been uttered in the knowledge that I could hear it. *He hasn't done anything new for ages.*

"I guess there's a lot I don't know," I said. "I'm really sorry if I—"

"Don't be so contrite," she said, "or I won't believe you. It's important that I believe you right now."

"I understand."

"Where are you staying? The Lake-Vue?"

"Yeah."

"Are you alone?"

"Yeah." Boy, was I alone.

"How long had you planned on staying?"

"Only as long as you wanted me to." I knew I was sounding like a whipped puppy again, but I couldn't help it. Her blindness notwithstanding, there was something about her carriage that was so commanding. "I could come back in the morning, Donna."

She shrugged with weary resignation. "What difference would it make now?"

It's funny how a little word like *now* can sow a subliminal seed that will grow into something unthinkable in a matter of minutes. It's not that I caught her implication—I didn't—but I could feel a new presence deep in my bones, already stirring to life, already sinking its terrible roots.

"I may be out of line," I said, "but I feel as if we've shared something. And I thought maybe if . . . you saw me . . . I mean . . . *met* me . . ."

A whisper of a smile. "I'm seeing you just fine."

I couldn't tell if this was sweet or sardonic—or a little of both. "I'm not nearly as stupid as I'm acting," I told her.

"Then don't I get a hug?"

This offer was so unexpected that I had to rummage for words. "Well, yeah . . . sure . . . of course." I moved closer and embraced her from the left side to avoid disrupting the dog. I caught a pleasant scent—lavender, I decided—and her cheek felt calmingly warm and smooth as it grazed mine. I imagined Pete meeting her for the first time, feeling the tender assurance of her touch, a sense that for her had surely been heightened by the absence of another. And one she'd been saving just for him.

"And this," she said, pulling out of the hug, "is Janus."

"I know." I stroked the dog's thick butterscotch neck. "We were introduced on the phone. He was attacking a vacuum cleaner at the time."

She touched my cheek appraisingly. "You're freezing your ass off, aren't you?"

"Well . . . yeah. Pretty much."

"C'mon." She jerked her head toward the house. "I'll put the kettle on."

Her living room was sparsely furnished and unadorned except for a portrait of Pete over the oatmeal sectional sofa. It was a blowup of the photo Donna had already sent me, the one with the startling beach-glass eyes. It took all my self-restraint not to ask where he was tonight, but I thought it wiser to let her call the shots. Still, my eyes wandered uncontrollably to the darkened hallway beyond the kitchen, where I knew the bedrooms must lie, where I could imagine Pete sleeping even as we spoke, a wheezing form in an oxygen tent. Unless he was back in the hospital again.

"Is this enough light?" she asked.

"Fine." There was just the glow from the Christmas tree, but I liked the kaleidoscopic play of its colors against her angular face. She was really quite lovely, I realized, in a rangy, rawboned kind of way.

She handed me a mug of peppermint tea, then sat on the sectional across from me, curling her corduroyed legs beneath her. I was sure she arranged herself just

303

that way when she listened to her patients; it somehow conveyed the very essence of informal concern.

"Did this surprise you?" she asked, sweeping her hand past her eyes.

Honesty seemed in order at this point. "Yes, actually . . . it did."

"Because it wasn't in Pete's book?"

"And because Ashe never mentioned it. It just wasn't . . . in the equation at all."

"You understand why, though." This was plainly more of a statement than a question.

"I think so, yes. For protective purposes."

She nodded.

"Have you been blind all your life?"

Another slow nod. "Almost."

"You mean since . . ."

"I remember what sky looks like. And a dollhouse I used to have. Things like that. But just barely."

"Well . . . it makes it even more impressive, you know . . . what you did."

"What do you mean?"

"You know . . . Pete . . . rescuing him."

"Is that what I did?" There was a note in her voice that was both wistful and ironic, a note I'd never heard before.

"It's obvious what you did, Donna. It's there on every page of Pete's book. Even without the mention of . . . your blindness."

She just nodded darkly.

"It's a shame he couldn't have used that detail. It would have made an even better story."

She heaved a sigh, then aimed those eyes at me like a sightless gun. "We weren't trying to make a story. We were trying to make a life."

"I know."

"No. I don't think you do."

"Look, if there's something I . . ."

"Has this always been just a story to you?"

"No," I replied in horror, wondering if Pete could hear us. "Not at all. It's been much more than that."

"I don't think so, Gabriel. Your mind has been engaged . . . but never your heart. Not really."

I was appalled at the hostility beneath this observation. "Donna . . . for heaven's sake . . . I love him."

She shook her head. "You loved the *idea* of him. There's a difference."

"I don't know what that means."

"He appealed to your vanity. This helpless kid who wanted you to love him. Wanted it so badly that he could ask you for it on the *telephone*. It made a wonderful story you could tell people, and you even got to be the hero of it. What could be nicer than that?"

"Well . . ." I took a moment to assemble my words. "What if that were true? What would be so awful about that? Most people would feel that way, wouldn't they?"

"But I didn't think you were most people. I thought you'd be different somehow. I thought you could look into his soul and see the whole child, with all his complexities and contradictions. I thought you saw him as your own flesh and blood. The way I do."

"I did, Donna. I do."

She shook her head. "You couldn't have. Or you wouldn't have discarded him so easily."

"What are you talking about? I've wanted nothing more than to keep him in my life. I've spent the last two days stumbling around in this fucking cold just so I could say I was—" I cut myself off, knowing that my confession would lose its power if it was offered in anger.

305

"Just so you could say what?" asked Donna.

Silence.

"That you were sorry, right? For thinking him a fraud."

She was staring at me—the only word that really works—in a way that suggested both disappointment and outrage. I was mortified at first, but that was unexpectedly swept away by a flood of relief. Then came anger at the realization that someone had cheated me of my chance to be honest. And I was sure I knew who that was.

"It wasn't Ashe's place to tell you that," I said.

She looked down, entangled in thought as she toyed with the cuff of her trousers.

I went on: "He knew how concerned I was about Pete's feelings. And *your* feelings as well. He had no right to tell you that."

"He didn't."

"What?"

"He didn't tell me anything. It's just something I've had a feeling about. I'm glad we've cleared it up."

I was cowed into silence again.

"No wonder you're so distrustful," she said. "You're always holding something back yourself."

"That's not true. I came here to tell you everything."

Can he hear me right now? I wondered. Is he pressed against a door somewhere, desperately in need of my reassurance?

"C'mon," said Donna. "You've been creeping after me for half an hour. That's hardly the mark of a forthcoming man."

"I was afraid you'd be pissed off. That you'd see me as somebody terrible. That you wouldn't invite me home."

"Well, you're right about the first part. That book was Pete's lifeline, you know."

"Look, I'm angry about that, too. This has been the worst time of my life. But I really can't take responsibility for what happened. That was Ashe's decision completely. I begged him not to do it."

"But you planted the doubt, right?"

My blood was beginning to rise again. "I didn't plant anything. I just raised the question. He already had doubts himself, he told me so."

"So why didn't you just come to me first? If we're as close as you say we are."

I hesitated. "I don't know, really."

"Yes, you do. You must."

"Well . . . I'm just not good at confrontations. I never have been."

"Oh, please. You can do better than that."

"But it's the truth . . ."

"Did you think I might be . . . unbalanced or something?"

"No," I lied, infusing my voice with indignation.

"Then why didn't you just ask?"

I shrugged helplessly. "I didn't want to hurt Pete. I didn't want to betray his belief in me."

Are you listening, son?

"Ah," said Donna. "So you went to his publisher. That makes sense. You cooked up this crazy storybook theory, and you went straight to the one man who could destroy—"

"Look," I said, leaning forward and lowering my voice so as not to be heard beyond the room, "I don't think it was that crazy, okay? It may have been unwise in retrospect, but a lot of people would have come to the same conclusion. Ashe never met Pete. I never met

307

him, and you wouldn't *let* me meet him. You wouldn't let *anybody* meet him, as near as I can tell. Frankly, if you hadn't been so obstinate—"

"*Obstinate?*"

"Well, yes, as a matter of fact. I know why you had your rules, but couldn't you have bent them a little when the question arose? This could all have been avoided, if you'd been willing to let one person in here to verify his . . ." I had started to say "his existence," but it sounded too brutal. And I'd seen the look of cold fury that was beginning to contort her features.

"How dare you?" she said. "What do you know about anything? That child couldn't eat off a plate when he came to me. He barely knew what a fork was for, or what it was like to sleep on anything but a pile of dirty rags. He wouldn't talk for a month, and he had scars in places you can't even imagine. Do you know what that's like? To live in terror for years—and to believe that it could happen again at any time?"

"Of course not."

"Well, I do, mister. I know that one very well. So don't be telling me what I should have done! Especially now!"

"I'm not laying blame," I said, softening my tone in the face of her rage, "but if being published meant so much to him, couldn't you have—"

"It wasn't being published that meant so much to him! It was being believed! And he lost that the minute you doubted him. Is that so hard to understand? How would you like it if somebody came to verify *you*? That book was his therapy, nothing more. It was the only way I had to bring him out of his blackness . . ." She stopped to swipe at her cheeks, and I realized with a stab of despair that there was still one function her eyes could readily perform. "What did you think?" she asked. "That *I* had written it?"

"Honestly, Donna, I didn't know. I just . . ."

"You should see how I write. I'm pathetic for someone with a doctorate. I can barely string two sentences together. Pete wasn't like that at all. It just flowed out of him like honey. He had a goddamned *gift*."

"I know that," I said gently. "And he still does."

"What?"

"I want him to keep writing, Donna. I'll find him another publisher, and I'll vouch for him myself. We could even do something together . . . a series of letters, maybe. Or I could write an introduction for him. I'll do whatever it takes to make this right again."

She absorbed this proposal with her mouth agape and her brow furrowed, as if I'd just said something inhuman. What had I done now? Did she think I was trying to exploit the boy? Or—worse—ride on his coattails?

"Jesus," she murmured. "You don't know, do you?"

"What?"

"You haven't talked to Ashe lately? In the last few days?"

"No. Not for a week, at least."

She looked away from me, then murmured "Fuck" so softly it might have been a prayer.

"What is it?"

"I just assumed that he'd called you, and that's why you came here . . . oh, shit, Gabriel, I'm so sorry . . . I thought . . . oh, Jesus . . ."

I could feel the blood draining from my head to make room for the shadowy enormity that had finally arrived.

"Pete died last Monday," she said.

*   *   *

There was enough irony for a lifetime in the curious reversal that followed. This woman who had lost her only child days before came and sat next to me on the sofa, the better to pour out her sympathy. By anyone's call I should have been consoling *her*, but there she sat with her hand on my knee, attending to my pain and confusion. No wonder Pete had treasured her.

"I'm sorry I snapped at you, Gabriel. I just thought . . ."

"I know."

"I probably shouldn't have turned off the phone, but . . . there were too many people to tell. I needed to feel it on my own and not spend my time . . . you know . . . explaining things."

I nodded.

"I called Ashe when I came out of it, and I figured he'd call you, but . . . I guess you've been on the road, huh?"

I pictured this woman's solitary anguish while I was out getting laid in a truck stop. This story had never been about me, I realized; it had always been happening somewhere else. "Was it his lungs?" I asked.

"Yeah. They just finally gave up. It wasn't unexpected."

I considered that for a moment, shuddering a little. "Was it . . . difficult for him?"

She shrugged. "He was on morphine at the end, so he was peaceful enough. He just drifted off in my arms."

I envied her the certainty of that moment, though I could already feel the weight of him in my own arms, the warmth ebbing from his body.

"I'm sorry you had to hear about it this way, but I'm glad you came." She squeezed my knee in gentle punctuation. "Really."

I wanted to cry, but I found myself unable. Part of me was still watching it all from a distance. There was safety in that, I suppose. But it also seemed indulgent, in the face of Donna's profound loss, to grieve for someone I'd never seen, however much he had meant to me.

"Do you want to see his room?" she asked.

I did, very badly. I needed something to make the past real for me. Not proof exactly—I was already beyond that—but a way to *feel* what had happened. And words were no longer sufficient.

"Would you mind terribly?" I asked.

"Of course not."

So she rose and led me down the hallway to his bedroom. It was the second door on the right, painted bright blue and emblazoned with a raft of impertinent bumper stickers. The one I remember said: PERHAPS YOU'VE MISTAKEN ME FOR SOMEBODY WHO ACTUALLY GIVES A SHIT.

"That's just like him," she said, tapping the stickers. "He wouldn't let us get too sentimental." Then, with a sigh, she swung open the door and switched on the light, and my heart seemed to stop altogether.

And here's the amazing part: the room was very close to what I'd imagined. (Or was I merely remembering Pete's description?) The shiny chrome bed was predictable enough, but even the other furnishings seemed properly placed: the bookshelf to the left of the bed, the dresser to the right, the cluttered desk where he kept his computer. And there was something I hadn't factored in: the faintest scent of boy, an

311

innuendo of adolescence. I flashed on my father forty years earlier, bursting into my room on a Saturday morning when my sheets were still sticky with discovery. "Jesus," he had boomed, "smells like a goddamn cathouse in here." He may have thought he was celebrating my manhood, but I'd felt exposed and humiliated, and I hated him for joking about something we had never once discussed. Five years later, when Josie was thirteen, the old man pulled a similar stunt with her. Having found a box of Kotex in her bathroom cabinet, he grilled her over breakfast about what it was for. And oh, the look my mother had given him.

"Check out the bulletin board," said Donna.

For the moment, I was lost in Charleston, circa 1962.

"Over there," she added, gesturing.

I finally saw what she meant. There was a small but ardent shrine to me in the form of photographs and yellowed press clippings. Elsewhere I saw printouts of E-mail from other writers and public figures, some of them very well known. For the first time ever I regretted my cyber-illiteracy.

"He loved you," said Donna. "Even before he met you."

I went to the window and gazed out into the snowy yard. There were two moons in the sky now: the real one, which had crept from behind the clouds, and the spectral blue globe of the water tank. I didn't bother to search for Roberta, because that game was finally over. If I needed proof of anything now, it was proof of my own humanity. I felt so utterly two-dimensional, as if I had been the impostor all along. Much as my father had done, when faced with the love of a child, I'd lost my nerve and retreated in panic and distrust.

"Did he know?" I asked, still staring out the window.

"What?"

"That I had . . . questions about him."

"No," she said. "He wasn't that kind of a person."

I wanted to know so much more—what his last thoughts had been, for instance—but I didn't feel I'd earned the right to ask. When all was said and done, I was just a peripheral character in this tragedy.

"Let me show you something," said Donna, crossing to the bookshelf. "This was under his sheets the night he died." Her fingers found the sturdy chrome uprights and climbed until they reached a stack of magazines just above her head. Then she smiled as she handed me the *Playboy*.

"Uh-oh," I said. "Busted."

She shrugged. "He kept it because it was from you."

I handed the magazine back to her.

"He was wearing the T-shirt you sent, too. The *Noone at Night* one. He asked for it specially that morning."

I nodded as the tears began to build behind my eyes.

"We sent him off in it when he was cremated. That was Marsha's idea, actually. She thought Pete would have wanted it."

I was glad to be reminded of Marsha. It helped to know that Donna wasn't alone, that she still had the friendship of someone sighted who had loved the boy as much as she had. "Thanks for that," I said.

Donna didn't reply; she just returned the magazine to its place on the shelf. As her slender arm extended, the sleeve of her blouse slipped to her elbow and I caught a glimpse of something I hadn't seen before: a long, pale scar down the underside of her arm. The skin there was smeared and poreless, like a very old burn mark, but the serpentine shape of the thing seemed less than accidental. I angled for a better look, but her arm fell back to her side and she shoved down the sleeve with a single efficient gesture.

Flustered, I scrambled for something to say. "Is . . . Marsha looking out for you?"

She didn't bother to turn around. "I don't need looking out for."

"I know. I'm sure. I just meant . . ."

"I've functioned on my own for a long time."

"I was thinking more in terms of . . . company."

She went to the door and turned off the light, leaving me in darkness. The snow outside the window was the only source of light, faintly reflecting the blue of the water-tank star. "I'm not at all lonely," she said, "if that's what you mean. He's everywhere I turn."

Back in the living room, we talked about other things: the bitter weather, that funky little coffee shop, the loyal creature dozing at Donna's feet. We both seemed to sense that we needed a break, a peaceful coming-down before we parted. And I wanted to show her we still had reason to communicate beyond the son we had lost.

"How are things with you and Jess?" she asked.

A sigh escaped from me like a death rattle. "Who knows? He had somebody with him when I called this afternoon."

Her brow creased sympathetically.

"It was probably just a friend, but . . . I have no way of knowing anymore. And that's the problem, I guess. For both of us."

"Why?"

"Well . . . he doesn't want to have to explain himself, and . . . I can't stand not knowing."

"Would it change the way you feel about him if you did know?"

I shook my head—which was lost on her, of course.

"Was that a yes or a no?"

"Sorry. No, it wouldn't. I'll always love him. It's a chronic condition."

"Does he feel that way about you?"

That one took me a little longer. "I think he does, yes. I'm sure he does."

"Then maybe it's only his needs that have changed. Not his love. Couldn't you look at it that way?"

"I try to, but I'm just . . ." I couldn't finish, so she did it for me.

"You're just the kind of guy who needs proof."

"Well . . . yeah."

"You need that body in the bed next to you. That child in your arms."

I shrugged. "Doesn't everybody?"

"Sure," she said, "until they grow up."

I was offended until I saw the sweetness of her expression.

"That's what it is, you know, growing up. When you've finally got this programmed"—she pressed her palm to her heart—"to carry everyone who's ever loved you. When the bliss becomes portable."

When I didn't reply, she continued:

"Jess has given you a gift, Gabriel: the chance to feel love without boundaries. Everything you've ever built with him is still in place. All you have to do is believe and let go, and you'll have all the proof you need. Maybe not in the way you planned, but it'll be there."

She leaned down to scratch Janus under his chin, then looked up at me with a wry smile. "No charge for that," she said.

Twenty-five

Giving Up The Ghost

Half an hour later, back at the motel, I phoned home and checked the messages on my machine. There, amid the usual procession of friends and strangers, I found the voice of Ashe Findlay, asking me to call him, please, as soon as possible, even if it meant calling him at home. It was clear from his somber tone that he had just heard about Pete from Donna. My heart went out to him, knowing we were finally in agreement about this child.

Then came a click on the line. I felt sure it was Jess, cutting in out of sheer curiosity. But the voice that said hello was female.

"Anna?"

"Oh, hi, Gabriel."

"It's late. What are you doing there?"

"Just working on the books. How's Wisconsin?"

"Cold."

"Did you meet him?"

I decided it was time to unload. "I met her," I said. "And we had a good talk. He died last week, Anna."

"Who?"

"Pete."

"Oh . . . really?" Her voice rose markedly on the second word.

"His lungs finally gave out on him."

"Oh."

"She cut off the phone because she couldn't handle telling people. And there were plenty to tell, apparently."

"Relatives, you mean?"

"No. Just friends. He had more than I realized."

"Like who?"

"Well, Stephen King, for one. And Tom Clancy. And Magic Johnson."

"You're kidding."

"No."

"Did he call them Dad, too?"

Her bluntness knocked me back, though I knew she hadn't meant to be cruel.

"Sorry," said Anna. "I just wondered . . ."

"I know. It's okay."

"Are you gonna stay for the funeral?"

"There isn't one. He was cremated."

There was a long pause. I knew what she was thinking, but I had no intention of going down that road. "She's blind, by the way."

"Who?"

"Donna."

"You mean, *blind* blind?"

"Yes."

"Then . . . how did she . . . take care of him and all?"

"That doesn't make her helpless, Anna."

"But . . . somebody had to drive him places."

"Yes. A friend. Across the street."

"Did you meet him?"

"Her. No, I didn't."

Another pregnant silence, and then: "Are you okay, Gabriel?"

"Yeah. More or less."

"Are you sad?"

"A little. And a little relieved that there's been a resolution."

Again, no response.

"Does that sound insensitive?"

"No. I just wondered if . . . I mean, if he was already cremated when you got there, how do you know if he actually . . ."

"I *know,* Anna. All right?"

"But how?" Her voice was more timid, but she wasn't giving up.

"I saw his room and his stuff. I saw *her*, for God's sake. I saw the look on her face. She was plainly grieving."

"Maybe she was grieving the loss of that personality."

"Anna, would you stop it, please?"

"But don't you see what—"

"You weren't here. You didn't feel what I felt. I could practically smell him in the room."

I realized how peculiar this sounded. "I had the same thoughts," I added in a quieter tone, "but they didn't last. Sometimes you have to stop doubting and trust your heart."

"My parents did that," Anna replied after a moment. "That's why we spent the first year of our lives in Jonestown."

I wasn't following her at all. "What? Who did?"

"Edgar and me. And Mom and D'or."

"Jonestown, Guyana? With Jim Jones, you mean?"

"We escaped to Cuba just before the big Kool-Aid thing. Then we lived in Cuba for three years because my moms trusted their hearts about Castro. Right up to the day he deported them as dykes."

The light dawned. I remembered headlines from the early eighties, when a couple of lesbians, long presumed dead in the massacre, showed up in San Francisco with their toddler twins. It had caused a minor uproar at the time. "Jesus," I murmured. "That was you?"

"That was us."

"Do you remember that?"

"No. Not the Jonestown part. But that doesn't mean I didn't learn from it."

"You've never even mentioned it before."

"It's embarrassing," she said. "Nobody should be that gullible."

I had a feeling she was talking about me again, but I didn't pick up the gauntlet. What I'd just experienced had been akin to a miracle or a flying saucer sighting. Not the sort of thing you could share with the uninitiated.

"I was just checking the messages," I said, by way of signing off. "Is there anything you need me to do?"

"Not really," she replied. "Just some checks to sign when you get back. Jess is coming over in a minute to help me prioritize them."

"Thanks for holding down the fort, Anna."

"No problem."

"Do me a favor, would you? When you talk to Jess, don't tell him what I just told you."

"About the kid being dead, you mean?"

"Any of it. I'd rather handle this when I get home."

"You got it," said Anna.

"Is Hugo okay?"

"Oh, he's fine. Sitting right here with me. He peed on the carpet this morning, but Jess cleaned it up."

Hugo hadn't done that since he was a puppy, so I could imagine the old dog's humiliation. Is that what it means to get old? I wondered. To revert to the helplessness of infancy without any of the fun?

"Give him a hug for me," I said.

"Who?" asked Anna.

"Both of them," I replied.

I took my second shower of the evening, just to make it easier to sleep. For the same reason I ordered a movie, but it was relentlessly stupid, so I scrounged a roach from the ashtray and managed to extract a few hits. In minutes I was buried in gray dreamless sleep, and I might have stayed that way until morning had I not been jarred awake by the phone at 2 A.M.

"I know it's late," said Jess.

"More like early." I was sure he'd somehow wheedled the news from Anna, but I had no intention of rehashing it at that hour.

"I just got a call from Josie," Jess said. "I thought you should know, babe. Your father's had a stroke."

Such a suitable word, *stroke*. I'd heard it since childhood without fully understanding its meaning, but it sounded, even through a haze of sleep and dope, just like itself: abrupt and brutal and irreversible.

A stroke of lightning, the stroke of midnight, the stroke of a pen.

Twenty-six

The Boo Daddy

When Josie and I were children at midcentury, I would terrorize her with tales of the Boo Daddy, a variation on the boogeyman I'd lifted from Gullah folklore. The Boo Daddy, it was said, would creep into your house late at night if your shutters weren't painted a certain prophylactic shade of blue. So I would watch for that color on trips to the country and point it out with perverse pleasure to my skittish little sister.

This memory came hurtling back to me some forty years later as Josie drove us into Charleston from the airport. These sprawling suburbs looked so numbingly alike now, but down there beyond the freeway, along the marshes of the Ashley, I thought I'd seen that color again—the eerie blue of a low gas flame—and I'd uttered the words "Boo Daddy" almost without thinking.

Josie corrected me. "That's a Blockbuster Video, sweetie."

"C'mon."

"Yep. Think so."

"Well, fuck. You're no fun at all."

She laughed. "You were awful to me back then."

"Was I?"

"You and your Boo Daddy."

What a telling name, I thought, as if hearing it for the first time. Down here the devil was just another difficult patriarch.

I hadn't been home—or rather to Charleston—for almost four years, when I came here, minus Jess, for Pap's eightieth birthday. Josie and Darlie had planned the event down to the last detail, renting a cottage on Sullivan's Island and hiring a troupe of decrepit bagpipers to serenade the old man. It was better than most of our reunions, but I'd eaten a bad oyster that night and ended up puking my guts out during a stirring rendition of "Loch Lomond." Since then, for reasons far beyond bad oysters, I'd resolved to stay on my own turf and let the family come to me.

"Is this weird for you?" my sister asked.

I shrugged. "Not in the scheme of things, no."

"I've told a few people you're coming. I hope you don't mind."

I smiled gamely.

"And Billy and Susan are flying in tomorrow."

"That's good."

"Would you like to freshen up first? We've done some new things with the house. I'm dying for you to see it."

Josie and her husband, Walker, had moved into our childhood home on Meeting Street in the early nineties when Pap and Darlie bought a two-bedroom condo in what had once been the Fort Sumter Hotel. Josie had given the house a thorough but sensitive remodeling, fussing over it in a way that seemed almost parental now that her kids were grown and gone.

"I think I should see him first," I said, "then freshen up. Smoke some crack, maybe. Shoot some heroin."

She turned to me and giggled. She was still so pretty. She had our mother's English coloring and kind hazel eyes, our mother's instinct to be strong when the menfolk might not be up to it. "He's handling it fine," she said. "And he looks okay, except for a droopy place on his face."

"Can he talk?"

"Oh, yeah. Now, *listening* is another matter."

I smiled.

"His personality hasn't changed. When he heard his nurse was named Clinton, he asked her if she was kin to that horny prick in Washington."

"Oh, God."

"And yesterday he told me his doctor is one helluva fine Jew."

"Right."

"He does it to get attention, as much as anything. What were you doing in Milwaukee, anyway?"

It was unsettling to be thrust back into that icy hallucination when it was almost seventy outside and a warm, spongy-soft breeze was rolling off the river. "I was visiting a sick boy," I said.

"Oh . . . how is he?"

"He died before I got there."

"Did you know him well?"

"Fairly."

"From where?"

324

"He was sort of a fan."

"A listener, you mean?"

"Yeah."

"God," she said. "You're catching some shit right now."

I wondered how much Jess had told her about the breakup, but I was too afraid to ask. He and Josie had always spoken freely, and he may well have told her what it was about me that had sent him packing.

"It's amazing," I said, peering out the window, "how many malls there are now."

"The whole damn place is a mall. It's just a theme park for Yankees. She-Crab Soup World."

Josie might be mostly our mother, but every now and then I could hear the old man loud and clear.

As we pulled into Roper Hospital I took another queasy somersault into the past. This was the very building where my mother had died twenty years earlier. I knew every detail of the place, even that ragged palmetto in the parking lot where my stepmother was standing, seemingly in an effort to intercept us. Josie took this as an ominous sign.

"Oh, fuck," she said. "Something's happened."

But when we got closer, it was clear that Darlie was just on a cigarette break.

"I didn't know she smoked," I said.

"Neither does Pap. So don't blab."

I snorted. "How could he not know something like that?"

"How could he not know *everything* he doesn't know? He's *arranged* it that way."

I frowned at her. "I'm surprised you're still humoring him. Why do you bother?"

"Because he's *here*, Gabriel." She didn't elaborate, but her larger message was clear enough: I had put a continent between Pap and me twenty-five years earlier; I was not to give lectures on handling him.

Josie swung past Darlie on her way to a parking space. "Caught ya!" she yelled.

"Oh, hey!" Darlie called back, twiddling her fingers. That strawberry-blond hair seemed more of a beacon than ever here in the low milky light of the Low Country. But even from a distance the worry and weariness were evident on her face. She tossed her cigarette onto the pavement, stubbed it out with her heel, and hurried toward us as we climbed from the car.

"I swear," she said, hugging me. "It's downright spooky."

"What?"

"You look more like him every time I see you. Just like he did when I fell in love with him."

I must have winced.

"Oh, c'mon now. He was a knockout when he was sixty-five."

"I'm fifty-four," I said.

"Oh, honey, same difference when you're our age." She took my arm and spun me around to face Josie. "Doesn't he look just like him?"

"Pretty much," said my sister.

I was deeply uncomfortable. Darlie and I were a year apart in age and had lived on different coasts since I'd known her, so she'd wisely never attempted an impersonation of motherhood. Still, it felt a little incestuous to be told, even jokingly, that she was turned on by my resemblance to Pap. I decided to change the subject: "How's he doing?"

"Oh, fine, right now. It was just a mini-stroke, and he's tough as an old boot."

Josie's brow furrowed. "What do you mean, right now?"

"Nothing. He's fine. C'mon, let's get up there before he starts goosing the lunch nurse."

His room was on the third floor and suitably large. There were flowers on every surface, suggesting that this crisis had already been something of a local event. The old man was lying on his side with his back to the door, an anonymous white mound tethered to an IV pole. Darlie approached him like a lion tamer testing the mood of her grumpiest cat.

"Honeypie?"

My father stirred but didn't turn around.

"Look who's here, sweetness."

He rolled over and grunted, then rubbed his eyes until he saw what she meant. "Well, I'll be god-damned . . ."

"Wouldn't doubt it at all," I said.

He hooted in appreciation, and right away I saw the distortion of his features. "You son-of-a-bitch. What the hell you doing here, boy?"

"Well, I heard there was this big sale on hoppin' John at the Piggly Wiggly . . ."

"Goddamn, it's good to see you." He sat up in bed and thrust out his hand, grabbing my shoulder with the other in the come-here-but-stay-away gesture I knew so well. "Seriously, son, you pushin' a book or something?"

I said I hadn't done that for a good long while.

"These crazy women didn't tell you something was wrong with me, did they?"

Darlie rolled her eyes at Josie. "Now why would we go and do a damn fool thing like that?"

"Hell, I don't know. Women get hysterical. That's just the way they are." The old man winked at me. "Right, sport?"

"Don't ask me," I said. "I'm still working on men."

The old man flinched in a broad Three Stooges sort of way, as if to make it clear that he was not really to be taken seriously. "Christ, don't be talkin' like that in front of your pore ol' sick father."

"Oh, *now* he's sick," laughed Josie.

"Help me up," said Pap, reaching for Josie. "I gotta piss before that little nigger gal gets here with my baloney sandwich."

"Lovely," said Darlie, glancing my way.

Pulling the IV stand, Josie steered the old man to the bathroom door, then let him navigate the rest on his own. When the door was closed, Darlie said: "That's just a blood thinner, by the way. It's standard for a stroke. Even a little one. He'll be off it tomorrow or the next day."

Josie glanced at the clock. "We're gonna leave you with him for a while. Is that okay?"

This proposal felt so prearranged that it made me nervous. "What's up?" I asked.

"Nothing. We just have to go pay our respects to the Edwardses. Libby Edwards died."

My father, now peeing noisily in the bathroom, boomed a footnote through the door: "Hateful old bitch!"

"Well," said Darlie, "his hearing's good as ever."

328

"What was that?" hollered Pap.

"Nothing, sweetums."

The old man flushed the toilet and came lumbering back with his pole. His skimpy striped hospital gown made his gruffness seem comical, like a polar bear who'd been rudely anthropomorphized by Disney. "You know it's the truth," he said. "She behaved atrociously after Bo's death."

"Bo Edwards died?" There was so much I didn't know about Charleston society these days.

Josie nodded, giving me a look I couldn't quite read. "About three years ago."

"He killed himself," Darlie added quietly.

I hesitated out of old habit, realizing how casually I'd led us into forbidden territory. I could feel my mother's eyes boring into me from across the years, but I managed to ignore them. "Why did he do that?"

Darlie replied with a single whispered word— "Prostate"—as if it explained everything. How thoroughly Southern that was: the assumption that an eighty-year-old who'd lost his "manhood" might naturally be driven to take his life.

"How did she behave atrociously?" I asked.

My father's mind had ambled off. "Who?"

"Libby Edwards."

"Oh, hell, she was just an angry bitch. Actin' so pissed off all the time. You'd think she was the one who died."

"Pap." Josie leveled those hazel eyes at the old man and spoke in a way that was both stern and gentle. "She had a perfect right to be pissed off."

"Well, she should've kept it to herself."

"Why? Why shouldn't she say how she felt if—"

"You don't make a public spectacle of yourself. Drag

the family name through all that crap. It's common."

Josie sighed, then caught my eye, obviously worried that I was about to say what I was thinking: that the family name had been dragging *us* through crap for years. But we were saved by the arrival of a nurse—middle-aged and inarguably white—bearing a tray with my father's sandwich.

When the women were gone, I took a walk around the block to clear my head. I returned to find my father propped up in bed, staring out the window. There was a look in his eyes I couldn't identify, but he blustered it away as soon as he saw me.

"Hey, boy! What's it like out there?"

I told him something I knew he'd like to hear: that I'd missed these old sideways houses, and the true ocean smell of the Atlantic, and the way the oaks made shady tunnels out of the streets.

"That's right," he said. "You ain't got many big trees out there, except for ... oh you know, what's that damn place called? Oh, hell, what is it? Named after that naturalist fella. Up north, across the bridge."

"Muir Woods."

"That's it! Muir Woods! Beautiful place."

Geography again. Hiding us from ourselves and each other.

"Remember when we took your mama up there?"

"Yeah, I do. That was nice."

"Duddn' seem that long ago, does it?"

I shook my head, smiling.

"It goes awful fast, son."

I told him I knew that already.

"But duddn' it bother you?"

I shrugged. "A lot of my friends died years ago. It seems like bad form to complain about getting older."

He paused a moment, assembling his words. "You know, I was mighty fucked up when your mama died. I didn't know what I was gonna do with myself. I thought it was all over until that little gal came along." He glanced toward the door as if he half expected to find Darlie hovering there, overhearing this endorsement. "Where the hell'd she go, anyway?"

"Just to that funeral."

"What funeral?"

"Libby Edwards."

"Oh, that awful old bitch. When she comin' back?"

"Libby? I seriously doubt she is."

It took him a moment to realize I was teasing. "I meant your mama, goddammit!"

He meant Darlie, of course, but his confusion was understandable. One person can easily be mistaken for another when you require insurance against solitude at any cost. And I resented him for that more than ever, the nearly constant companionship that had allowed this wounded fledgling to impersonate an eagle all these years. He'd had it so easy, really.

"She'll be back," I said. "You can do without her for an hour or so."

"I wanna tell her something."

"You can do that later."

He's just as scared as I am, I thought. He hates the thought of being alone with me and what we would do with the silences.

"So when do you have to go back?"

I shrugged. "A few days, I guess. I dunno. I'm on my own schedule."

"You're a lucky son-of-a-bitch, you know."

"Yeah, I guess so."

"Oh, hell, almost forgot: Dick Burbage called. Wants you to come to the Centurion Feast."

This was the annual Christmas party of my father's club, a quasi-military hereditary society that I joined on my return from Vietnam, mostly out of deference to the old man. The Centurions did a lot of drinking and ancestor worship but not much else. I'd remained a member in absentia when I moved to California, but they'd quietly asked me to resign in the late seventies when *Noone at Night* made my open queerness apparent.

I frowned. "Did you tell him I was here?"

"Hell, no. He called *me*, I didn't even know you were coming. Must've heard it through one of Walker's friends."

I found myself grinning idiotically and sounding a lot like my father. "Well, if that don't beat all."

"You wanna go, then?" The longing in his eyes was palpable. That damned club still mattered to him more than anything.

"Sure," I said. "Just as soon as Dick Burbage comes out of the closet."

"Now, wait a goddamn—"

"And I want you to put it just that way."

"I won't do anything of the kind!"

"And while they're at it, a written apology would be nice."

"That was twenty years ago, for God's sake!"

"So?"

"So a lot's changed."

"Yeah. I'm famous now. That's what's changed. So Dick Burbage gets to kill two birds with one stone: do

332

you a favor and impress the twinkies he picks up down at Arcade."

"He's not doing me a favor, I told you that."

"Fine. He's not doing me one either."

"And you don't know anything about . . . his private life."

"I wouldn't lay money on that, Pap."

He regarded me with a wary scowl, obviously wondering if I spoke from personal experience. I didn't bother to disabuse him, though Dick Burbage's homohood was probably more aesthetic than carnal. Like a number of queers, he was drawn to the club by its lovely old house full of lovely old things. These guys were discreet around the dinosaurs, but even my father's beloved Centurions had its own secret coterie of girly-men.

"Jesus," the old man muttered, "you've got the biggest goddamn chip on your shoulder."

I smiled at him. "I kind of enjoy it, too. I see why you like yours so much."

He let that pass. "The Centurions have been my life, you know."

"I know, Pap. *Your* life, not mine."

"Would it kill you to go down there and have a drink with them?"

And would it have killed you, I thought, to defend me? To tell your buddies to go to hell when they ostracized your son for his honesty?

"It seems like a compliment to me," he added. "You should be happy they asked."

I *was* happy they had asked. It felt great to realize that these people no longer mattered to me at all. "Look," I said. "I could easily go down there and be Scarlett O'Hara in my red dress, but there's no point in . . ."

"Red dress? What the hell you talkin' about?"

"Relax. It's just a metaphor."

"Thank God."

"When is it, anyway?"

"When's what?"

"The Feast."

"Oh . . . tomorrow night."

"Well, that settles it, then. I'd rather be here with you."

The old man sighed. "So what am I spose to tell Dick Burbage?"

"Don't worry about it. I'll tell him myself."

"Jesus, don't tell him to come out of the closet!"

I laughed. "All right. I promise."

"You'll give the ol' fruit a heart attack."

I just shook my head and smiled, recognizing one of his oldest oratorical tricks: a bait and switch that allowed his audience the briefest glimpse of what he really knew to be true.

Twenty-seven

No Epiphanies

Another nurse arrived—the "little nigger gal," I presumed—and began fiddling with my father's IV line.

"This is Sondra," my father said in his best courtly fashion. "She's a helluva fine nurse, and she comes from good folks out on Edisto."

"Hey," I said.

"Hey," she said.

"That's my son, that distinguished-looking fella. He lives out in California, and he's famous as all get-out. Just ask him."

"Pap . . ."

"What do you do?" asked Sondra.

"I'm a writer."

"What's your name?"

"Same as mine," said my father. "Gabriel Noone. Embarrasses the hell out of him."

This clearly rang no bells for Sondra, but she was gracious enough not to ask what I'd written. She gave me a friendly, knowing look as she plumped the old man's pillow. "He's a pistol, isn't he?"

"More like an Uzi."

"Lemme ask you this," said my father. "Why do folks always talk about me like I ain't here?"

"Wishful thinking, I guess."

Sondra looked a little horrified at my wisecrack. "Now don't be talking about your daddy that way."

"That's right," said the old man. "You tell him, Sondra. He's got no respect for his elders."

"I'm outa here," she said, heading for the door. "Too many roosters in this barnyard."

My father winked at me as soon as she was gone, as if our sparring exhibition had been staged for Sondra's benefit alone. "She's a sweet little gal," he said. "And I'll tell you something else: she's a damn sight more efficient than the white ones."

It always touched me when he tried this hard to prove he wasn't a racist. "She does seem nice," I said.

An awkward silence followed. My father looked nervous, fiddling with his sheet, glancing toward the window and back again. "You don't have to stay, boy. The gals'll be back in a little while."

"I'd like to stay."

"You gotta have some friends you wanna visit."

"Nope," I said, smiling.

A longer silence followed. There was nothing left to save us, nothing to muffle the taunts of things left unsaid. Then my father noticed the scab on the palm of my hand. "What the hell did you do to yourself?"

"Oh . . ." I shrugged. "Just a roadside mishap."

"Does it hurt?"

"Little bit."

"Least you can feel something. Lookee here." His

hand popped up from the sheets, as if he were about to recite the Boy Scout Pledge.

"What is it?"

"Damnedest thing. It's all numb down one side."

"Was this from the stroke?"

He grunted yes.

"I thought it just affected your face."

"Well, I had another little one last night."

"Jesus, Pap."

"It wasn't a big one."

"Does your doctor know?"

"Oh, yeah."

"Did you tell Darlie and Josie?"

"Hell, they don't need to know everything. They just get hysterical."

I gaped at him in amazement. "I'm gonna get that way myself in a minute."

"It's nothing, I tell ya."

"So why tell me at all?"

No answer.

"Talk to me, Pap."

"I'm talking, goddammit. I talk all the time."

"Yeah. About stuff that doesn't matter—communists and liberals and scenery. But you never talk about your feelings. If you're scared, why don't you just say so? I'd really like it if you could."

He grunted. "You've been out there way too long."

"No, Pap, this has been going on forever. I've accommodated your embarrassment for so long that I actually feel it myself. And that makes me crazy, because you're the only person on earth I do this with."

"Embarrassment? What the hell are you talking about?"

"Maybe that's not the word, I don't know. There's

just this stiffness that happens. This dance of avoidance we do. You're not comfortable with me. I used to think it was because I was a sissy and you knew it."

"That's not true at all. Ask your mama . . ."

"She's dead, Pap."

"Well, she'd be glad to tell you if she was here."

"I want you to tell me. Were you afraid I'd just be a bigger sissy if you held me from time to time?"

"Held you?"

"Yeah. Held me." How pathetic it felt to be having this overwrought *East of Eden* conversation so late in both our lives.

"I held you all the time, goddammit."

"When I was a baby, maybe. When you were posing for pictures. But I've never had so much as a hug from you that didn't feel like an uncomfortable duty. I just waited for the moment when you'd have to pull away."

"That's a damn lie."

"No, Pap. It always got to be too much for you."

"Well, I'm sorry if it seemed that way."

"It was that way. It is that way."

"Well, case closed. I guess I'm just a sorry bastard."

"No. Nobody thinks that. Why do you always do that?" (Jess did this too, I realized, retreating in a cloud of righteous anger whenever we swerved too close to the tender heart of things.) "Can't you just say that it's hard for you to be intimate?"

"Well, that's a fascinating theory, but—"

"You wanna hear the rest of it?"

"Hell, no."

"Well, yell for the nurse then, because you're gonna get it."

"What the hell is the matter with you, anyway?

338

You're fifty years old, and you still care what your father thinks."

How mean he could be sometimes. And how accurate.

"And you don't?" I asked.

"Don't what?"

"Care what your father thought?"

His eyes turned as flinty as arrowheads. Gathering my courage, I free-fell into the abyss. "Why don't you ever talk about him, Pap?"

He stayed surprisingly calm. "So that's where you're heading."

"Yeah. I guess so. Do you mind?"

"No. But it's not gonna happen."

"What?"

"Whatever it is you're expecting. There'll be no epiphanies on this deathbed."

I smiled at him. "This isn't your deathbed."

"How the hell do you know?"

"You're right. We better talk fast."

He just grunted at my effort at levity. After a moment of awkward silence he said: "Go ahead then. Shoot."

Shoot.

"Well," I began, "do you know why he did it?"

"No sir, I don't."

"He didn't leave a note or anything?"

"No."

"That must have been terrible. Not knowing for all this time. I can't imagine."

There was no response for a while, and then he shrugged. "You can't spend your life fretting about something like that."

Can't you? I thought.

"Did he do it in your room?" I asked.

"My room? Hell, no. Where'd you hear that?"

"Just . . . around."

"It happened in the garden shed."

"Where was that?"

"Back where we put the lych-gate. Christ, do you want a map?"

"And you were . . . how old . . . seventeen?"

"Something like that."

Something like that? Who wouldn't remember exactly?

"It was during the Depression, right?"

"Yep."

"So it could have been about money."

"I doubt it seriously. He was just depressed, that's all. There was nothing crazy about him."

"Is that what people said?"

"No. Hell, no."

"Then why did you say that?"

"Well, some folks just automatically assume . . ." He couldn't finish, so I did it for him:

"That anyone who commits suicide is crazy. Or gay or something."

His face was afire in a matter of seconds. "How dare you say such a thing?"

"Oh . . . maybe because I don't see anything wrong with it."

"Well, he wasn't. Ask anybody."

"And I wasn't suggesting that he was."

"The whole damn world's not that way, you know."

"Oh, I know."

"He was a decent family man."

"Fine. Thanks for sharing. I'm glad we've cleared him of that shameful possibility."

"That's not what I meant, goddammit. Don't twist

my words. We weren't even talking about you."

"No." I mustered all my calm. "You're right. Tell me what he was like."

He sulked for a while. "He was a good man, like I said. A gentleman. You would have liked him, if you'd met him."

It was an odd moment, this hypothetical introduction to someone who'd been gone for sixty-five years. Still I fleshed out my grandfather, giving him colors and textures and smells the way I'd done with Pete, building someone out of nothing, because a ravenous mind demanded it.

"Did he look like us?"

My father thought about that for a moment. "He was a good-sized man."

I gave him a crooked smile.

"So that's one thing you can't keep blaming me for."

I studied him soberly for a moment. "I don't blame you for anything."

He grunted. "Sure as hell feels like it sometimes."

"I got a lot of good things from you, Pap. Your sense of humor, your love of an audience. Your political indignation."

His eyes narrowed dubiously at the last point.

"It's the same instinct," I added, "just aimed in a different direction. I wouldn't be who I am if it weren't for you, Pap."

This was too much for him. "Now I know I'm dying."

"I wish you hadn't been angry all the time. I do wish that. And I wish it for Mummie, too. She walked on eggshells for you, Pap."

"What the hell are you talking about?"

"That," I said quietly. "That's what I'm talking about.

It's not easy to deal with, you know. The way you're always ready to explode."

"You don't know the slightest goddamn thing about—"

"I do, Pap. I was there. And I know what it's like to accommodate someone else's anger, because I ended up marrying you."

"What?"

I grew almost feverish with mortification. Where had that come from, and why had I decided to put it into words?

"Forget it, Pap."

"No, you said something."

"It's just that . . . you and Jess are both wound so tight. And I dealt with it the same way Mummie did."

"Which was?"

"Always smoothing things over. Eating my own anger, because two pissed-off people is more than one marriage can bear."

"Your mama and I loved each other deeply."

"I know that, Pap."

"So if you're comparing us to you and that fella . . ."

"Jess, Pap. His name is Jess. And I *am* comparing you, because you two were the only model I had. You should be flattered, because Jess was just a younger version of you. He was just as stubborn and protective and just as mushy on the inside, but he didn't keep me at arm's length. And that felt so damn good, I have to tell you."

There were tears in my eyes, and the old man saw them.

"Christ, son. Did he die?"

"No."

"I don't understand."

I swiped at my eyes, composing myself. "He moved out a few months ago. I haven't been dealing with it very well."

"Why didn't you tell me?"

"I didn't want you to tell me I was better off."

My father studied me for a long time, then slapped the bed with the flat of his hand. I could tell this wasn't an angry gesture, but its meaning eluded me at first. Funny, considering how often I used that semaphore myself to let my dog know it was all right to join me on the sofa.

I stood my ground, pretending I hadn't read him. His hand came down again, slamming the sheets even harder.

"Goddammit, I haven't got all day."

I went to the bed and crawled onto it without a word. One of his hands jostled me to his side as if we were shipmates meeting in a bar. The other, the one that had lost its feeling, stroked my head with clumsy tenderness.

I know that this happened, because I was there, gazing down on those two old men as they braved the terrors of love.

343

Twenty-eight

My Old Room

That night Josie put me up in my old room. It was gussied up for guests these days, but a phantom of its former self remained, like an image lingering on the retina behind closed eyes. With very little effort I could erase that walnut "entertainment center" and sketch in my old bunk bed and the cubbyhole near the ceiling that my father had built for my radio. (To show him what an unrepentant rebel I was, I had used my wood-burning kit to brand the words FORGET, HELL! into the bottom shelf.) And still there for real: that early indicator of the man to come, the stained-glass window I'd commissioned at fourteen.

I opened the door and went outside to the piazza, just to catch the effect of those dark green shutters against the pink stucco walls. There was a lemon wafer of a moon in the sky, and the wrought-iron gates next to the streetlight cast a familiar filigree on the garden path. I was awash with memories that seemed to belong to someone else entirely. The person I had been in this place was more of a stranger to me now than my father.

"Sweetie?"

I turned to find my sister standing in the room with a cordless phone in her hand. "There's a call for you," she said.

I came in from the piazza with a sense of growing dread. "The hospital?"

She shook her head with a thin reassuring smile. "I don't recognize the voice. She sounds young."

Anna, I thought. Being motherly again.

Josie handed me the phone and left the room, pausing briefly at the door. "Come down for some eggnog if you'd like."

I watched as she eased the door shut, then sank to the edge of the bed with the phone. "This is Gabriel."

"Thank God," said the voice on the other end, a voice so distinctive it could only be one of two people.

"Donna?"

"No . . . it's Pete."

I couldn't summon a response.

"Don't freak out, okay? I know what Mom told you, but she was just trying to get people off our backs. She told Ashe I was dead, so we could get our lives back again. Mom hated all this attention to begin with. She just went along with the book because of me. And after the book fell through I figured you didn't trust me anymore, so I just . . . I dunno . . . but then Mom told me you came to see me, and I realized how bad you felt, and I couldn't stand the thought of you thinking I was dead. You're the only reason I even feel alive." He paused, waiting for a reaction. "You there, Gabriel?"

"I'm here."

"Are you mad at me?"

I said my feelings were more complicated than that.

"Jess told me about your dad," he said. "Is he okay?"

"No. I don't think he has much time left." It was hard to put that into words, but Pete was still my confessor, for better or worse.

"I'm really sorry, Dad."

I sighed for so many different reasons. "This is weird, Pete. I have to tell you."

"I know, but I miss you so much, Dad. I just want another chance." He was weeping now—extravagantly—so I waited for him to stop.

"Look," I said at last, "I'm not going anywhere. I just don't understand. Were you hiding when I came to your house?"

"No," he said emphatically. "I didn't even know you were there. I was in Milwaukee with Marsha."

"At the hospital?"

"Yeah. Getting my fucking tests done. It was just a coincidence that I wasn't at home, but Mom sort of . . . went with it. She'd already told Ashe I was dead, so she didn't have any choice but to say it again."

"Where's Donna now?"

You're talking to her, you sentimental fool.

"Down at the post office," said Pete. "Closing out our account."

"Why?"

"We're leaving day after tomorrow."

"For good, you mean?"

"Yeah."

"Where are you going?"

"I don't know yet. Mom won't say. Marsha's driving us to the airport. Mom just wants out of here."

"And what do you want?"

"It's okay with me, I guess. One place is pretty much like another for me. As long as there's a telephone I'm fine."

"Will you give me your number when you get there?"

He didn't answer.

"What's the matter, Pete?"

"I think it's better if I just call you. Mom would be really upset if she knew we were still in touch."

"Why?"

"She doesn't trust you anymore. She got really weirded out when you followed her home."

I told him I was ashamed about that.

"I kind of understand it," said Pete, "but it really bothered her. She thinks you're obsessed with me or something."

That took me aback. "What do you think?"

He didn't hesitate. "I think you just love me."

I knew I was supposed to confirm this, but I just couldn't find the words.

Pete kept on: "I didn't know that for sure, you know, until you came to see me. When I heard that, man . . ." His voice cracked pitifully.

"Are you all right, kiddo?"

"Yeah. I'm fine."

"I want to ask you something, okay?"

"Okay," he said warily.

"Did something happen to your mom when she was little?"

Silence.

"Do you understand me?"

"Yeah, but . . . I just don't know. She never talks about her childhood."

"Have you ever asked her?"

"No. It's hard, man, when you know she doesn't want to talk."

I hear you, I thought. I've been there myself.

"And she's done so much for me, you know."

"But maybe that's why, Pete. Maybe her life was as bad as yours, and she wanted to make things easier for somebody else. Did she ever tell you what caused her blindness?"

"Some disease, I think, when she was little."

"What about that scar on her arm?"

"She fell down the stairs."

"It doesn't look like that. It looks like it was—"

"Oh, shit!"

"What's the matter?"

"She's coming back. The post office must have been closed."

"Well, can't you just—"

"I gotta go, Dad." His voice had lowered to a frantic whisper. "I'll call you as soon as I can, okay?"

I didn't have a chance to answer before he hung up. Or to reflect on the possibility that I might never hear from him again.

I awoke the next morning at nine, when Josie arrived at my room with a lavishly laid-out breakfast tray. I was on the verge of praising her when I noticed the ruined state of her eyes.

"You heard something," I said, leaving off the question mark.

She nodded. "Several hours ago. I didn't want to wake you. You looked so peaceful."

Her lip began to tremble, so I pushed the tray aside, and held her in my arms while she cried.

Twenty-nine

Father, Son, and Holy Ghost

The funeral was held at St. Michael's and drew a standing-room-only crowd, a fact that would have pleased Pap no end. There were two former governors in attendance and ol' Strom himself, thrilled to be working such an aristocratic crowd. The reception at the house began on an appropriately stately note and deteriorated sharply from there. By late afternoon it was just another shrill Charleston cocktail party, and it was hard to believe that Pap could no longer be found at the center of that cacophony. I stayed long enough to catch up with my brother and help Darlie evict the last mourners, then retreated to my room to check the airline schedules. As I'd expected, there were no available flights to San Francisco until Christmas Day.

I actually didn't mind travelling then. Had I stayed on either coast that day someone would have tried to make it merry for me, and the effort would have been more painful than no Christmas at all. I did wonder what sort of reception awaited me, what I'd be asked about Pete. After all, I'd told Anna emphatically that Pete was dead, while Jess had apparently talked to him the following day, when Pete called the house looking for me.

I found signs of Jess's brief reoccupation when I arrived home: a bag of potato chips in the cupboard, a new box of treats for Hugo, a general tidying-up of the items on the bulletin board. It felt sweetly reassuring to see his imprint on the house again, though that feeling was promptly trampled by errant thoughts of the men who might have been there with him.

Hugo didn't greet me at the door, so I assumed he was out walking with Jess. But when I climbed to my writing room under the eaves, I found the dog curled in a ball on the sofa. Finally sensing my presence, he rose on wobbly legs and tried to wag his tailless rump, but this only sent him toppling to the floor with a whimper. I scooped him up in my arms and restored him to his spot on the sofa, where I stroked him carefully and nuzzled his graying face. "I know what you mean," I said.

I heard the front door open and close. Jess, upon spotting my luggage, hollered up the stairwell at me.

"Where are you?"

"All the way up."

He appeared in my aerie sporting a new accessory: a gleaming gold nose ring. And not one of those prissy little wires either; this was a meanest-bull-in-the-pasture number that pierced the middle of his nose and dangled like a door knocker out of both nostrils. "Wow," I said with less enthusiasm than the word usually demands. "That's new."

Jess, of course, could tell what I was thinking, so he

shrugged off the matter as unworthy of discussion. "Yeah. Fairly." Then he stepped forward and embraced me, kissing me lightly on the lips. "You okay?"

"Yeah. I'm fine."

"I'm sorry about Pap."

I'd never heard him call the old man that, and I was moved by the sound of it, the suggestion that he'd just lost an in-law.

"I guess it was time," I said.

"I spoke to Josie this morning. She said you got to talk to him."

"Yeah."

"Well, that's good."

He gazed out the window toward the tree line of Sutro Forest, where a pair of turkey vultures was making drunken figure eights above the valley. "She also said you were depressed about some kid who died."

I nodded.

"She couldn't have meant Pete," he added.

I sighed in concession and headed for the stairs. "Let's make coffee first."

He let me tell the story without interruption, nodding me along while I shaped its themes and refined its details. The star in the east. The sightless Madonna. The empty manger. That miraculous resurrection.

"Father, son, and holy ghost," said Jess.

I didn't get it.

"Pap and you and Pete."

"That's good," I said absently. "Clever."

"Use it, then. You're the writer."

"Is that what you think?"

"That you're a writer?"

351

"No. That he's a ghost. That he's imaginary."

He shrugged. "That's the fun of it, isn't it?"

I said it wasn't fun anymore.

"Oh, I think it must be, or you would've tried to meet Marsha. Or gone to that hospital and asked if he was ever a patient there."

"I had to go see my father, for God's sake. And I don't even know which hospital Pete was in."

"And you never once asked him, did you? Or her."

I shook my head.

"See? You never wanted to know. You *require* mystery, babe. It's like oxygen to you."

"Forget about me," I said irritably. "Tell me what *you* think."

"Well . . . that it was probably a hoax of some sort, and once she knew you'd gotten wind of it, she killed him off."

"But he called back."

And he cried and said he missed me.

"So," said Jess. "She's not an evil person, and you're not an easy person to hurt. She probably felt bad, and this was her way of making it easier on you. She went for the slow fade-out instead."

Like you, I thought. Leaving without ever saying it was over. You knew that was one more thing I don't want an answer about.

"But why would she do that?" I asked. "If it made her look like a liar in the process?"

"Because," said Jess, "she's not the one you have to believe. Pete is."

I brooded for a moment, then made a feeble stab: "I saw his room, remember. His bed."

"You saw *a* bed. It could have been a prop. She must've expected that sooner or later someone would

come looking for him. Or maybe it had been his bed—
or someone's bed—once upon a time."

Another silence betrayed my decision to surrender.
Finally, I asked, "Has Findlay called again?"

"Not that I know of," said Jess.

"He still thinks Pete is dead. He hasn't even heard
the latest."

"Why don't you just leave it that way?"

"Why?"

He shrugged. "What's the point? It's not gonna
change his mind about publishing the book. It just
makes the whole thing more suspect than ever. And
Findlay will just think you're—" He cut himself off.

"What? Being gullible again?"

"Something like that."

He was right, of course.

"Besides," said Jess. "You don't want to give away
your best material. You're gonna use all this in your
book."

I flashed him a dead-eyed look.

"You need to write, Gabriel. You'll feel better when
you do. You know that as well as I do."

"I do, do I?"

"I bought you some paper." Jess nodded toward
the computer. "And there's several more reams in the
closet."

"I'll be writing about you," I said darkly.

"Fine," he replied with a smile. "I trust you."

I holed up in the aerie for two weeks, extracting the
first chapter of this book. During that time, Hugo kept
me constant company, hardly leaving his shepherd-
shaped dent on the sofa. His efforts to pee outside were

rarely successful, and the tortuous descent to the garden only made him yelp with pain. There was no longer any valid excuse for postponement, so I made a few inquiries with friends, then called Jess.

"I can't do this alone," I said.

"I wouldn't let you," he said. "Where do we go?"

"This guy comes to the house, apparently."

"Well, that's civilized."

"Yeah," I said with a sigh. "Dr. Kerbarkian."

Jess laughed weakly, and the joke distracted us until the day of the deed, when I could no longer suppress the feeling, however irrational, that I was betraying Hugo. (A day earlier I'd been chiding myself for having held off too long.) To make it even harder, the dog was more active than usual that morning, shambling out to greet the gardener—his friend of more than fourteen years—who'd come to dig his grave beneath the tree ferns. I didn't cry, though, until Jess arrived in his best leathers bearing a pretty Tibetan prayer cloth. "I thought we could wrap him in this," he said solemnly, and the floodgates burst for both of us.

Were we mourning more than Hugo that day? I don't recall ever feeling that kind of primal, scouring grief. Maybe our other losses were just too vast to articulate, so Hugo, in his sweet simplicity, became the safest repository for our pain. Or maybe it had more to do with our fading dream of coupledom; this dog, after all, had been the closest witness to our bliss.

Dr. Kerbarkian turned out to be a soft-eyed Chilean with a comically droopy mustache. There would be two shots, he explained, one to relax the dog, the other to do the job. So we spread the prayer cloth on the bed and lay on either side of Hugo, stroking him gently as the first shot was administered. Almost immediately his muscles relaxed and his face fell into what we chose to interpret as a smile. This gave us a minute to say our goodbyes, to fill his deaf ears with endearments and let him soak up the smells of his family.

On the second shot, as we'd been warned, Hugo's body stiffened in one brief, horrific spasm. When it was over, I glanced up at the doctor, who was holding the syringe in one hand and crossing himself with the other. Jess, thank God, missed this overt display of popery because his eyes were still fixed on Hugo. My own were lost in the gossamer web of tears dangling from Jess's nose ring, the loveliest, silliest collision of tough and tender.

I continued to write into February, extruding the details of my breakup with Jess, the solace I'd received from those first playful exchanges with Pete. I still didn't have a clue about the end, but I refused to lose faith. An ending could be forced, I believed, the way a bloom can be forced if you keep it out of the wind and shine enough light on it.

Then, on the day after Valentine's Day, when the plum trees along the street were a volley of pale pink detonations, a letter appeared in my mailbox. Five words were written on a sheet of Days Inn stationery: "Roberta Blows. I love you." The postmark said Tacoma, Washington. He was on this side of the continent now.

I told no one.

By April I had written five chapters. I asked Jess to read them and give me his thoughts, which he did with extraordinary detachment, considering the nature of the material. He spent a day with it, then called me in tears to say it was my best work yet and that we should start looking for an outlet. He pressed hard for his earlier scheme—a televised reading on the Curtain Call network—but I immediately rejected the idea.

"But it's a done deal," he argued. "They're all set to go as soon as we give them the word."

"I understand that," I said, "but I'd rather do radio."

"Why? You're good with cameras."

"I want this to be just my voice, Jess."

"But you'll reach a whole new audience."

"I don't want a new audience," I told him. "I want my old one."

He knew what I was up to, but he didn't give me a hard time. In a matter of days he was talking to my producers at NPR about a brand-new show with a brand-new name. They liked what they'd read so far, but were understandably nervous about starting a series that had yet to be completed. I reminded them that I work best under pressure and promised to deliver on time. So Jess contacted our local station— the site of my infamous meltdown—and set up a date for the first recording session.

When that day arrived, the two of us held court in the studio while a succession of engineers and secretaries made gracious remarks about my re-emergence. "Jesus," said Jess, when the last one had gone. "It's like Norma Desmond returning to Paramount."

"Thanks," I said with a grin. "But that makes you Max, you realize."

It felt good to be joking again, to feel the easy, immovable love beneath our jokes. And later, in the moment before we began to record, I relished the sight of him in the control room (his nose ring pushed into its cave for this professional moment), nodding his support through the glass.

The engineer signalled, so I took a sip of water and began to read:

"I know how it sounds when I call him my son. There's something a little precious about it, a little too wishful to be taken seriously. I've noticed the looks on people's faces, those dim indulgent smiles that vanish in a heartbeat. It's easy enough to see how they've pegged me: an unfulfilled man on the shady side of fifty, making a last grasp at fatherhood with somebody else's child. That's not the way it is . . ."

THE END

Afterword

The first chapter of *The Night Listener* aired on NPR on May 16, 1999. An early broadcast this time—8 P.M.—to herald my return. I made a point of staying home that evening, but not to listen to the show. No, that's not entirely true; I always listen to the show; my work doesn't seem real to me until I hear it the way the public does, properly announced and placed in the context of "legitimate" programming. But mostly I stayed home to wait for the phone call I was almost certain would come later that night.

I wasn't obsessive about it. I went about my usual rituals after the reading was over, washing dishes and sorting laundry and tidying up. And a few thoughtful friends did call to say that they'd heard the broadcast and couldn't wait to find out where this new plotline was heading. But an hour passed and that hoped-for call never came, so I smoked a joint and went out to the hot tub for a moonlight soak.

A spring's worth of bamboo shoots, some as fat as broomsticks, had made a benign jail cell of the big redwood barrel. As I floated there in its amniotic warmth, watching a Japanese woodblock moon dawdle in the new leaves, I savored the thought that my story was finally out there in the ether, a self-sufficient organism beyond my control, changing shape in every new mind that absorbed it. And I was so much less afraid about everything, even my solitary state. It felt fine to be there, middle-aged and single, soft in the gut and long in the scrotum, keeping watch over my own little acre of stars.

When I was a boy, my father swapped daylily bulbs with an English professor named Preston Stamey. I knew that Preston was gay, because I'd once heard Pap describe him to my mother as "a fairy nice fellow." He had a tiny jewel box of a carriage house over on Tradd Street that he shared with a three-legged spaniel named Sumter. Preston was a bull-necked old nancy, jolly as a pirate, but while my father seemed to enjoy his company, privately my parents expressed pity for the professor. "How lonely he must be," my mother would say. "No wife and no children to carry on."

Long after I'd discarded my own requirements for wife and children, I still bought that melancholy assessment of Preston's life. I might be gay, but I would never be *that* kind of old queen: alone in my fifties, fussing over my flowers and my Williamsburg weather vane; I would find a lover to protect me against such emptiness. It had never occurred to me that Preston might have been more evolved than the rest of us, that he might have treasured his own company. And there could well have been students who idolized him, exlovers who still loved him, sailors he met on the

Battery who followed him home and swung on his friendly old dick and called him Daddy. He could have been having a life, in other words—and a damn good one at that.

All you have to do is believe and let go, and you'll have all the proof you need . . .

A ringing phone yanked me back into the moment. Remembering that I'd turned off the answering machine, I scrambled out of the hot tub and blotted myself hastily with my sweatpants.

Hang on, son, I'm coming.

Naked and dripping, I raced down the steps to the terrace, swung open the sliding door, barreled through the house and up the stairs to the office. On the last turn I whacked my knee sharply on the banister.

"Fuck, fuck, fuck." I did a little war dance of pain as the phone rang for the fifth time.

I grabbed the receiver and dropped into a chair.

"Hello!"

"Well, damn," my father said. "There you are. Thought you'd be out gettin' drunk."

"Oh, hey, Pap."

"Listen, son. That was one helluva first chapter you read tonight."

It had been a while since I'd received such a call from the old man. "Well, thanks, Pap. That's nice of you."

"No, it ain't. It was just a damn good piece. Was that the little boy you told us about on our way to Tahiti?"

"Yeah . . . pretty much."

"What do you mean? He either is or he ain't."

"Well, I changed his name, of course, and a few identifying details."

"Like what?"

"Oh, you know. Where he lives and what he looks like. Some of the things that happened to him."

"So the whole goddamn thing's a lie."

I laughed. "That's what fiction is for, Pap. To fix the things that have to be fixed."

"Well, you had me going there."

"Good. That was the idea."

"Then . . . all that stuff about you and Jess . . . you fellas are okay, aren't you?"

"Oh, sure. We'll always be okay."

"So when are you gonna come see us? We ain't seen you since you threw up on that bagpiper at my birthday party."

I laughed. "I've got some stuff to do, but I'll come as soon as this series is done."

"How long is this one gonna be?"

"I'm not sure yet. It's not done."

"Jesus. You're cuttin' it close. How much you got left to do?"

I began to feel a sort of low-grade anxiety. "I don't know. A hundred pages or so. Don't ask."

"Am I in it?"

"Are you in what?"

"You know what I'm talking about, you little son-of-a-bitch. What have you done to me this time?"

I told him I hadn't decided yet.

GN
San Francisco

Acknowledgments

My sister, Jane Yates, lives in the nether reaches of New Zealand but inhabits many hectares of my heart. Likewise, Ian McKellen and James Lecesne make me feel loved and valued from afar. Pam Ling and Judd Winick provide family here in my own valley. Robert Jones is a gifted writer with a generous nature, which makes him the best of all possible editors. Patrick Janson-Smith has championed my work longer than anyone. Binky Urban took me under her wing long before she became an agent, let alone mine. Steven Barclay is a master at providing what I love the most: a stage. The extraordinary Patrick Gale helped me to unravel my past before I twisted it back into fiction. Tony Maupin and I have just learned what it means to be brothers, which fills me with joy. Tim McIntosh makes me laugh and listens beautifully. Cheryl Maupin has my admiration and affection more than ever. Don Bachardy continues to inspire me by his remarkable self-discipline. David Hockney and Barry Humphries help me to remember to play while I'm working. My friends Stephen McCauley, David Sheff, Karen Barbour, Darryl Vance, Louise Vance, Peggy Knickerbocker, Anne Lamott, Thomas Gibson, Cristina Gibson, Buddy Rhodes, Susan Andrews, Jake Heggie, Steven Lippman, and Davia Nelson read an early draft of this novel and offered invaluable insight and support. Maggie Hamilton brought me light when I needed it. Nicolas Sheff makes me dote like an old gay godfather. Gary Lebow felt like family far sooner than I expected. Nick Hongola is my swell new friend. David Wong has the gentlest of hearts. Barry Jones, Liz McKereghan, and Lawrence Jenkins remind me to live in my body. Ben Shaw, Todd Hargis, and Jose Landes have brought me all the comforts of home. Alan Poul's dedication and good taste have kept *Tales of the City* on television. The incandescent Laura Linney is both the woman I would want and the woman I would want to be. Olympia Dukakis has always been a goddess-send. Terry Anderson, who keeps our cottage industry on course, gave me his unequivocal blessing, then cajoled, encouraged, and tolerated me until this novel was finished. When all is said and done, he's still the one.

AM
San Francisco

MAYBE THE MOON
Armistead Maupin

'WONDERFUL, FUNNY POIGNANT AND GUTSY . . . YOU
CAN FEEL THE AUTHOR'S HUGE AND HURT AND
LOVING HEART BEAT ON EVERY PAGE'
Anne Lamott, *Mademoiselle*

All of thirty-one inches tall, Cadence (Cady) Roth is a true
survivor in a town where – as she says – 'you can die of
encouragement'. Her early leading role as a lovable elf in a
smash-hit American film proved a major disappointment since
moviegoers never saw the face behind the rubber mask she had
to wear. After a decade of hollow promises from the Industry,
she is still waiting for the miracle that will make her a star.

Through a series of bracingly frank journal entries, Armistead
Maupin tracks his spunky heroine across the saffron-hazed
wasteland of Los Angeles – from her infrequent meetings with
agents and studio moguls to her regular, harrowing encounters
with small children, large dogs and human ignorance. Then
one day a lanky piano player saunters into Cady's life,
unleashing heady new emotions, and she finds herself going
for broke, shooting the moon with a scheme so hare-brained
and daring that it might just succeed. . .

Maybe the Moon, Armistead Maupin's first novel since his
bestselling *Tales of the City* sextet, is the tale of an outsider
told from the inside. It is a work that speaks to the resilience
of the human spirit.

'DELIGHTS, AMUSES, MOVES AND ANGERS YOU WITH THE
LIGHTEST OF TOUCHES. IT IS, AS MIGHT BE SAID OF
CADENCE HERSELF, A SMALL MASTERPIECE'
Simon Callow, *Vogue*

'*MAYBE THE MOON* WILL DISAPPOINT ONLY THE ENVIOUS.
RICH, MOVING, SEXY AND FUNNY, IT ALSO HAS A
PLEASINGLY ANGRY STREAK'
Patrick Gale, *Daily Telegraph*

0 552 99875 3

BLACK SWAN

A LIST OF OTHER ARMISTEAD MAUPIN TITLES
AVAILABLE FROM BLACK SWAN

99876 1	TALES OF THE CITY	£6.99
99877 X	MORE TALES OF THE CITY	£6.99
99878 8	FURTHER TALES OF THE CITY	£6.99
99879 6	BABYCAKES	£6.99
99880 X	SIGNIFICANT OTHERS	£6.99
99881 8	SURE OF YOU	£6.99
99875 3	MAYBE THE MOON	£6.99